Writing Race Across the Atlantic World

SIGNS OF RACE

General Editors: Philip D. Beidler and Gary Taylor

Volumes Already Published

Writing Race across the Atlantic World: Medieval to Modern, edited by Philip D. Beidler and Gary Taylor

Buying Whiteness: Race, Culture, and Identity from Columbus to Hip-hop, by Gary Taylor

Future Volumes

English and Ethnicity, edited by Janina Brutt-Griffler, Catherine Davies, and Lucy Pickering

Women and Others: Racial and Gender Difference in Anglo-American Literature and Culture, edited by Celia R. Daileader, Rhode Johnson, and Amilcar Shabazz

Race, Nationality, and National Literatures: The Institutionalization of English, edited by Peter Logan

Postcolonial Otherness and Transnational Capitalism: Contexts, Contests and Contradictions, edited by Robert Young

WRITING RACE ACROSS THE ATLANTIC WORLD
MEDIEVAL TO MODERN

Edited by
Philip D. Beidler and Gary Taylor

WRITING RACE ACROSS THE ATLANTIC WORLD
© Philip D. Beidler and Gary Taylor, 2005.

First published in 2005 by
PALGRAVE MACMILLAN™
175 Fifth Avenue, New York, N.Y. 10010 and
Houndmills, Basingstoke, Hampshire, England RG21 6XS
Companies and representatives throughout the world.

PALGRAVE MACMILLAN is the global academic imprint of the Palgrave Macmillan division of St. Martin's Press, LLC and of Palgrave Macmillan Ltd. Macmillan® is a registered trademark in the United States, United Kingdom and other countries. Palgrave is a registered trademark in the European Union and other countries.

ISBN 0–312–29596–0 hardback
ISBN 0–312–29597–9 paperback

Library of Congress Cataloging-in-Publication Data

Writing race across the Atlantic world : medieval to modern / ed. Philip D. Beidler and Gary Taylor.
    p. cm.
    Papers from a symposium held at the University of Alabama in 2001.
    ISBN 0–312–29596–0—ISBN 0–312–29597–9
    1. America—Race relations—Congresses. 2. Great Britain—Race relations—Congresses. 3. Great Britain—Colonies—America—History—Congresses. 4. Slavery—America—History—Congresses. 5. Racism—America—History—Congresses. 6. Racism—Great Britain—History—Congresses. 7. Acculturation—America—History—Congresses. 8. Racism in literature—Congresses. 9. English literature—History and criticism—Congresses. 10. American literature—History and criticism—Congresses. I. Beidler, Philip D. II. Taylor, Gary, 1953–

E29.A1W75 2004
305.8'0097—dc22   2004053929

A catalogue record for this book is available from the British Library.

Design by Newgen Imaging Systems (P) Ltd., Chennai, India.

First edition: January 2005

10 9 8 7 6 5 4 3 2 1

Printed in the United States of America.

CONTENTS

General Editors' Preface

> I have never been to Alabama before, but it is and will forever remain seared in my memory as the place where black Americans challenged America to live up to the meaning of her creed so as not to make a mockery of her ideals.
>
> —August Wilson (September 26, 2001)

The first thing you see when you enter the permanent exhibits at the Birmingham Civil Rights Institute is a pair of drinking fountains. Over one hangs a sign that says "White." Over the other hangs a sign that says "Colored."

As an inquiry into the cultural history of race, the series "Signs of Race" has its own obvious historical origins. It springs from a series of symposiums at the University of Alabama—the place where George Wallace made segregation's last stand. But the series finds its larger cultural and intellectual impulses in a deeper and wider history that surrounds us here. Black, brown, red, and white; African American and Afro-Caribbean; English, French, and Spanish; Celtic and Jewish; native American and northern European, creole and mestizo: such cultural categories, wherever they are found, in whatever combinations, and in whatever arrangements of historical interaction and transmission, constitute the legacy of the oceanic intercultures of race in the early modern era. In Alabama, the very landscape is steeped in such history. Twenty miles to the south of the town of Tuscaloosa, the home of the University, is a vast city of pre-Columbian mounds, the capital of a Mississippian empire that flourished at the time of the Norman Conquest and then disappeared two centuries later. The town of Tuscaloosa itself is named for a great Chief of the Alabamas, known as the Black Warrior, who engaged the Spanish explorer DeSoto in the 1540 battle of Maubila, to this day thought to be the largest single combat ever fought by native Americans against Europeans. The European settlement of the Gulf Coast pitted English, French, Spanish, and American colonizers against each other well into the nineteenth century. The Revolutionary War found native tribes, their ruling families frequently intermarried with Scots-Irish traders, allied with loyalists against American nationalists? The early-nineteenth-century wars of extermination and removal against native peoples—Creeks, Choctaws, Cherokees, Chickasaws, and Seminoles—and the filling up of the rich agricultural lands thereby opened to a vast slave empire, were determining events in the southward and westward expansion of slavery eventuating in civil war.

In more recent historical memory, particular words and phrases constitute a litany of particular racial struggle. Jim Crow. Ku Klux Klan. Separate but Equal. The Scottsboro Boys. Autherine Lucy. Rosa Parks. The Schoolhouse Door. The names of major cities and towns ring forth as the Stations of the Cross of the Civil Rights Era: Selma, Montgomery, Birmingham, Tuscaloosa. Most recently, Alabama, like much of America, finds itself newly Hispanic, with large influxes of population from Mexico and the Caribbean, South and Central America.

To the extent that every social identity is to some degree local, the meanings of race in Alabama necessarily differ, in some demographic and historical particulars, from the meanings of race in North Dakota and Northern Ireland, New York and New South Wales, Cape Town and Calcutta. But the same questions can be asked everywhere in the English-speaking world.

How do people signal a racial identity?

What does that racial identity signify?

This series examines the complex relationships between race, ethnicity, and culture in the English-speaking world from the early modern period (when the English language first began to move from its home island into the wider world) until the postcolonial present, when it has become the dominant language of an increasingly globalized culture. English is now the medium of a great variety of literatures, spoken and written by many ethnic groups. The racial and ethnic divisions between (and within) such groups are not only reflected in, but also shaped by, the language we share and contest. Indeed, such conflicts in part determine what counts as "literature" or "culture."

Every volume in the series approaches race from a global, interdisciplinary, intercultural perspective. Each volume in the series focuses on one aspect of the cross-cultural performance of race, exploring the ways in which "race" remains stubbornly local, personal, and present.

We no longer hang racial signs over drinking fountains. But the fact that the signs of race have become less obvious does not mean that they have disappeared, or that we can or do ignore them. It is the purpose of this series to make us more conscious, and more critical, readers of the signs that separate one group of human beings from another.

Philip D. Beidler and Gary Taylor

INTRODUCTION: *E PLURIBUS VERUM*

Philip D. Beidler and Gary Taylor

> Civilization does not have one color, one religion, or one geographical orientation.
>
> —August Wilson (September 26, 2001)

The following essays speak for themselves. One need not patronize authors or readers with attempts at summation and paraphrase. This introduction reflects briefly on their significance as part of an ongoing attempt to trace out both a discourse and a subject of investigation in a rapidly evolving field of multidisciplinary inquiry. The immediate focus of this collection is constructions of race in the early modern Atlantic world. But that needs to be understood within the larger study of race, literature, and ethnicity, projected in the "Signs of Race" symposia and volumes—and within the wider world which affects us all, as scholars and human beings.

In the first year of the twenty-first century, organizers of the University of Alabama Symposium Series, "Signs of Race," proposed and received approval for an ongoing set of multidisciplinary conferences on race, ethnicity, language, literature, and cultural difference. From the beginning, the programs were envisioned as bringing together speakers from a wide array of disciplines: literature, critical theory, linguistics, history, cultural studies, sociology, anthropology, religious studies, and so on. Several were also projected to feature eminent keynote speakers and performers from the contemporary arts—literature, drama, film, music, dance—whose careers and major achievements had centered on cultural representations of race.

The events of September 11, 2001, were still in the future when these plans were made, and the first symposium was innocently scheduled to begin on September 26, 2001. Since the speakers were coming from as far away as Hawaii, the grounding of all commercial air traffic in the United States in the immediate aftermath of the Al Qaeda attacks threatened to make the projected gathering of minds and disciplines physically impossible. But planes began to fly again, in time, and all but one of the invitees—already, as that person put it, "a nervous flyer," who would have been departing from, of all places, New York—arrived. The symposium began in Morgan Hall, a building erected in 1911 and named for J. T. Morgan (1824–1907), Alabama secessionist, Brigadier General in the Confederate Army, and United States Senator for thirty years. From the stage of the restored Edwardian theatre in that building, dedicated to one of the architects of segregation, the eminent American playwright August Wilson told a spellbound, overflow, interracial audience something about his own experience, as an artist and a citizen of African heritage, with race and cultural difference in contemporary America. Even before the rigorous security measures imposed at airports in the wake of the 2001 attacks, Wilson noted wryly at one point, he had already found himself invariably selected from boarding passengers on flights for "random" screening. "I guess I'm just a random kind of guy," he concluded.

There was nothing random about Wilson's condemnation of "the politics of exclusion, damning and damaging to our global world." The rhetoric and practice of exclusion has, since Wilson spoke, only intensified, lengthening the roll-call of victims of real or putative randomness. Whatever the differences between George W. Bush and Osama bin Laden, they both apply righteous and violent binaries to the thick complexity of interactions between the world's many peoples. "The present is the consequence of history," Wilson reminded us, "given form and function." The contributors to this collection describe some of the forms and functions that the righteous, violent binaries of race have historically taken, and some of the effects of that past upon our present. The anthology of stories this volume tells should teach us the colossally tragic consequences of any division of the world into black and white, good and evil, us and them.

Much of the importance of such a volume as this lies, beyond its specific content, in the collaborative framing of an investigatory enterprise. When the coeditors—one of us a specialist in early modern England, the other an early Americanist—first envisioned this project, we began with the simple idea of making sure we represented both sides of the Atlantic. This may seem elementary, but in fact the fault-lines of academic disciplines usually confine a scholarly career, or a classroom, to one side or the other of "the pond."

This is not to say we were without major points of reference in contemporary scholarship. Focusing on the legacy of African slavery in British postcolonial experience, Paul Gilroy's *The Black Atlantic* stood as a model of inquiry into the sociology of race as a function of Anglo-American transatlantic cultural exchange. Similarly, Ira Berlin's *Many Thousands Gone* revealed the depth to which cultural constructions of race in the slave world of the British Caribbean and colonial North America intertwined themselves from the outset with complex administrative, legal, and ethnological myths of color and heredity. An abundant general literature existed concerning the English, American, Dutch, French, Portuguese, Spanish, and Islamic participations in the African slave trade. An important tradition of intellectual history involving well-known writers as diverse as Winthrop Jordan, David Brion Davis, Toni Morrison, David Eltis, and Orlando Patterson had also traced out the western racialization of blackness in its relation to corresponding myths of whiteness attendant upon African slavery and its cultural legacy. And a number of texts had begun to enlarge our previously limited knowledge of complex constructions of race erected by major early modern nationalities as a result of the colonial enterprises bringing them into contacts with New World native peoples—Caribbean as well as North, Central, and South American. In Early American colonial studies there was Jill Lepore's *In the Name of War*; in French, Gordon Sayre's *Le Petit Sauvages*, and in English, Karen Ordahl Kupperman's *Indians and English: Facing Off in Early America*. In early modern English studies on literature and race, there were Kim Hall's *Things of Darkness* and Arthur Little Jr.'s *Shakespeare Jungle Fever*. We were fortunate enough to attract three of these authors as symposium participants and contributors to this volume.

What we believed we might bring newly to such conversation was an attempt to locate such historical questions of race within the particular cultural-studies context that Joseph Roach, another of our contributors, has described as the world of early modern oceanic intercultures—that is, a space of transatlantic interchange in which early modern colonial cultures may have frequently devised models of their interaction with each other and with enslaved and conquered peoples according to emergent theories of racial difference; but a transatlantic intercultural space as well in which they frequently conceived and reconceived such difference within the ranks of their own populations and others both at home and abroad. In the wake of the reconquest of the Iberian peninsula, for instance, formerly Moorish Spain, now redesignating itself a Christian empire, found a need to redefine previous ethnicities according to new religious categories. Newly converted Islamic believers became *moriscos*; newly converted

Jews became *conversos*. Meanwhile, in New Spain Creoles distinguished themselves on one hand from *peninsulares*—European Spaniards— and *mestizos, negros,* and *indios*. Similarly, in the outpost of New France soon to be known as the Haiti of the black revolutionary Toussaint L' Overture, four major racial groupings—*gran blanc, petit blanc, mulatto, negro*—provided the contours of political struggle in a colony that *in fact* administratively acknowledged 128 separate racial definitions. Vernacular categories likewise followed the course of empire. In English, the definition of "moor" became increasingly dissociated from the idea of the North African region of Mauritania. A new coinage came into being: blackamoor. Shakespeare's Othello (1603) is repeatedly called "black" as well as a "moor." A similar eliding of terms appears in Samuel Purchas' 1625 voyage collection. By the eighteenth century, a "moor" had simply become "black." Even the visual evidence is there: in the engravings of Hogarth, addressed at some length by Joseph Roach in these pages, a blackamoor, frequently depicted in arabesque haute couture as a decorative adjunct of conspicuous wealth, is clearly no longer a North African but a subsaharan Negro.

Simultaneously, oceanic interculture provided a space of realignment within racial terms of international relationships and colonial rivalries between and among western nationalities themselves. The English "race" distinguished itself from the Spanish "race" according to the quasi-religious post-Reformation myth of the Black Legend. Meanwhile, at home, there was the nagging problem of Ireland, again dividing itself along lines mixing religion, race, and ethnicity. For the English, French, and Spanish alike there was frequently the need to accommodate both within and without older cultures of difference such as Judaism and Islam.

On these issues *Writing Race across the Atlantic World* offers a kind of progress report. It makes a contribution to our collective search for some measure of meaning in the past. We are proud of what is here. By virtue of it, at the same time we are also made distinctly aware of what could be here and what needs to be part of the future record. All fields of knowledge, at whatever stage of definition they happen to have reached, are porous. They construct themselves continuously from within and without, with each addition or subtraction reconfiguring the field. They take shape by virtue of an attempt to comprehend what has been said, what is being said, and what has yet to be said—even as the prospect of knowledge envisioned critiques the deficiencies of knowledge current and past. To acknowledge this, too, is an important function of collaborative scholarship.

A book or essay by a single author almost inevitably conveys an impression of autonomous, directed, fulfilled purpose. By contrast, any collaboration is necessarily and evidently a story of purposefulness and randomness. We regard this mix as a strength, not a weakness, because the apparent randomness introduced by collaboration forces purpose into new channels, which might never have been explored by a single purposed mind in isolation. "As an African American," August Wilson emphasized at the outset of our collective enterprise, "improvisation is the keystone, the hallmark of my aesthetics." As mentioned above, one of the invited speakers—who would specifically have addressed the experience of African slavery in the Atlantic world—found herself forced to withdraw because of the events of September 11. As symposium codirectors, we attempted to address the problem with two improvised contributions. Philip D. Beidler's response—stimulated directly by the Al Qaeda attacks, and included here—addresses the historical role of the Islamic slave trade in early modern conceptions of race and slavery in Anglo-European and early American African slave culture. Gary Taylor's response, an examination of the interacting co-construction of white and black identity, grew into the book *Buying Whiteness*, concurrently issued as the second volume in the Palgrave *Signs of Race* series.

For all this print production arising from a three-day symposium—both a collection of essays and a related single-author volume—the account of discovery even here would be incomplete should we not acknowledge a profound awareness of what continues to be missing. We were unable to address significant representations, for instance, both originally in English and in contemporary translation, of the French colonial enterprise, with regard to enslaved Africans and to conceptions of native peoples. None of the essays significantly addressed race in the early modern Caribbean world. Even more curiously, none of them addressed the critical role played by the geography of the Atlantic itself in the interaction of circumatlantic peoples, sometimes as obstacle, sometimes as facilitator, but always as an overwhelming physical reality.[1]

Between the symposium meeting and the issue of this book, the conversation on race in the Atlantic world has been enlarged and invigorated by Ira Berlin, Mary Floyd-Wilson, Joyce Green MacDonald, and James H. Sweet, whose recent contributions have joined the working bibliography of any serious investigator.[2] It is our hope that this and further texts in the Palgrave *Signs of Race* series will continue to enlarge the discourse and to serve what Wilson called every writer's—and we would add, every reader's—"grave obligation to the truth."

NOTES

1. Gary Taylor hopes to address that issue in a future volume in the series.
2. Ira Berlin, *Generations of Captivity: A History of African American Slaves* (Cambridge: Harvard University Press, 2003); Mary Floyd-Wilson, *English Ethnicity and Race in Early Modern Drama* (Cambridge: Cambridge University Press, 2003); Joyce Green MacDonald, *Women and Race in Early Modern Drama* (Cambridge: Cambridge University Press, 2003); James H. Sweet, *Recreating Africa: Culture, Kingship, and Religion in the African-Portuguese World, 1441–1700* (Chapel Hill: University of North Carolina Press, 2003). Mary Floyd-Wilson was a participant in the 2001 symposium, and we had hoped to include her lecture on the construction of race in *Othello* in this collection, but it reached print as a chapter of her book before our own volume was published. We strongly recommend it to anyone interested in the issues addressed here.

1

NATIVE EUROPEANS AND NATIVE AMERICANS

1

A MIRROR ACROSS THE WATER:
MIMETIC RACISM, HYBRIDITY, AND
CULTURAL SURVIVAL

Barbara Fuchs

It is my contention that the complexities of race in the New World cannot be adequately understood without a concomitant understanding of metropolitan, European racism. This essay first traces these transatlantic connections through the racial system in the Spanish Americas and then examines their refraction in the writings of an indigenous critic of the Conquista, Guaman Poma de Ayala. Finally, it takes Poma's denunciation of hybridity as the occasion to interrogate our own critical fascination with the term, and with such figures as Poma himself.

In its focus on genealogy, the racial system in the Spanish colonies in the New World can be traced partially to the obsession with "limpieza de sangre," or blood purity, in the Iberian peninsula.[1] What began in Spain as religious and cultural intolerance gradually became, over the course of the sixteenth century, an essentializing obsession with genealogy and blood that marginalized even those Jews and Moors who converted, however unwillingly, to Christianity. This ideology, honed and exacerbated over the same decades in which the Spanish were carrying out their conquest of the New World, translated into a system of white/Spanish privilege in the colonies that persisted despite the increased frequency of interracial unions over the generations.

The situation in Spain was very complex. After 700 years of cohabitation by Moors, Jews, and Christians, el-Andalus, as southern Spain was known, was a multicultural society with much mingling among groups. Religion and phenotype by no means coincided: there were, for example, Moors of all colors, including blondes. In an inventory of Moriscos (Christianized Moors) captured in the rebellion of the Alpujarras (1568–71), they are described as "de color moreno," "de color negra," "de color blanco que tira un poco a membrillo cocho," and even, frequently, "de color blanca" ["tawny," "black," "white tending to cooked quince," and "white"].[2] The linguist Manuel Alvar notes that there were no specific terms to name the offspring of mixed unions in this period, which suggests that they were not perceived as particularly different from the rest of the population.[3] With the fall of Granada to the Catholic Kings in 1492—the same year in which Columbus reached the New World and the Jews were expelled from Spain—the territorial and political unification of Spain seemed viable. In this context, the myth of the Reconquista, or "reconquest" of territory from the Moors, by an ancestral Gothic, Christian nation provided a sense of cohesion and purpose for the newly centralized state. But it was largely a convenient fiction, one that ignored the myriad exchanges and points of contact between Christians and Semitic peoples over hundreds of years. As Ferdinand and Isabella—and the Hapsburg monarchs after them—harnessed the power of religion to the new state, Spain's Semitic strains were ever less welcome. With the Reformation, the Crown increased its efforts to equate Spain with the one true religion, as Defender of the Faith. And where the defeated Moors had initially been offered broad assurances of tolerance and respect for their culture, as the century wore on they found themselves increasingly persecuted for their origins. Much like the *conversos* (converted Jews), the Moriscos (Moors who had been converted to Christianity) were persecuted not only for their anomalous cultural practices, but for their heredity. As Deborah Root has convincingly suggested, it was the opacity and unknowability that resulted from the forced conversions of "New Christians" that eventually led to this degree of persecution.[4] Because the true conviction of the convert could never be known, he or she always represented a threat to the homogenizing state. Whereas *conversos*, especially, had once occupied positions of great power and social prominence, over the course of the sixteenth century "New Christians" were generally prevented from occupying civil and ecclesiastical offices, attending university, emigrating to the New World, and so forth.[5]

All Spaniards, even those who boasted most loudly of their Old Christian blood were vulnerable to accusations of unclean blood. There was even a legal process, the *averiguación de limpieza*, or inquiry into cleanliness, which served to establish that all of one's ancestors were Christians. That elusive chimaera, "pure" or "clean" blood, was never written on the face of an individual subject, so that it was often possible for New Christians to confound the exclusionist system that oppressed them. Literary representations by writers sympathetic to the Moriscos suggest that these passed routinely for Spanish Christians, which, of course, many of them *were*.[6] And whatever their innermost conviction, the Moriscos could perfectly approximate Spanishness. Moved in part by their profound mistrust of New Christians, the Crown turned to controversial and extreme measures: in 1609, the Moriscos, Moors who had lived in Spain for countless generations and had converted a century earlier, were summarily expelled from Spain.

CONSTRUCTING RACE IN THE NEW WORLD

In the New World, the first stages of the Conquista were not marked by the same racism as the later sixteenth century. The Spaniards were initially quite willing to marry native women, especially if they were part of the indigenous nobility. The early *cédulas* (official proclamations) promoting marriages between Spanish men and Indian women recognized that these unions could be hugely advantageous for the conquerors—and sometimes also for the indigenous nobility—in political, social, and economic terms. Elizabeth Kuznesof has demonstrated that race itself was assigned differently to men and to women in the New World, with many examples of "racial drift"—women noted as *mestizas* or Indians in baptismal records, but white in marriage records—through the eighteenth century.[7] As Stuart B. Schwartz argues, in the earliest stages of the Conquista parental recognition—that is, legitimacy—and lineage seem to have mattered more than "race."[8] Some of the children of these early unions were completely assimilated into Spanish society in the New World, holding *encomiendas* and other privileges; some even lived out their lives in Spain. In many cases, they were simply known as Spaniards. The key distinction, of course, was the status of the Indian women who participated in these unions. For the undistinguished, and unrecognized, offspring of what were often forced unions, there was little chance of recognition by Spanish society. These mestizos lived most often in Indian society or drifted uncomfortably between two worlds. Because this latter scenario was actually the norm, mestizos quickly became equated with illegitimacy. As the Spaniards consolidated their presence in the New World, mestizos suffered a further loss of status, as their loyalty to the Spaniards became increasingly suspect.

It is important to note that, as for the Moriscos who passed as Christians in Spain, identity was for these mestizos partly a matter of choice, as it would to a certain extent be for all subjects in Spanish America. The Spaniards had mapped a medieval social organization onto the New World, with the Spaniards and Indian notables as the nobility, the remaining Indians as tribute-paying vassals, and the blacks as slave labor. Within this racist social organization, passing presented clear advantages. By avoiding identification with the indigenous population, a mestizo—or even a "pure" indigenous subject—could avoid tribute payments. As Scharwtz reminds us, the racial categories in the New World were social constructs, ripe for manipulation by subjects intent on fashioning their own identity, especially by the broad category of the *castas*, or people of color existing between the most clearly defined races in this system. This involved anyone from that first generation of mestizos who lived as Spaniards, to the Spanish soldier who passed as a Mapuche Indian to avoid further conscription on the Chilean front, to the myriad subjects who, though culturally Indian, loudly voiced their Spanish or mestizo origins in order to avoid tribute.[9] Black Africans, who were forcibly carried to the New World as slaves, were most savagely discriminated against based on the color of their skin, as well as their legal status. Despite their oppression, however, many blacks and especially mulattos managed to improve their position, often by acting as intermediaries between the Spaniards and the native peoples or by applying the fruit of their labor to their own manumission. Thus, in the construction of identity, legal and social status did not always coincide.[10]

The Spaniards gradually set up a detailed system of genealogical classification for the various kinds of racial hybrids that ensued from the Conquista—a system that had social, if not legal, force. Its visual epitome is the eighteenth-century genre of the *casta* painting, which catalogues both proper and miscegenated couplings, the latter leading, in a sadly predictable fashion, to the "degeneration" of darker skin.[11] As these artifacts suggest, more than two centuries after the Conquista, the racial picture in Spanish America was very complex. After generations of intermingling among the principal groups in the colonies, any definite racial classification was necessarily suspect. A baroque exuberance of terms gradually appeared to describe the racial genealogies of New World subjects, but the categories themselves betray the prejudice and uncertainty that inhere in the system. Beyond the better known terms, such as *mestizo* (the offspring of a Spaniard and an Indian) or mulatto (born of a Spaniard and a Black), this racial system spawned a plethora of recondite categories: *castizo, zambaigo, albarazado, barcino, cambujo, chamizo, zambo, chino,* and so forth. Some of the terms, such as *lobo* (wolf) and *coyote*, frankly animalize the *castas*. Other, particularly colorful ones (all puns intended) mark the impossibility of the very project of classification: categories such as *tente en el aire* (hold yourself in mid-air), *no te entiendo* (I don't understand you) or *tornatrás* (turn back) all seem to indicate confusion rather than Enlightenment certainty. Indeterminacy and unknowability lay at the heart of the system.

The detailed hierarchy that granted whites the lion's share of privileges even included a knowing provision by which money could whiten subjects of an indeterminate hue: by purchasing certificates of whiteness called "*gracias al sacar*" (something along the lines of "graces that remove one"), *castas* could access white privileges and escape racist ordinances. These certificates were socially effective fictions that served to counter the fiction of race. Scholars have speculated that they served to buy the Crown the loyalty of economically powerful *castas*, or to counter the power of the *criollos*, or American-born whites.[12] Over the course of several generations, the system became increasingly complex, even as racial boundaries became more and more blurred.

The racial nomenclature strikingly reveals its ideological premises. Note, for example, how it superimposes race and nationality at the top. The category for whites is "Spaniard,"—a conflation that both whitens Spain and erases the presence of other European subjects from Spanish America. The casta paintings also record the pragmatic exceptions to genealogical determinism in the first generations of the Conquista: the initial union of a Spaniard and an Indian produces a *mestizo*, the union of a Spaniard and a *mestiza* produces a *castizo*, but the union of a Spaniard and a *castiza* magically produces another Spaniard, effectively erasing all traces of indigenous blood.[13] There are also interesting lexical traces of the Peninsular obsession with blood that underlies so much of this New World pigmentocracy.[14] Most notably, the union of a Spaniard and a mulatto produces a *morisco*, in a fascinating translation to the Americas of the Spanish word for a converted Moor.[15]

In the wake of Linnaeus's *System of Nature* (1735), the casta paintings and the complex genealogies they map may be read as an Enlightenment attempt to catalog and contain the racial variety of the New World—several sets of paintings were sent to museums and scientific collections in Spain as specimens. But the plethora of terms—which often vary from one set of paintings to the next—signals the futility of the effort. *No te entiendo, tente-en-el-aire*—these are hardly anchors for an Enlightenment hierarchy.

As literary scholars trained within deconstructive and Foucauldian paradigms, we have been conditioned to read the aporias and contradictions in hierarchies as spaces for subversion. I myself have pointed out the extent to which racial identity was not only constructed but also a matter of subjects' choice. But to what extent did these choices actually exist? How were they circumscribed by material considerations? The casta paintings are relentless in charting the social and material degradation that accompanies racial "degeneration" away from the white, Spanish apex of colonial society. One way to address these vexed questions is to consider how a subaltern subject in that society views race relations. Instead of considering the transgressive possibilities of deconstructing the hierarchy, as I have briefly sketched above, I will examine instead a pointedly anticolonial manifesto that depends on an *exacerbation* of Spanish racism, ably harnessing it to indigenous concerns.

A NEW CHRONICLE: MESTIZOS, MOORS, AND JEWS

In the late years of the sixteenth century, the Spaniards' own disdain for mixed blood affords the Andean writer Felipe Guaman Poma de Ayala a powerful rhetorical weapon against the Spanish presence. In his *Nueva corónica i buen gobierno*, a pointed retelling of the conquest of Peru and prescription for its "good government," Poma argues passionately against *mestizaje* and for the survival of "pure" Andean peoples, emphasizing in particular the gendered violence that augments the mestizo population. As I will show, his mimetic strategy complicates our own critical romanticization of hybridity, *mestizaje*, and creolization, by underscoring the huge price that the colonized pay for such admixtures.

The *Nueva corónica*, probably completed in 1615, is a fascinating document. An undelivered, nine-hundred-page letter addressed to Philip III, King of Spain, it is replete with syncretic illustrations that locate the Spanish regime within Andean representational and symbolic traditions.[16] As far as we know, the letter never reached its destination. It was only discovered in a Copenhagen archive in 1908. (Given its powerful indictment of Spanish abuses, it was probably acquired by Protestants as supporting evidence in the construction of the "Black Legend" of Spanish cruelty.) The *Nueva corónica* combines several historical genres, such as the *crónica* and the *relación*, which the Spaniards themselves used to narrate the Conquista.[17] While Poma rehearses the story of the conquest in his own terms, his narrative also includes a history of the peoples of Peru before the arrival of the Spaniards and, most original of all, a prescriptive set of recommendations for the "good government" of the region. Beyond its recombination of Spanish genres, the text intersperses Quechua with the Spanish, presenting a striking formal hybridity that contrasts tellingly with its own prescriptions for racial separation. In what follows, I focus on Poma's reformulation of Spanish racial and religious ideology.

One of the key challenges for the author is to construct a voice of sufficient stature to allow him to address the Spanish sovereign. Poma claims close ties to the Inca rulers: his father, he tells us, was ambassador for the Inca Huáscar to the Spaniards in the early days of the *conquista*, and saved a conquistador's life on the battlefield, while his mother was the daughter of the Inca Tupac Yupanqui. What little we know of Guaman Poma suggests that his claims to nobility are far inflated. Records show that he was a Yarovilca of no particular distinction who had worked as an interpreter for the Spaniards, even collaborating in early campaigns against native resistance. His command of Spanish and interactions with the Spaniards made him an *indio ladino*, or acculturated Indian. Yet the *Nueva corónica* resolutely condemns the Spanish administration in Peru.

Poma's account of his father's felicitous encounter with the conquistador Luis de Avalos de Ayala on the battlefield is a striking attempt to confer upon himself the stature of Spanish *hidalguía*, or nobility. In Poma's story, when his father, Martín, saves Avalos de Ayala from a rival Spaniard in an internecine battle, the conquistador confers upon him a kind of honorary Spanishness, by transferring to him his name, which will, of course, become Poma's own. Yet this transaction is shadowed by a far less heroic one. Poma introduces Avalos de Ayala as "padre de dicho santo hermitaño Martín de Ayala, mestizo"[18] [father of the said holy hermit Martín de Ayala, mestizo], whom the author has earlier described as his half-brother. If we reconstruct the tangled web of real and honorary paternity in Poma's story, it becomes clear that Avalos de Ayala does more than confer his name on the chivalrous Martín. He also sires a son with the Indian's wife. It is impossible to know whether the conquistador passed his native concubine on to his Indian retainer, as was sometimes the case among Spaniards of greater and lesser status, or whether the mestizo half-brother was the result of even more egregious colonial violence.

It is ironic, given Poma's wholesale denunciation of *mestizaje* elsewhere in the text, that the mestizo Martín de Ayala—who shares Poma's father's name—occupies a crucial position in his introduction. As the one who teaches both Poma's father and the author himself Christian doctrine, Martín de Ayala enables Poma's own Christianity, and thus his moral authority. As "holy hermit," the mestizo also provides an exemplary model for the clergy in Peru, which is a particular target of Poma's critique.[19] The drawing that illustrates Poma's relationship with the mestizo makes his importance clear: a huge "Padre Martín de Ayala, Santo de Dios amado" [Father Martín de Ayala, Saint beloved of God] towers over the young Guaman Poma and his Christian parents (13).

Poma's critique of abuses by the Church allows him to voice his opposition to *mestizaje*. The preachers, Poma complains, keep the women for their own sexual use, despite ordinances to the contrary:

> Ni con color de la dotrina no lo ajunte por los daños y pleytos y no multiplicar, acauarse los yndios y acauarse la hazienda del servicio de Dios y de su Magestad...
> Y ancí multiplica muchos mestizos y cholos en este reino. (536)
>
> [Nor with the excuse of teaching doctrine should they get close to them, for all the harm and disputes it causes, and the Indians do not multiply and they disappear and the servants who are the wealth of God and His Majesty disappear...
> And so the mestizos and *cholos*[20] multiply in this kingdom.]

Given that the Indians are the ones who pay tribute, Poma can back up his moral outrage with a purely economic argument. If the Indians fail to reproduce and their towns are depopulated, the King will lose their tribute: "Y ací se uan acauando los yndios deste rreyno y se acauarán y perderá su Magestad su rreyno" [And so all the Indians of this kingdom will disappear and His Majesty will lose his kingdom, 550].

In a more sophisticated rhetorical move, Poma repudiates the Spaniards' abuses—and, indeed, their very presence—in Peru, by appealing to the Spaniards' own ideas about blood purity. Poma's familiarity with these ideas, and his reliance on them to make his argument, suggests their currency in the very different racial context of the New World. In a daring move, Poma equates the Spaniards in the New World with the Moors or the Jews they themselves persecuted in Spain, as consummate outsiders. In a linguistic aside, he succinctly demolishes Spanish claims to primacy in the Americas, by showing how, for the native peoples, a foreigner is a foreigner. "Como dicen *uira cocha* le llaman en común al castellano estrangero, judío, moro, turco, ynglés y francés, que todos son españoles *uira cochas*" [The name *viracocha* they use generally for the Spanish "foreigner,"

Jew, Moor, Turk, Englishman, and Frenchman, for all are Spanish
viracochas, 96]. Note how devastating this list is: the Spaniards are
equated with not only the Jews and Moors from whom they try so hard
to distinguish themselves, but also the English and the French, their
imperial rivals. Poma thus introduces into the New World mix those
other Europeans that were so deftly excluded in the racial genealogies,
where "Spaniard," and not "white" or "European," stood at the apex.
Poma paints Peru as a world-upside-down, in which traditional pro-
prieties have been undone by the Conquista. The Spaniards themselves
participate in the unseemly dissolution of hierarchy:

> Que los dichos coregidores y padres o españoles y caualleros y los
> dichos caciques prencipales, ciendo señor de título desde sus antepasa-
> dos, se acienta en su mesa a comer y a conbidar y conuersar y beuer,
> jugar con personas figones y rrufianes y salteadores, ladrones, men-
> tirosos, ganapanes y borrachos, judíos y moros y con gente baja, yndios
> *mitayos*. Y a estos dichos descubren sus secretos y tienen conuersación
> con estos mestizos y mulatos y negros.
>   Y ancí hay en esta uida muy muchos dones y doñas de calauasas.
> (468–70)

> [For the magistrates and priests or Spaniards and knights and the prin-
> cipal Indian lords, legitimate lords since the time of their ancestors, sit
> down to eat and entertain and talk and drink and game with riffraff,
> ruffians, highwaymen, robbers, liars, laborers and drunkards, Jews and
> Moors and lowly persons, Indian menials. And they tell these people
> their secrets and converse with these mestizos and mulattos and blacks.
>   And so there are in this life many lords and ladies not worth a fig.]

The inclusion of Jews and Moors in this list is intriguing. Jews and
Moors in Peru—and it is clear that many *conversos*, at least, managed
to travel to the New World—certainly would not have openly pro-
fessed their identities, for the Inquisition soon followed in the conquistadors' footsteps.[21] They appear on this list, I would suggest, in
order to tap into a particularly Spanish sense of outrage. The conquest wreaks havoc not only with native hierarchies—an issue that
does not particularly concern the Spaniards—but with the general
social order. Mestizos are equated with Jews and Moors as the unclean
products of mixed blood. Poma applies the Peninsular obsession with
blood purity to the New World, arguing,

> El hombre tiene la culpa hazer hijo judío o mestizo y sus parientes tiene
> la culpa. Y ci fue el hombre gente baja o judío y la muger fue de la casa

de caualleros y de cristiano biejo, de todo se echa a perder, parientes y
linages y sus hijos, son de rruyn casta, peor que mestizo. (470)
[It's a man's fault if he has a Jewish or mestizo son, and it's his relatives'
fault. And even if the man was lowly or a Jew and the woman was of a
noble house and an Old Christian, everything is lost, relatives and
lineages and their children are of the lowliest class, worse than mestizos.]

Yet the passage ends on a curious note, as Poma demurs: "Aunque
sea negro o español o yndio, tiene que le honrre ci es caballero de título
desde sus antepasados y linajes" ["Whether he is Black, or Spanish, or
Indian, he should be honored if he is a legitimate lord since the time of
his ancestors and lineages" 470]. Poma seems more interested in status, and in keeping apart different peoples, than in any inherent notion
of European superiority. His racism, if we can call it that, is oddly
abstract, privileging purity rather than any particular hierarchy. Of
course, Poma is also quite sardonic when discussing the difficulty of
determining who has a clean lineage, especially at such a remove from
Spain: "que cómo se ha de sauer ci tiene mancha de un poco de judío
o moro u turco, englés" [for how is one to know if he is stained with a
bit of the Jew or Moor or Turk or Englishman, 878]. The only solution is loudly to proclaim one's own lineage: "Harto mejor es dezir que
soy cristiano biejo" [Much better to say I am an old Christian]. In the
chaos of colonial Peru, anyone may reinvent him or herself.

Poma's emphasis on the value of different races, as long as they are
kept apart, leads him to his most radical recommendation for redress,
as he claims that, "todo el mundo es de Dios y ancí Castilla es de los
españoles y las Yndias es de los yndios y Guenea es de los negros" [all
the world belongs to God and so Castile belongs to the Spaniards and
the Indies to the Indians and Guinea to the Blacks, 857]. In this
world view, the Jews and Moors, though persecuted, are oddly incorporated into Spain, where they are fittingly repressed by Spanish laws:
"Que uien puede ser esta ley porque un español al otro español,
aunque sea judío o moro, son españoles, que no se entremete a otra
nación cino que son españoles de Castilla" [For this law may well
exist, for a Spaniard [rules] another Spaniard—even if a Jew or a
Moor, they are Spaniards, for he is not intruding into another nation
for they are Spaniards from Castile]. In a provocative move, Poma
now insists on the common origins of both Jews and Spaniards, the
better to emphasize the Indians' difference:

Conzedera que la nació de español fue judío: Aunque tubieron otro ley
y tubieron letra y trage, áuito y rrostro, barbas, cudicia, aunque fueron

gentiles deferencia en el sacrificio, los judíos conocieron muy de ueras
a Dios y tubieron ley de Muyzén y mandamiento. Lo qual no las
tubieron los yndios su ley ni áuito ni rrostro ni letra. (882)

[Consider that the Spaniard's nation was once Jewish: even though they
had another law, they had letters and costume and appearance, beards
and cupidity; although they had a different ritual, the Jews knew God
very well and had Moses' law and commandments. Which the Indians
did not have, neither the law nor the costume, nor the appearance nor
the letters.]

Poma describes a Judeo-Christian continuum that by no means
includes the Andean peoples, even though he had earlier argued for
their Christianity. The separation of the races, despite their religious
similarities, becomes his principal goal. Thus Poma manipulates the
Spaniard's own racial ideology, in often contradictory terms, in order
to emphasize the outrage of their presence in Peru. In his most
impassioned moments, he goes as far as to equate them with Jews and
Moors, if only to underscore the disorder that they represent in an
Andean polity.

Poma offers the King a grand solution: native rulers for each of the
four parts of the globe, with Philip III himself as monarch of the
whole world, ruling over them. Again, racial differences organize his
thinking, as he nominates his own son, who he claims is a descendant
of the Incas, to rule over Peru, and proposes a "Black prince of
Guinea," the "King of the Christians in Rome," and the "Great Turk,
King of the Moors," for their respective lands (889). (Where the Jews
would be located in this scheme, we are never told.) Poma's solution
is not as fanciful or utopian as might at first appear: it recalls older
models of coexistence between Moors and Spaniards within Spain,
and reflects contemporary progressive Spanish ideas for the restitution of the Incas.[22] It also echoes the Hapsburgs' self-presentation as
universal rulers. Presumably this model would entail some kind of
parallel state, with Spaniards ruling over Spaniards and the Incas over
the indigenous peoples (and perhaps mestizos?). But Poma's formulation depends above all on the conscious refraction of Spanish racial
ideology, as it operated within Spain, in a powerful argument for the
separation of the races and against any kind of interracial unions in
Peru.

It is not my aim here to indict Poma as a racist, but instead to show
how he manipulates and mimics the Spaniards' own construction of
racial categories. His emphasis on the separation of races that are, the-
oretically at least, equal in his scheme, suggests that his is a strategic

racism that harnesses Spanish prejudice to an anticolonialist cause. (It must be said, however, that his discussion of blacks in the text is often far less sophisticated and more straightforwardly prejudiced.[23]) What I find particularly interesting as a theoretical and methodological point is Poma's general refusal of hybridity, and his equation of it with the disappearance of Andean cultural forms. His uncompromising rejection offers an important corrective to the critical fascination with creolization, *métissage*, and other variants of hybridity, an attraction that bears closer investigation.

HYBRIDITY AND ITS DISCONTENTS

Postcolonial theory is largely responsible for the wholesale reevaluation of culture that has attuned us to the prevalence of hybrid forms and persons in the wake of European expansion. In the early modern period, critics have become fascinated with such hybrid figures as the mestizo Inca Garcilaso de la Vega, the Morisco Leo Africanus, the exiled Spanish Jew Leone Hebreo, and, of course, Guaman Poma himself. The centrality of hybridity in cultural theory stems from the Bakhtinian notion of linguistic hybridity—the "mixture of two social languages within the limits of a single utterance"—which already implies a contestatory, dialectical interaction.[24] Bakhtin prioritizes this deliberate, challenging hybridity, but recognizes also a more inert version, an "unintentional, unconscious hybridization" akin to creolization or the merging of cultures.[25] Yet, as I shall suggest, this distinction between intentional and "organic" hybridity is itself problematic.

Bakhtin's concept of intentional hybridity, crucial for deconstruction, has been productively expanded to the colonial sphere, most notably by Homi K. Bhabha. In his seminal essay, "Signs Taken for Wonders" Bhabha extols the force of hybridity as a means of subversion.[26] While hybridity, he argues, "is the sign of the productivity of the colonial power," it also fundamentally destabilizes that power's discourse of authority: "[hybridity] unsettles the mimetic or narcissistic demands of colonial power but reimplicates its identifications in strategies of subversion that turn the gaze of the discriminated back upon the eye of power." Hybridity thus "enables a form of subversion, founded on the undecidability that turns the discursive conditions of dominance into the grounds of intervention."[27] As Robert Young has argued, both intentional hybridity (in Bakhtin's initial formulation or Bhabha's deconstructive version) and organic hybridity, with its fusion and recombination, are central to a contestatory cultural politics. Hybridity "works simultaneously in two ways: 'organically', hegemonizing, creating new spaces, structures, scenes, and 'intentionally', diasporizing, intervening as a form of subversion, translation, transformation."[28] In this analysis, hybridity is granted a tremendous power of progressive cultural transformation, despite what Young notes are its heterosexist biases—biases clearly evinced by the *casta* paintings that I discussed above.

This dialectical account of the power of hybridity sheds an interesting light on the *Nueva corónica*. Whatever its author's claims, Poma's highly critical text is the product of a hybrid culture and a hybrid subject: Felipe Guaman Poma de Ayala writes in Spanish and Quechua, combining Spanish genres and Andean beliefs. He bases his authority partly on his own cultural hybridity: his Christianization via an actual mestizo and his literacy in Spanish. And he writes in a world marked by "organic" hybridity, not only as a result of the Spanish conquest but also of the earlier Inca empire, the Tawantinsuyu. Even within the Andean world, that is, cultural purity—as opposed to some sort of purely indigenous hybridity—is never really an alternative.[29] Nonetheless, Poma argues stridently for the separation of peoples and cultures as the only way to ensure cultural survival, and generally espouses racial purity despite the intentional hybridity of his own voice. The urgency of Poma's claims raises some rather uncomfortable questions about our own fascination with hybridity: what is lost when we emphasize the constructedness and choice involved in cultural identity? In our critical celebration, are we not surreptitiously imposing a Western regard for the self-fashioning subject on other cultures, or romanticizing the effects of colonialism? What does a hybrid culture sacrifice? To whom does it appeal? Who controls the terms of its hybridity? As I suggest below, these questions are especially pressing for the Andean nations that inherited the long-term effects of the abuses that Poma catalogues.

In the case of these Latin American nations, the cultural construction of *mestizaje* challenges the critical distinctions between intentional and organic hybridity. As J. Jorge Klor de Alva points out, the meanings of *mestizaje* "have always been politically charged and . . . have always held a culturally ambiguous place in nation-building projects throughout the American hemisphere."[30] Our conceptual map of hybridity now looks very different. No longer do the distinctions between intentional and organic seem as clear-cut, for what Bakhtin views as an inert, organic melding can in fact be culturally manipulated to take on a broad range of political meanings. As Klor de Alva argues, the celebration of *mestizaje*—the specific version of "organic" hybridity that Poma rejects—is central to Latin American nationalist discourse:

> Throughout much of the core of Spanish America, however, a glorified memory of local precontact states, especially in the eighteenth- and early nineteenth-century criollo imaginations, led numerous members of the controlling sector, who nonetheless disparaged the mixed and unmixed descendants of the original natives, to identify themselves as legitimate heirs of the ancient indigenous empires. And in our century, claims to authentic ethnic (and moral) precedence over the conquering Europeans, made by those who identified themselves as *indígenas* (indigenes), transformed Amerindian symbols and cultural practices into critical building-blocks for many nation-building narratives defining modern nation-state identities.[31]

Yet these narratives of idealized *mestizaje* have in fact displaced any real progress for indigenous and subaltern peoples within the framework of the creole state. The glorification of *mestizaje* does as little for actual mestizos as the state promotion of a stylized "Indianness" does for the remnants of indigenous populations.[32]

Obviously, I do not mean to suggest that we should romanticize cultural purity as an alternative to *mestizaje*. This is especially fraught in the case of Latin America, where the very category of the "Indian" is part of the colonialist legacy.[33] And the quest for an essentialized pure alternative to hybridity seems as misguided as it is futile. As scholars have pointed out, it is much easier to identify what is hybrid than its opposite.[34] Yet I do think that we need to interrogate further the concept of hybridity, and to be more careful in our own (un)critical celebration of it.

Part of the reevaluation is conceptual. One important corrective comes from Anthony Easthope, who, in a wholesale critique of Bhabha's version of hybridity makes the important point, following Ernesto Laclau, that "no single ethical or political consequence such as the end of hierarchy is *necessarily* imposed by openness to alterity."[35] Easthope's larger critique tars Bhabha's deconstructive analysis of the colonial scene with the same brush as deconstruction itself, arguing that ambiguity or indeterminacy in themselves offer no solution to the dilemmas of identity.

A second important dimension of this reevaluation has to do with the scope of the term hybridity. As we have seen, within Latin America the local variant—*mestizaje*—has taken on a range of complex and often contradictory political meanings in the centuries since the Conquista. In general, the individual and collective lived experiences of *mestizo* subjects bear little relation to the often hyperbolic exaltation of the term in national discourses. Moreover, the term is often used as a shorthand for an achieved transformation instead of an ongoing cultural and political struggle. From within Latin American Studies, Antonio Cornejo Polar passionately argues that the emphasis on *mestizaje* celebrates a "falaz armonía" [fallacious harmony]:[36]

> el concepto de mestizaje, pese a su tradición y prestigio es el que falsifica de una manera más drástica la condición de nuestra cultura y literatura.En efecto lo que hace es ofrecer imagenes armónicas de lo que obviamente es desgajado y beligerante, proponiendo figuraciones que en el fondo sólo son pertinentes a quienes conviene imaginar nuestras sociedades como tersos y nada conflictivos espacios de convivencia.

> [the concept of *mestizaje*, despite its tradition and prestige, is the one that most drastically falsifies the state of our culture and literature. What it in fact does is to offer harmonious images of what is obviously frayed and belligerent, suggesting figurations that are only relevant for those who benefit from imagining our societies as smooth and non-conflictive spaces of coexistence.]

Cornejo Polar's denunciation suggests what might be our own stake in romanticizing the processes of cultural contact and declaring them resolved through hybridity. It is not only the powerful elites in Latin America that manipulate notions of hybridity; scholars within the Western acedemy also misuse the concept, albeit unwittingly, in ways that paper over social rifts that are far from resolved.

The point then is not to take Poma's recommendations for racial separateness at face value, or to read his mimicry of Peninsular racism as an implicit acknowledgment of its merit. The dangers of essentialism are far greater than anything I have described in this critique. Instead, it behooves us to recognize the unevenness of the mix in hybridization—the power differentials, the uneven distribution of agency, the selective preservation of certain cultural forms over others—and, most importantly, the uses and abuses of hybridity in diverse cultural arenas.

NOTES

1. In "The Iberian Roots of American Racist Thought" (*William and Mary Quarterly* 54.1 [Jan. 1997]: 143–166), James H. Sweet traces "the foundations of racism in modern Western thought," but focuses almost exclusively on prejudice against black Africans. Inexplicably, "limpieza de sangre" is barely mentioned.

2. *Documentos notariales referentes a los moriscos 1569–1571*, coll. Nicolás Cabrillana from the Archivo Histórico Provincial de Almería (Granada: Universidad de Granada, 1978). The reference to "membrillo cocho" ("cooked quince") is from Document 304, the others are repeated throughout the collection.

3. Manuel Alvar, *Léxico del mestizaje en Hispanoamérica* (Madrid: Ediciones Cultura Hispánica, Instituto de Cooperación Iberoamericana, 1987), 73.

4. Deborah Root, "Speaking Christian: Orthodoxy and Difference in Sixteenth-Century Spain," *Representations*, 23 (Summer 1988): 118–134.

5. On *limpieza*, see Henry Kamen, *Inquisition and Society in Spain in the Sixteenth and Seventeenth Centuries* (Bloomington: Indiana University Press, 1985); Julio Caro Baroja, *Los judíos en la España moderna y contemporánea*, 3 vols. (Madrid: Istmo, 1978); Albert Sicroff, *Los estatutos de limpieza de sangre: Controversias entre los siglos XV y XVII*, Mauro Armiño, trans. (Madrid: Taurus, 1985); and Antonio Domínguez Ortiz, *Las clases privilegiadas en el Antiguo Régimen* (Madrid: Istmo, 1973).

6. See my *Passing for Spain: Cervantes and the Fictions of Identity* (Urbana: University of Illinois Press, 2003).

7. Elizabeth Anne Kuznesof, "Ethnic and Gender Influences on 'Spanish' Creole Society in Colonial Spanish America," *Colonial Latin American Review*, 4.1 (1995): 153–176.

8. Stuart B. Schwartz, "Colonial Identities and the *Sociedad de Castas*," *Colonial Latin American Review*, 4:1 (1995): 188.

9. Schwartz, "Colonial Identities," 186.

10. On the contradiction between legal and social status, see Magnus Mörner, *Race Mixture in the History of Latin America* (Boston: Little, Brown & Co., 1967), 60–62.

11. On the casta paintings, see the catalog for the Americas Society Art Gallery 1996 exhibit, *New World Orders: Casta Painting and Colonial Latin America*, Ilona Katzew, curator (New York: Americas Society, 1996), especially Katzew's essay, "Casta Painting: Identity and Social Stratification in Colonial Mexico," and J. Jorge Klor de Alva, "*Mestizaje* from New Spain to Aztlán: On the Control and Classification of Collective Identities."

12. Mörner, *Race Mixture*, 45.

13. By implicitly whitening the *castiza* women who marry Spaniards, the *casta* paintings provide evidence for Kuznesof's claim that gender crucially affected racial categorizations.

14. The term was coined by Alejandro Lipschütz, in his *El indoamericanismo y el problema racial en las Américas* (Santiago de Chile: Nascimento, 1944), second edition.

15. Mörner, *Race Mixture*, 58 cites a royal decree prohibiting the use of the term.

16. For the visual dimension of Poma's text, see Mercedes López Baralt, *Guaman Poma, autor y artista* (Lima: Fondo Editorial de la Pontificia Universidad Católica del Perú, 1993).

17. See Rolena Adorno, *Guaman Poma: Writing and Resistance in Colonial Peru* (Austin: University of Texas Press, 1986).

18. Felipe Guaman Poma de Ayala [Waman Puma], *El primer nueva corónica y buen gobierno*, critical ed. John V. Murra and Rolena Adorno, trans. and textual analysis of Quechua Jorge L. Urioste (Mexico: Siglo Veintiuno, 1980), 4. All references are to this edition and appear in the text by page number only. Translations are my own.

19. For the problems of clerical misbehavior and its implications for the newly converted Andean population, see Kenneth Mills, "Bad Christians in Colonial Peru," *Colonial Latin American Review*, 5:2 (1996): 183–218.

20. *Cholo* may mean variously mestizo, descendant of a mulatto, or descendant of a black and an Indian (Alvar, *Lexico*, 128–129).

21. For the persecution of New Christians in the New World, see *The Jewish Experience in Latin America: Selected Studies from the Publications of the American Jewish Historical Society*, ed. Martin A. Cohen (New York: Ktav, 1971), 2 vols.; and Martin A. Cohen, *The Martyr: The Story of a Secret Jew and the Mexican Inquisition in the Sixteenth Century* (Philadelphia: The Jewish Publication Society of America, 1973).

22. Adorno, "Colonial Reform or Utopia? Guaman Poma's Empire of the Four Parts of the World," *Amerindian Images and the Legacy of Columbus*, eds. René Jara and Nicholas Spadaccini (Minneapolis: University of Minnesota Press, 1992), 357–358.

23. For a survey of Poma's attitude toward blacks in the *Nueva corónica*, see J. P. Tardieu, "L'Integration des noirs dans le discours de Felipe Guaman Poma de Ayala," *Revue du CERC*, 4 (1987): 40–60.

24. M. M. Bakhtin, *The Dialogic Imagination: Four Essays*, trans. Caryl Emerson and Michael Holquist (Austin: University of Texas Press, 1981), 358. For the hybridity of Bakhtin's own notion, see Robert J. C. Young, *Colonial Desire: Hybridity in Theory, Culture and Race* (London: Routledge, 1995).

25. Bakhtin, *The Dialogic Imagination*, 358; Young, *Colonial Desire*, 21.

26. Homi K. Bhabha, "Signs Taken for Wonders: Questions of Ambivalence and Authority under a Tree outside Delhi, May 1817," *Race, Writing and Difference*, ed. Henry Louis Gates, *Critical Inquiry*, 12:1 (1985): 144–165. The essay is reprinted in Bhabha's *The Location of Culture* (London: Routledge, 1994), from which I cite.

27. Bhabha, *The Location of Culture*, 112.

28. Young, *Colonial Desire*, 25.

29. For the relations between Cusco and the provinces colonized by the Incas, in comparison to Spanish practices, see Irene Silverblatt, *Moon, Sun, and Witches: Gender Ideologies and Class in Inca and Colonial Peru* (Princeton: Princeton University Press, 1987) and her later article,

"Becoming Indian in the Central Andes of Seventeenth-Century Peru," in *After Colonialism: Imperial Histories and Postcolonial Displacements*, ed. Gyan Prakash (Princeton: Princeton University Press, 1995), 279–298.

30. J. Jorge Klor de Alva, "The Postcolonization of the (Latin) American Experience: A Reconsideration of 'Colonialism,' 'Postcolonialism,' and 'Mestizaje,'" in *After Colonialism*, 243.

31. J. Jorge Klor de Alva, "The Postcolonization of the (Latin) American Experience," 243–244.

32. On the cultural uses of the "pure Indian," Michael Taussig writes: "But while the phantom figure of the pure Indian becomes the object of desire by the First World, that same Indian tends to be the cause of unease if not the object of erasure in the Third World—as in Guatemala, to cite a well-known instance—no matter how much a certain style of Indianness may be appropriated and promoted by the State in the designs on the currency, a concern for archaelogy, and in the promotion of weavings by Indian women for tourism" (*Mimesis and Alterity: A Particular History of the Senses* [New York: Routledge, 1993], 142–143).

33. J. Jorge Klor de Alva, "The Postcolonization of the (Latin) American Experience," 248–249. See also Silverblatt, "Becoming Indian," which explores the process by which "Spaniards tried to make 'Indians' out of Andeans" (279).

34. As Alan Sinfield points out, "it is quite hard to envisage a culture that is not hybrid" ("Diaspora and Hybridity: Queer Identities and the Ethnicity Model," *Textual Practice*, 10:2 (Summer 1996), 278.

35. Anthony Easthope, "Bhabha, Hybridity and Identity," *Textual Practice*, 12:2 (Summer 1998): 346.

36. Antonio Cornejo Polar, "Mestizaje e hibridez: los riesgos de las metáforas. Apuntes," *Revista de Crítica Literaria Latinoamericana*, 22:47 (1998): 8. My translation.

ANGELLS IN AMERICA

Karen Ordahl Kupperman

On the morning of March 22, 1622 in a highly coordinated attack, the Pamunkey Indians of Virginia and their allies fell upon the English settlements that had been spreading alarmingly on both sides of the James River for the preceding four years and wiped out or took captive about a third of the English population. Edward Waterhouse in London compiled the official Virginia Company account of the "Barbarous Massacre in the time of peace and League" out of the letters and personal reports that made their way home. The reports affirmed that the "utter extirpation" of the English had been the Pamunkeys' goal, "which God of his mercy (by the meanes of some of themselves converted to Christianitie) prevented." The planters had encouraged "daily familiarity" with their American neighbors "for the desire we had of effecting that great master-peece of workes, their conversion. And by this meanes that fatall Friday morning, there fell under the bloudy and barbarous hands of that perfidious and inhumane people, contrary to all lawes of God and men, of Nature and Nations, three hundred forty seven men, women, and children, most by their owne weapons; and not being content with taking away life alone, they fell after againe upon the dead, making as well as they could, a fresh murder, defacing, dragging, and mangling the dead carkasses into many pieces, and carrying some parts away in derision, with base and bruitish triumph." Robert Beverly argued that the Pamunkeys' reason for trying to destroy all the English was to leave "none behind to bear Resentment."

"Lyons and Dragons . . . (as Histories record)" have spared their benefactors, but "these miscreants . . . put on a worse and more then unnaturall bruitishnesse" and killed those who had been kindest to them. The worst example was the fate of "that worthy religious Gentleman, Master George Thorpe."[1] George Thorpe, M. P. and gentleman of the king's privy chamber, had gone to Virginia in March 1620 to inaugurate an Indian college and a program of religious conversion. The context of the college plan was the Virginia Company's reorganization in 1618 and the offer of land to all prospective planters. With tobacco established as a cash crop, that land was valuable and the settlers spread over the terrain in wave after wave.

A call went out from the bishops, and pious donors in England contributed £1,500. The money, combined with Virginia Company allotments, financed a 10,000-acre plantation at Henrico to be worked by fifty servants, with the proceeds going to support the college. Indian children, backers hoped, would come to board at the college and experience total immersion in English culture; trade goods, judiciously distributed, would encourage parents to send their children. John Rolfe, back in Virginia after his wife Pocahontas's death in England, reassured Virginia Company backers: "The Indyans very loving, and willing to parte with their childeren. My wives death is much lamented; my childe much desyred . . ." Young Thomas Rolfe had been left in England.[2]

William Strachey, colony secretary, had urged "that holie Cause" of conversion in his *Historie of Travell into Virginia Britania*, which circulated in manuscript from 1612. Playing on the theme that the Americans resembled England's Anglo-Saxon ancestors, and punning on the resemblance between "Angles" and "Angels," he wrote:

> Wild as they are, accept them, so were we,
> To make them civill, will our honour bee,
> And if good workes be the effects of mindes
> That like good Angells be, let our designes
> As we are Angli, make us Angells too
> No better work can Church or statesman doe.[3]

As Waterhouse wrote, Thorpe "did so truly and earnestly affect their conversion, and was so tender over them, that whosoever under his authority had given them but the least displeasure or discontent, he punished them severely. He thought nothing too deare for them." Thorpe himself described his strategy in a letter home to Virginia Company leader Sir Edwin Sandys. He would teach first from "the booke of the worlde as beinge nearest to theire sence," and he expected "the winning of them by degrees." He was pleased to see that the Powhatans "begin more and more to affect English ffassions." As they "wilbe much alured to affect us by giftes," Thorpe hoped the

Virginia Company would send apparell and "househouldestufe" for them, "I meane the Kinges." Colony secretary John Pory wrote home that "the cominge hither of that vertuous Gentleman Capt Thorpe, was to us in many respects as of an Angell from heaven.... I pray god send more like unto him."[4]

Waterhouse wrote that Thorpe had especially favored the Pamunkey leader, Opechancanough, spent time with him, and gave him presents. "And whereas this king before dwelt onely in a cottage, or rather a denne or hog-stye, made with a few poles and stickes, and covered with mats after their wyld manner, to civilize him, he first, built him a fayre house according to the English fashion, in which hee tooke such joy, especially in his locke and key, which hee so admired, as locking and unlocking his doore an hundred times a day, hee thought no device in all the world was comparable to it."

Thorpe talked often with Opechancanough about Christianity and "the Pagan confessed, moved by naturall Principles, that our God was a good God, and better much then theirs, in that he had with so many good things above them endowed us." Thorpe replied that if Opechancanough would "serve our God, hee should bee partaker of all those good things wee had."

Pious promoters argued that Virginia's early troubles were God's judgment on the colony for neglecting the work of conversion. As Thorpe wrote, "God is displeased with us, that wee doe not as we ought to doe, take his service alonge with us by our serious endevours of converting the Heathen that live rounde about us." The Reverend Patrick Copland, minister with the East India Company ship the Royall James, collected over £70 at the Cape of Good Hope for the work of conversion in Virginia. He brought the money to London and, in his subsequent sermon before the Virginia Company, he preached that in Virginia, that "Heathen-now Christian Kingdome," "all difficulties are swallowed up." God had "sayd to the destroying angel, It is sufficient, hold now thy hand." Virginia historian Robert Beverly, writing at the end of the seventeenth century, said the colonists had begun "to think themselves the happiest People in the World."

Ironically Copland's sermon, on April 18, 1622, was delivered just a month after the great attack, news of which had not yet arrived in London; his claim that "the feare of killing each other is now vanished away" would soon be proven hollow. Moreover, the easy assumptions behind the conversion campaign would also soon be overthrown.[5] The Pamunkeys were said to have expressed great love and admiration for Thorpe, yet on that morning in March 1622, "they not only wilfully murdered him, but cruelly and felly, out of devillish malice, did so many barbarous despights and foule scornes after to his dead corpes, as are unbefitting to be heard by any civill eare." By these events, Waterhouse wrote, Thorpe had earned a glorious martyr's crown, but the Pamunkeys would now feel God's "justice" rather than his bounteous love.[6]

Although Waterhouse stressed the unreasoning bestiality of the attack, he also supplied the reason for it: The "true cause of this sur-prize was most by the instigation of the Devill, (enemy to their salvation) and the dayly feare that possest them, that in time we by our growing continually upon them, would dispossesse them of this Country, as they had beene formerly of the West Indies by the Spaniard." He recorded the spreading out of the plantations in various directions "as a choyce veyne of rich ground invited them."

Those fears would now be realized. Waterhouse argued, as did many in Virginia, that the colonists' hands had previously been tied "with gentleness and faire usage," but were now "set at liberty by the treacherous violence of the Savages." They could now "invade the Country, and destroy them who sought to destroy us." They could then "enjoy their cultivated places ... possessing the fruits of others labours." Captured Pamunkeys "may now most justly be compelled to servitude and drudgery."[7]

The great surprise attack of 1622 and its transformative effect on the English settlements and their relations with all Indians in Virginia is well known to modern readers. This essay is, in part, an attempt to explore how it would have been read by contemporaries. An early modern English audience might have made different connections than our contemporaries do, as these accounts paralleled so exactly Tacitus's account of the revolt of the ancient Britons against their civ-ilizing Roman masters. In his analysis, it was the Romans' turn to milder seductive ways that provoked the greatest rebellion. Tacitus's *Life of Julius Agricola* was translated into English for the first time in the 1590s, and historians and national leaders argued strongly that it contained important lessons for early modern descendants of the Britons.

Cornelius Tacitus was a Roman senator, a consul, and a provincial governor. Though he is best known for his *Histories* and his *Annals*, chronicling events at the center of power in Rome, Tacitus's first books dealt with the empire's margins. He wrote of the conquest of Britain through his biography of his father-in-law Julius Agricola, gov-ernor of the Roman colony in Britain, and he wrote an ethnographic account of the Germans; both manuscripts are dated to +98 and both offer an oblique commentary on the evolving imperial state in Rome. Authentic manuscripts of both books were uncovered and published in the fifteenth century.[8]

Like English writers who promoted American colonialism, Tacitus presented the Britons as ripe for incorporation in the civilizing mission of Rome: "The Britans endure levies of men and money and all other burdens imposed by the Empire patiently and willingly if insolencies be forborne, indignities they cannot abide, being already subdued as to be subjects, but not to be slaves." But a series of weak rulers caused the Britons to consider the creeping encroachments of the Romans and how their own patience had yielded nothing but greater burdens. Leaders argued that the Romans "had nothing to moove them to warre, but their owne covetousnesse and wanton lust: and that they would doubtlesse depart, as Caesar Julius had done, if the Britans would imitate the vertues of their progenitours." They resolved "to take arms under the conduct of Voadica (marg. Beodicia or Boudicca) a lady of the blood of their Kings: for in matter of governing in chiefe they make no distinction of sexe." They attacked "the seate of their slaverie: in sacking whereof no kinde of crueltie was omitted, which either anger or the rage of victorie might induce a barbarous people to practise."

Agricola was sent to lead the Roman presence in Britain in the continuing conflict after Boudicca's revolt. Like George Thorpe in Virginia, he sought to lure the conquered Britons to peaceful ways, "to induce them by pleasures to quietnesse and rest," beginning with a program of building "temples, and houses, and places of publicke resort." Educating carefully chosen children was central to both men's plans. Of Agricola, Tacitus wrote, "the noble mens sonnes he tooke and instructed in the liberall sciences" and found them now "curious to attaine the eloquence of the Roman language." At the same time, just as the Chesapeake Algonquians began "to affect English ffassions," the Britons took up wearing the toga. This campaign was, as Tacitus wrote, "a most profitable and polliticke devise."

Young men among the colonized were enticed into civility/docility through education. Women were seduced in other ways. Although British women were not "violently forced as in open hostilitie," they were "under the colour and title of guests often abused" by the Romans. Pocahontas, a child of ten or eleven when Jamestown was founded, had befriended the straggling settlers. Her father, Powhatan, employed her as go-between as did the plantation's leaders, and Captain John Smith was convinced that she had saved the infant colony. As Pocahontas became a woman and warfare between English and Indians became endemic, she moved away from Jamestown and cut her ties with the English. Her whereabouts were discovered quite by accident when Captain Samuel Argall, conducting one of the settlers' ever more widely ranging quests for corn, discovered her among the Patowomekes on the Potomac River. Argall captured her, but not by force; rather he employed the implicit threat that underlay friendship. Argall approached Iopassus, brother and subchief under "the great king Patowomeke" and a man whom Argall considered "an old friend, and adopted brother." Argall told Iopassus that he must "betray Pokahuntis unto my hands" or their friendship would end. Iopassus, acting with the consent of the Patawomeke chief and his council, then devised a ruse through which Pocahontas was tricked onto Argall's ship and into his hands. In this way all the Patawomeke leaders learned the costs of civility and friendship. And Iopassus's malleability aroused contempt rather than gratitude among his English friends.[9]

Pocahontas lived the rest of her life among the English. Governor Sir Thomas Dale personally undertook her conversion with the support of the Reverend Alexander Whitaker and finally, after he "had laboured along time," Pocahontas "renounced publickly her countrey Idolatry" and "openly confessed her Christian faith."[10] Her conversion was followed by her marriage to John Rolfe and the birth of their son Thomas. When the Rolfes went to England, they were accompanied by Uttamattamakin (aka Tomocomo), leading priest among the Powhatans and Pocahontas's brother-in-law, and several men and women of high rank. After her death many of her attendants remained in England. One man went to live with George Thorpe; his parish register records the baptism of Georgius Thorpe and his burial as Homo Virginae just over two weeks later in 1619. Thorpe's biographer points out that in giving his own name to his "Virginian boy" Thorpe emulated the ancient Roman custom.[11]

Powhatan accepted Pocahontas's marriage, but absolutely refused when governor Dale, having heard "the bruite of the exquisite perfection of your yongest daughter," asked for a second daughter for himself. In his reply Powhatan turned the language of friendship back upon the English: "I holde it not a brotherly part of your King, to desire to bereave me of two of my children at once." Powhatan did release William Parker, an Englishman who had been held by him, and insisted that Dale compensate him by sending a long list of tools; he also insisted that Ralph Hamor, Dale's ambassador on this occasion, write down his requirements.[12]

The centrality of goods, possessions, in the civilizing process is remarkably similar in the ancient and early modern cases. The book of the world, the lure of superior products, was frankly presented as the main attraction of the civilized world. Moreover, greater material possessions lured potential converts to Christianity; missionaries promised things, commodities, to those who believed in God sincerely. Two months before the Virginia attack, the governor and council wrote home to the company that Opechancanough had "confessed" to George Thorpe "that god loved us better then them." But whereas Thorpe and his contributors earnestly believed that they brought only a better life to the Americans, Tacitus's understanding of the meaning of this cultural transformation was more frank and profound: "...and so by little and little they proceeded to those provocations of vices, to sumptuous galleries, and bathes, and exquisite banquettings; which things the ignorant termed civilitie, being indeede a point of their bondage."[13]

Simplicity, even poverty, could mean a kind of independence, as Indians sometimes pointed out. Moreover, they could turn the language of friendship against the English. Powhatan told Captain John Smith in his "discourse of peace and warre" that if the Jamestown colonists pressed the Pamunkeys too hard, the Indians would simply "hide our provisions and fly to the woods." If they did that they would be uncomfortable, "forced to lie cold in the woods, feede upon Acornes, rootes, and such trash," but they would survive. The English, for their part, would "famish by wronging us your friends".[14] Later, in New England, in the heat of King Philip's War, Nipmucks left a note pinned to a tree at Medfield that made the same point. The Indians, with "nothing but our lives to loose," could go on fighting as long as necessary, but the English were tied to their possessions—"many fair houses cattell & much good things"—which they would lose in protracted warfare.[15]

English promoters allowed themselves to make easy assumptions about their enterprise and seemed quite comfortable with the association of commodities and Christianity. The Reverend Patrick Copland, urging on the Virginia Company to greater conversion efforts, assured his listeners that "when you advance religion, you advance together with it Your owne profit."[16] In reality commercial relations marred the image of an uplifting mission through which naive virtue would be perfected by civility. Tacitus wrote of the Germans, "we have taught them also to receive money." Colonists introduced the Americans to the concept of a medium of exchange, and converted native wampum, spiritually charged and emblematic beads, to a form of currency. William Bradford described how Dutch entrepreneurs from the colony of New Netherland began the transformation that was soon taken up by the English; "And strange it was to see the great alteration it made in a few years among the Indians themselves."[17]

Puns linking the antique gold coin known as an angel to the elevating/corrupting power of money were common on the English stage, as was representation of America as a source to be mined for riches. Falstaff, in Shakespeare's *The Merry Wives of Windsor*, couched his aspirations for the seduction of Mistress Ford and Mistress Page in these terms. Calling the two women his "East and West Indies," Falstaff claimed that Ford controlled her husbands's "legions of Angels." Mistress Page, he crowed, was "a Region in Guiana; all gold, and bountie!" and he went on, "I will be Cheater [escheator] to them both, and they shall be Exchequers to me."[18] Such rough talk about America's resources sat uneasily with promoters' claims that the lives of Americans would be enhanced when the new and old worlds were linked by merchandise. But both discursive lines put possessions in the forefront of the relationship.

Exchange of furs and other commodities was soon followed by transfer of lands, and American natives quickly saw loss of their planting and hunting territories coupled with threats to their traditional culture. As Agricola pushed the frontiers of Roman Britain farther and farther north in annual campaigns into Caledonia, "the Britans" united in resistance; their fate would be "revenge or servitude." Galgacus, "for vertue and birth of all the leaders the principall man," addressed the armies before battle, picturing the North Britons as the only people still "free from all contagion of tyrannie. Beyonde us is no lande, beside us none are free." Galgacus warned against attempting to placate the Romans "whose intollerable pride in vaine shall you seeke to avoide by service and humble behaviour: robbers of the world, that having now left no lande to be spoiled, search also the sea." Savile's translation of Tacitus presented his comment on imperial schemes and their civilizing mission in a classic statement of rhetorical redescription: "To take away by maine force, to kill and to spoile, falsely they terme Empire and government: when all is waste as a wildernesse, that they call peace."[19]

The English translation of Tacitus's *Agricola* frankly presented the extreme cruelty visited by the wronged and courageous British on the invading Romans. But in describing the Powhatan uprising in Virginia English writers adopted the Roman identity and denounced the "cruelty" and "savagery" of the Indians who had been forced, through the stripping of their land, into the ancient British role. For the Virginia Company the treatment of George Thorpe was testimony to the Americans' innate savagery, but Tacitus would have been able to explain the Indians' rejection of the "bondage" wrapped up inproferred "civility."

Tacitean wisdom, as redacted by Thomas Gainsford, offered a hard-headed statement on human relations: "It is the property of mans nature to hate those, whom they have hurtt."[20] Virginia Company strategists drew on Tacitus's *Life of Agricola* in planning their future relationship to the Virginia Algonquians. Rebellion, they thought, had been aroused not by harsh treatment but by leniency. Waterhouse, describing the complacence in which the colonists lived, summed up: "yet were the hearts of the English ever stupid." William Capps, an "ancient planter," wrote a year after the attack that "Thorp he hath brought such a misery upon us by letting th' Indians have their head and none must controll them."[21] Like Vectius Bolanus and other weak Roman leaders, the English, they asserted, had made the mistake of "governing in a gentler & milder manner, then was fit for so fierce a cuntrey."[22]

Strategies employed in the ensuing decade-long Anglo-Powhatan War derived from Tacitus. Waterhouse, pointing to the success of the Spanish, advocated forcing the Pamunkeys and their allies into their enemies' territories and then aiding those enemies. Quoting Tacitus, he argued that this tactic had allowed the Romans to conquer "this Iland of Great Britayne." As Savile's translation said, the Romans' best advantage lay in Britain's division into "partialities and factions" under "petty Princes." Rome, Waterhouse argued, "rose upon the backe of her enemies."[23]

Classical sources advocated matching the enemy's mode of war, even if that meant violating the precepts taught in European armies. Julius Caesar had written that his British foes "never fought thick and close together, but thin, and at great distances." Like the colonists' own British ancestors, the Indians were reported to have adopted a style of war by stealth in small groups rather than massed battles, and Gainsford counseled emulation: "Itt is requisite to match the enemy in the same manner of Fight, as he accewstometh, as if he devide the army into many battailes."[24]

Gainsford's observations from Tacitus also outlined the precise tactics the Virginia planters would employ: "Although the cawse of the greatest fear is want of provision in a cuntry wasted with wars: yet is itt sometimes pollecy to cutt of the storehowses of a province to procure famine; wherby dissentions may arise amongst the people, and so a way made open to the army intending to invade the same, or otherwise to suppress the insolency of rebells: so have I seen in Ireland their corne cutt down with our swordes."

Robert Beverly recorded how English Virginians employed this strategy in the decade of warfare following 1622. Because their efforts to pursue Pamunkeys, "who cou'd too dexterously hide themselves in the woods," were ineffective, the colonists chose to make "use of the Roman maxim (Faith is not to be kept with Hereticks) to obtain their ends" and "pretended Articles of Peace, giving them all manner of fair Words and Promises of Oblivion." Their goal was to "draw the Indians back, and intice them to plant their Corn on their Habitations nearest, adjoining, to the English; and then to cut it up when the Summer should be too far spent to leave them Hopes of another Crop that Year; by which Means they proposed to bring them to want Necessaries, and starve." This strategy was successful, according to Beverly, and gave the English "an Opportunity of repaying them some part of the Debt in their own Coin."[25]

As Virginians planned their response they preferred to forget another perspective Tacitus offered on the behavior of the ancient planters. Agricola put down rebellion in Britain, but he also dealt with the roots of discontent in exploitative Roman behavior: "armes avayle little to settle a new conquered state if injuries and wrongs be permitted." He disciplined his own people, "cutting away those pettie extortions" in the collecting of taxes, and regulating the food supply. The 1622 attack in Virginia provoked the investigation of the Virginia Company's record that ultimately led to revocation of its charter. But Virginia's becoming a royal colony ironically freed the settlers of oversight, and allowed them to use the government to support their own interests.[26]

After the recovery of Tacitus's works his writing occupied a central position in humanist scholarship. Nigel Smith places him at "the centre of the historiographical revolution of the early sixteenth century" from which his influence extended for centuries.[27] The popularity of Tacitus reached a peak as the sixteenth century gave way to the seventeenth. English readers found him uncannily relevant to their own concerns, and to the mixture of pride and fear with which they viewed developments in contemporary government and society and the economic activities of the new merchants tying England to the world. The perceived concentration of power at the court with its attendant flattery, manipulation, and corruption matched the picture of Tiberius's Rome in Tacitus's pages, which offered a warning of future decline.[28]

Riches earned through opening England to the world offered sophistication and variety that could easily degenerate, as in Rome, into mere novelty and luxury. Tacitus encapsulated the ambivalence with which English leaders looked forward to a stronger, richer, worldly nation.[29] American ventures played a large part in this set of expectations. England had taken a back seat to the Iberians and France in efforts to exploit the fabled treasure of America, but the period when the English rage for Tacitus began also saw the first tentative efforts to found a permanent English presence across the Atlantic. In fact America, both as place and as concept, offered thoughtful Tacitists unique ways of thinking about the problems the nation faced, and posed solutions to those problems.

In the sixteenth century's last decade, members of the newly formed Society of Antiquaries translated Tacitus into English, making his work widely available for the first time. William Camden emulated Tacitus's history of Rome in his *Annals* of the reign of Elizabeth. His colleagues Sir Henry Savile, Warden of Merton College, Oxford, and Provost of Eton, and Richard Greneway translated Tacitus's history of Rome and his *Life of Agricola* and *Germania*. Their work was published in one volume in 1598.[30] Historians in the Society of Antiquaries were joined by national leaders such as Francis Bacon and William Cecil in their interest in the study and dissemination of Tacitus's works; members of the Earl of Essex's circle were deeply involved in this enterprise in the 1590s.[31]

All this activity contributed to a growing body of thought with skeptical and neoStoic roots at a time when education was increasingly seen as necessary for a gentleman. A very high proportion of those who wrote about direct American experience in the founding decades of English colonies were university-educated men. Even those who had only grammar-school educations participated in the prevailing humanist mental world with its emphasis on study of the classics. Captain John Smith prepared himself for his chosen life by reading "Machiavills Art of warre, and Marcus Aurelius" under the tutelage of "Seignior Theadora Polaloga...a noble Italian Gentleman" at the Earl of Lincoln's Tattershall Castle, and he and his admirers compared Smith to Julius Caesar, who held "it no lesse honour to write, than fight." Some, like Smith, had spent time in Europe and the eastern Mediterranean. Writers sprinkled their books with Latin tags and references to classical authors.[32]

Among English scholars, Tacitus had special relevance because the recovery and popularity of his works paralleled the rise of the notion that the English were descended from the ancient Germans he described. And this association carried a powerful political message. America offered English Tacitists ways of thinking about the challenges facing England. One analytical line held that engagement in productive new world enterprises would allow the nation to achieve wealth and stability without the corruption and degeneration seen on the continent. Another implicitly argued that the English could better understand the sources of their own unique virtue and vigor by looking at the American Indians and their society through the lens of Tacitus's descriptions of the ancient Germans and Britons, the ancestors of the English nation whom the American natives seemed uncannily to resemble.[33] English descent from the virtuous barbarians described by Tacitus was a truism, summed up in Nathanael Carpenter's claim that the Britons and Germans were "little different from the present Americans." Tacitist Hugo Grotius argued that the Americans who lived north of Central America were actually descended from an ancient German migration.[34]

The idea that the Americans resembled the ancestors of early modern Europeans was not unique to English writers. Marc Lescarbot, writing about early French experience in Acadia, for example, said sedentary agriculturalists in America lived "just as the Germans in the time of Tacitus, who has described their ancient way of living." Moreover, it was the American Indian bands living by hunting and fishing, those "who have nothing of their own," who resembled most closely French forebears. "We have nothing to jest about, for our old Gallic ancestors did the same thing, and even dined from the skins of dogs and wolves, if Diodorus and Strabo tell the truth."[35]

But Tacitus's descriptions of the ancient Germans and Britons had particular resonance with English readers because, like the ancient hero Galgacus, they believed that they lived in the last free nation. Other European nations were equally descended from liberty-loving and virtuous Saxons and Celts, but continental nations had lost their way and had succumbed to absolute monarchy. Britain now stood in danger of absolutism as well. The program of bringing Tacitus to a wide audience in the early seventeenth century was designed to alert the political nation to the dangers of passivity in the face of deterioration in the provinces and concentration of power at the center. John Fletcher's play *Bonduca: Queene of Brittaine*, written in the 1610s, drew on Tacitus to present the story of British resistance to tyranny on the stage, as Thomas Middleton's contemporaneous *Hengist, King of Kent* dramatized the establishment of the Saxons and their traditions in England.[36]

The Saxons, as described by Tacitus, loved liberty and lived simply. They were governed by powerful chiefs, but chiefs who consulted their leading men before making any important decisions: "the Kings power is restrained, and not to do what he listeth." John Speed argued that among the Saxons, whom he called the strongest and most courageous of the Germans, the king's power was restricted by an ancient parliament of twelve nobles. This, according to the Tacitists, was the original model of English government; the witenagemot of "the Anglo-Saxons our ancestors," was "An assembly of the wise."[37] Specially trained orators persuaded leaders to action rather than forcing them through coercion. Colonial promoters such as Lord Saye and Sele sought a clear and separate role for the nobility in the contemporary English government and avidly read European interpreters of Tacitus. Saye would ultimately take a leading role in the resistance to Charles I.[38]

That the Angles and Saxons were progenitors of the peculiarly free British constitution became a commonplace of early modern discourse. Thomas Jefferson wrote that the "antient Saxon laws" were "the wisest and most perfect ever yet devised by the wit of man." John Adams, who was on the committee with Benjamin Franklin and Jefferson to design a Great Seal for the United States in August 1776, recorded that Jefferson suggested a two-sided medal: "The Children of Israel in the Wilderness, led by a Cloud by day, and a Pillar of Fire by night, and on the other Side Hengist and Horsa, the Saxon Chiefs, from whom We claim the Honour of being descended and whose Political Principles and Form of Government We have assumed."[39]

Virtue, personal and collective, was the foundation of Saxon society as described in the *Germania*. Selfishness and other vices were not tolerated or condoned, and hospitality was freely given. Germans thought first of the public good. The roles of both genders were regarded with respect and were carried out fully and well. Plain living eliminated covetousness.

In establishing the ancient Britons and Saxons as their true ancestors, the English rejected the once-accepted idea that they descended from Trojans who had come to Britain with their leader, Brutus.[40] In a further twist on these complicated inheritances, Thomas Morton argued that the American Indians were descended from Trojans. Some of the departing Trojans, Morton theorized, might have been scattered by storms at sea. Once out of sight of land and lacking a compass, "they might sayle God knoweth whether, and so might be put upon this Coast, as well as any other." Drawing on the common opinion that language was the best indicator of cultural origins, he argued that the Algonquians of southern New England used many words derived from Greek and Latin.[41]

The Trojan foundation myth had been propagated for England by Geoffrey of Monmouth in the twelfth century. The campaign to replace it with the Saxon story of English origins bore rapid and convincing results. As Gary Taylor has demonstrated, late sixteenth-century drama was full of the image of the English as "Troynovant," but no writer who emerged in the early seventeenth century employed this reference. Moreover, through plays such as Middleton's *Hengist*, the Saxons came to be celebrated on the stage.[42]

In rejecting the Trojan myth, the protestant English sought to strip away associations with the corruption of the Medieval church. Many argued instead for an apostolic foundation for the English church, and an unbroken, though hidden, religious tradition that had persisted throughout the period of Roman Catholic dominance only to reemerge when the Welsh, therefore British, king Henry VIII severed the tie with Rome.[43] Thomas Middleton's anti-Spanish play *A Game at Chesse*, performed to popular acclaim in 1624, punned on the word "angle" to celebrate English religious independence. The play opened with a speech by Jesuit founder Ignatius Loyola, who appeared in England with "Error at his foote as asleepe." He began with the question, "what Angle of the world is this?" and lamented that he could not see the "politick face" nor could his "refinde Nostills" discern the traces of any of his followers. He went on, "I thought theyde spread over the world by this time coverd the Earths face and made darke the Land like Aegiptian Grassehoppers." England had resisted Roman tyranny twice over.[44]

This free religious tradition had combined with the liberty-loving traditions the Saxons brought to England and rendered the island nation unique among European states. But now the search for novelty and luxury, the decline of hospitality and public-spiritedness among the richer sort, and the concentration of power at the center threatened to end England's liberties. Virtue, the necessary foundation of liberty, was vanishing. The campaign to seduce the Americans into a kind of decadent dependence on the products and culture of civility was replicated in Britain, as imports from ruffs to over-fancy foods became staple items. Thomas Harriot, for example, wrote admiringly of the Indians' simplicity; they were "verye sober in their eatinge, and drinkinge, and consequentlye verye longe lived because they doe not oppress nature." A few pages later he returned to the subject: "I would to god wee would followe their exemple. For wee should bee free from many kynes of diseasyes which wee fall into by sumptwous and unseasonable banketts, continuallye devisinge new sawces, and provocation of gluttonye to satisfie our unsatiable appetite."[45] Thomas Morton, the New England puritans' antagonist, also lamented jaded English palates and their need for "variety of Sauces to procure appetite".[46]

At the same time that Opechancanough delighted in his new English-style house and young Algonquians began to prefer English clothes, in the "Rude Partes" of Britain, Scottish and Irish lords caught up in the civility machinery were driving themselves deeply into debt in furnishing their families and houses in the latest fashions.[47] Luxury and ornamentation was the underpinning of the absolutism so many English leaders feared. As Thomas Gainsford, drawing on Tacitus, wrote, "Though curtesy, moderatt behaviour, affabillity, and other vertues enoble the name of a Prince: yett are the common people caried away with outward shoes: so that a Prince had the better maintaine his estate with ornaments of majesty, pompous attendancy, and all other observations of greatnes..."[48]

Tacitus's translators highlighted these themes in rendering the contrasts he drew between the ancient French and Britons. The war-like Britons were strong, "not mollified yet by long peace," but absence of war had made the French cowards, so that "shipwrack was made both of manhood and libertie togither."[49] Leaders who sought to enlist the Stuart government to support the European wars in defence of protestantism, and who argued for American colonization as a way to weaken the power of Spain, believed they saw early warnings of such decline at home.[50]

Because so much was at stake in English claiming and celebration of their Tacitean ancestors, it is significant that these English writers saw the same qualities of savage simplicity and virtue in the Americans. Writer after writer argued that the Indians lived well because they were satisfied with little; they were not yet subject to artificially created demand for useless goods. They loved their children intensely and fulfilled homely roles with dedication. Their government was powerful and proud, yet responsive to the wishes of the people and subject to restraint. Not only did English writers portray the Americans as resembling the ancient peoples of whom Tacitus wrote, but the very categories for describing an alien culture, the traits that mattered, came from his *Germania* and *Agricola*. Tacitus furnished the template for descriptions of the other; he provided the categories from chiefly power to methods of storing food.[51] The eighteenth-century historian William Robertson, acknowledging that writers on America employed the same categories as Tacitus, argued that the validity of his portrayal of the ancient Germans could be verified by reading reports of the American natives.[52]

And yet, the doubleness of vision through which English promoters looked to America could never be held down for long in a single line of argument. At the same time they wrote longingly of the virtuous and free lives of their own forebears who resisted the slavery embodied in preferred civility, they also wholeheartedly assumed and embraced the Roman role. This is the further meaning of William Strachey's pun on Angels and Angles. Against those who argued that colonization "is injuryous to the naturall Inhabitants," he pointed to England's situation before the Romans came. Citing Tacitus he wrote that Agricola "reduced the conquered partes of our barbarous Island into Provinces...teaching us even to know the powerfull discourse of divine Reason." "Had not this violence, and this Injury, bene offred unto us by the Romanis," he argued, "we might yet have lyved over-growne Satyrs, rude, and untutred, wandring in the woodes, dwelling in Caves, and hunting for our dynners (as the wyld beasts in the for-rests for their prey,) prostetuting our daughters to straungers, sacri-ficing our Children to our Idolls, nay eating our owne Children, as did the Scots in those dayes." Strachey referred to William Symonds's sermon *Virginia*, preached to the departing America-bound fleet in 1609. Symonds argued that England was a paradise compared to its pre-Roman state because of the "civill care of conquerors and planters." England's status as a godly nation depended on this cam-paign, according to Arthur Lake, who preached in England during the warfare following 1622, that "We should take another course for their conversion, yea the same that was taken for ours." Then God might continue to regard the British as "his people."[53]

The Indians as described in the later sixteenth and early seventeenth centuries were not Noble Savages; English colonists could not afford that luxury. The Noble Savage is necessarily a defeated culture.[54] Rather, the Tacitist theme in writings about America reflected the powerful currents of Neostoicism that underlay much Tacitist thought, and drew on the tradition of pastoral literature, in which descriptions of a simpler, more virtuous life offered an ironic commentary on the writers' own society. Tacitus, according to Simon Schama, depicted Germany as "not-Rome"; English travelers presented the Indians as not English, but as proto-English. Drawing in part on the georgic theme as presented by Hesiod and Virgil, these writers rejected the pastoral tradition's celebration of retirement from involve-ment in human affairs. Instead, they preached engagement in a course of restoration and improvement, embodying what Patrick Cullen calls pastoralism's "longing to regress coupled with its longing to progress."

In traveling to America, English men and women could renew their own society and, building on the foundation of native integrity, could bring the Indians to a higher plane of understanding without corruption.[55] But underlying all these aspirations was the knowledge that civility brings the corrupting desire for ownership of things.

And ambivalence about the choice between primitive freedom and virtue and the blessings of civility continued to surface as colonists forged ahead. Robert Beverly's *History and Present State of Virginia*, looking back from the end of the seventeenth century, concluded Book III, "Of the Indians, their Religion, Laws, and Customs, in War and Peace," in this way: "Thus I have given a succinct account of the Indians; happy, I think, in their simple State of Nature, and in their enjoyment of Plenty, without the Curse of Labour. They have on several accounts reason to lament the arrival of the Europeans, by whose means they seem to have lost their Felicity, as well as their Innocence. The English have taken away great part of their Country, and consequently made every thing less plenty amongst them. They have introduc'd Drunkenness and Luxury amongst them, which have multiply'd their Wants and put them upon desiring a thousand things, they never dreamt of before."[56] Tacitus could not have put it better.

NOTES

1. Edward Waterhouse, *A Declaration of the State of the Colony and Affaires in Virginia* (London, 1622), 14–15; Robert Beverly, *The History and Present State of Virginia*, 1705, ed. Louis B. Wright (Charlottesville: University of North Carolina Press, 1947), 51.

2. Rolfe to Sir Edwin Sandys, June 8, 1617, in *Records of the Virginia Company of London*, ed. Susan Myra Kingsbury, 4 vols. (Washington, D.C.: U.S. Govt. Printing Office, 1906–1935), III, 70–73, quote 71.

3. William Strachey, *The Historie of Travell into Virginia Britania 1612*, ed. Louis B. Wright and Virginia Freund (London: Hakluyt Society, 1953), 3, 6.

4. Waterhouse, *Declaration of the State of the Colony and Affaires in Virginia*, t.p., 11–27; Virginia Company, Instructions to George Yeardley, November 18, 1618, in *Records of the Virginia Company*, ed. Kingsbury, III, 102; Virginia Company Court, May 26, 1619, ibid., I, 220–221; George Thorpe to Sir Edwin Sandys, May 15–16 1621, ibid., III, 446–447; John Pory to Sir Edwin Sandys, June 12, 1620, ibid., III, 305. On Thorpe see Eric Gethyn-Jones, *George Thorpe and the Berkeley Company: A Gloucestershire Enterprise in Virginia* (Gloucester: Alan Sutton, 1982) and J. Frederick Fausz, "George Thorpe, Nemattanew,

and the Powhatan Uprising of 1622," *Virginia Cavalcade* (Winter 1979), 111–117.

5. George Thorpe to Sir Edwin Sandys, May 15–16 1621, *Records of the Virginia Company*, III, 446; Patrick Copland, *Virginia's God be Thanked, or A Sermon of Thanksgiving for the Happie successe of the affayres in Virginia this last yeare* (London, 1622), 2, 9–10, 24 and Patrick Copland, *A Declaration how the monies (viz. seventy pound eight shillings sixe pence) were disposed* (London, 1622); Beverly, *History and Present State of Virginia*, ed. Wright, 49–50.

6. For an interpretation of these events see Fausz, "Thorpe, Nemattanew, and the Powhatan Uprising of 1622," *Virginia Cavalcade*, Winter 1979, 111–117.

7. Waterhouse, *Declaration of the State of the Colony and Affaires in Virginia*, 16–17, 21–24.

8. See Benedetto Fontana, "Tacitus on Empire and Republic," *History of Political Thought*, XIV (1993), 28–40; Simon Schama, *Landscape and Memory* (New York: Knopf, 1995), 76–78; Mark Morford, *Stoics and Neostoics: Rubens and the Circle of Lipsius* (Princeton: Princeton University Press, 1991), 144–147.

9. Cornelius Tacitus, *The Life of Agricola*, trans. Henry Savile (London, 1598), 196; "A Letter of Sir Samuell Argoll touching his Voyage to Virginia, and Actions there, 1613," in Purchas, *Pilgrimes* XIX 92–93; Hamor, *True Relation*, 4–6; Captain John Smith, *The Generall Historie of Virginia, New-England and the Summer Isles* (London, 1624), in *The Complete Works of Captain John Smith*, ed. Philip L. Barbour, 3 vols. (Chapel Hill: University of North Carolina Press for the Omohundro Institute of Early American History and Culture, 1986), II, 243–244.

10. Hamor, *True Discourse*, 4–7; Dale to "the R. and my most esteemed friend Mr. D. M." ibid., 55–56; Whitaker to "my verie deere and loving Cosen M. G." ibid., 59–60. See Peter Hulme, *Colonial Encounters: Europe and the Native Caribbean, 1492–1797* (London: Methuen, 1986), chap. 4.

11. Gethyn-Jones, *George Thorpe and the Berkeley Company*, 53–60.

12. Hamor, *True Relation*, 38–46.

13. Tacitus, *Life of Agricola*, trans. Savile, 189–193; Council in Virginia to the Virginia Company, January 1622, in *Records of the Virginia Company*, III, ed. Kingsbury, 584.

14. Smith, *Generall Historie*, in *Works*, II, ed. Barbour, 196.

15. Nipmuck note reproduced in Jill Lepore, *The Name of War: King Philip's War and the Origins of American Identity* (New York: Knopf, 1998), 94–95.

16. Copland, *Virginia's God be Thanked*, 28.

17. Tacitus, *The Description of Germanie*, trans. Grenewey, 262; William Bradford, *Of Plymouth Plantation, 1620–1647*, ed. Samuel Eliot Morison (New York: Knopf, 1952), 203.

18. William Shakespeare, *The Merry Wives of Windsor* (1602), act 1, scene 3. I thank Barbara Fuchs for bringing this reference to my attention.

19. Tacitus, *Life of Julius Agricola*, trans. Savile, 190, 195–196. Benedetto Fontana argues that this "brilliant epigram" may represent Tacitus's commentary on the consolidation of power within the Roman state itself; "Tacitus on Empire and Republic," *History of Political Thought*, XIV (1993), 29. On redescription, see Quentin Skinner, *Reason and Rhetoric in the Philosophy of Hobbes* (Cambridge: Cambridge University Press, 1996), 161–172, esp. 163 note 148. Philip Vincent employed Galgacus's words as he described the depredations of the Thirty Years' War in Germany, as did Fernández de Oviedo in commenting on the destructive record of the Spanish in the Caribbean; Philip Vincent, *The Lamentations of Germany* (London, 1638); Anthony Grafton, *New Worlds, Ancient Texts: The Power of Tradition and the Shock of Discovery* (Cambridge, M A: Harvard University Press, 1992), 55.

20. Thomas Gainsford, "Observations of State, and millitary affaires for the most parte collected out of Cornelius Tacitus," 1612, MS Huntington Lib. EL 6857, 36. Tacitus's original is in Savile's translation of *The Life of Julius Agricola*, 201.

21. Waterhouse, *Declaration of the State of the Colony and Affaires in Virginia*, 18; Capps to John Ferrar, March 31, 1623, in *Records of the Virginia Company*, IV, ed. Kingsbury, 76.

22. Henry Savile, *The Life of Agricola*, published in *The Ende of Nero and the Beginning of Galba* (London, 1591), 241.

23. Waterhouse, *Declaration of the State of the Colony and Affaires in Virginia*, 25, 27; Tacitus, *Life of Agricola*, 189.

24. *The Commentaries of C. Julius Caesar, Of his Warres in Gallia, and the Civile Warres betwixt him and Pompey*, trans. Clement Edmonds (London, 1655), 106; Gainsford, "Observations...out of Cornelius Tacitus," 1612, MS Huntington Lib. EL 6857, 62, 66. On native warfare in America see Patrick M. Malone, *The Skulking Way of War: Technology and Tactics Among the New England Indians* (Plimoth Plantation, 1991; Baltimore, 1993) esp. chap. 1 "The Aboriginal Military System."

25. Beverly, *History and Present State of Virginia*, ed. Wright, 54. On this tactic see Edmund S. Morgan, *American Slavery, American Freedom: The Ordeal of Colonial Virginia* (New York: Norton, 1975)

26. Tacitus, *Life of Agricola*, 192; David Thomas Konig, "Colonization and the Common Law in Ireland and Virginia, 1569–1634," in *The Transformation of Early American History: Society, Authority, and Ideology*, ed. James A. Henretta, Michael Kammen, and Stanley N. Katz, (New York: Knopf, 1991), 90–92.

27. Nigel Smith, *Literature and Revolution in England, 1640–1660* (New Haven: Yale University Press, 1994), 337–352, quote 337. See also Grafton, *New Worlds, Ancient Texts*, 43.

28. Donald R. Kelley, "*Tacitus Noster*: The *Germania* in the Renaissance and Reformation," in *Tacitus and the Tacitean Tradition*, ed. T. J. Luce and A. J. Woodman (Princeton: Princeton University Press, 1993), 152–167; J. H. M. Salmon, "Seneca and Tacitus in Jacobean England," in *The Mental World of the Jacobean Court*, ed. Linda Levy Peck (Cambridge: Cambridge University Press, 1991), 169–188; and Salmon, "Stoicism and Roman Example: Seneca and Tacitus in Jacobean England," *Journal of the History of Ideas*, 50 (1989): 199–225. Markku Peltonen, while acknowledging the influence of Tacitus, argues that Cicero's influence remained strong; see *Classical Humanism and Republicanism in English Political Thought, 1570–1640* (Cambridge, 1995), 15, 280, 311.

29. Blair Worden, *The Sound of Virtue: Philip Sidney's Arcadia and Elizabethan Politics* (New Haven: Yale University Press, 1996), chapter 14.

30. David Womersley, "Sir Henry Savile's Translation of Tacitus and the Political Interpretation of Elizabethan Texts," *Review of English Studies*, new ser., XLII (1991): 313–314. On Savile's position, see also Salmon, "Precept, Example, and Truth: Degory Wheare and the *Ars Historica*," in *Historical Imagination in Early Modern Britain: History, Rhetoric, and Fiction, 1500–1800* ed. Donald R. Kelley and David Harris Sacks (Cambridge: Cambridge University Press, 1998), 17–18.

31. D. R. Woolf, *The Idea of History in Early Stuart England: Erudition, Ideology, and "The Light of Truth" from the Accession of James I to the Civil War* (Toronto: Toronto University Press, 1990), 115–125; Perez Zagorin, *Francis Bacon* (Princeton: Princeton University Press, 1998), 136, 206–210; Debora Shuger, "Irishmen, Aristocrats, and Other White Barbarians," *Renaissance Quarterly*, 50 (1997): 495–497. The core texts are available in recent scholarly editions of the *Germania* by J. B. Rives (Oxford: Clarendon Press, 1999) and of *Agricola and Germany* by Anthony Birley (Oxford: Oxford University Press, 1999).

32. *The True Travels, Adventures, and Observations of Captaine John Smith*, in *Works*, ed. Barbour, III, 156. Philip Barbour argues that Smith must have read the Peter Whitehorn translation of Machiavelli (1560) and that his Marcus Aurelius must have been Thomas North's translation of Antonio de Guevara's *The Diall of Princes* (1557), as the Meditations of Marcus Aurelius were not available in English until Casaubon's translation was published in 1634. Theodore Paleologue was riding master to the earl of Lincoln. For comparisons of Smith to Caesar, see Barbour, ed., *Works*, II, 41, 50; III, 47 (quote). On the way in which men on the public stage studied the art of rhetoric and the classics, particularly Livy and Tacitus, as guides to action, see Skinner, *Reason and Rhetoric*; Peter Burke, "A Survey of the Popularity of Ancient Historians, 1450–1700," *History and Theory*, 5 (1966): 135–152, quote p. 151, and "Tacitism, scepticism, and reason of state," in *The Cambridge History of Political Thought, 1450–1700*, ed. J. H. Burns (Cambridge: Cambridge University Press, 1991), 484–490; Anthony Grafton and Lisa Jardine, "Studied for

Action: How Gabriel Harvey Read His Livy," *Past and Present*, 129 (1990), 30–78; and Alan T. Bradford, "Stuart Absolutism and the 'Utility' of Tacitus," *Huntington Library Quarterly*, 46 (1983): 127–155. On the use of classical rhetorical form in tracts promoting America see Andrew Fitzmaurice, "Classical Rhetoric in the Literature of Discovery," unpub. PhD diss., Cambridge University, 1995.

33. For the argument for Saxon origins, and for the description of the ancient German polity, see William Camden, *Britaine, Or A Chorographicall Description of the most flourishing Kingdomes, England, Scotland, and Ireland*, trans. Philemon Holland (London, 1610; first pub. 1586), 127–141; Richard Verstegan, *A Restitution of Decayed Intelligence: In antiquities. Concerning the most noble and renowmed English nation* (Antwerp, 1605), 2 and passim; John Speed, *The History of Great Britaine Under the Conquests of the Romans, Saxons, Danes and Normans* (London, 1614), 287–289; ed. Robert C. Johnson, Mary Frear Keeler, Maija Jansson Cole, and William B. Bidwell, *Proceedings in Parliament 1628*, 6 vols. (New Haven: Yale University Press, 1977–1983); *Commons Debates 1628* II, 330, 333–334, *Lords Proceedings 1628*, V, 162, 172–173, 180. For modern treatments of the issues see Hugh A. MacDougall, *Racial Myth in English History: Trojans, Teutons, and Anglo-Saxons* (Hanover, NH: University Press of New England, 1982); Christopher Hill, "The Norman Yoke," in *Puritanism and Revolution: Studies in Interpretation of the English Revolution of the Seventeenth Century* (London: Schocken, 1958); Joyce Chaplin, *Subject Matter: Technology, the Body, and Science on the Anglo-American Frontier, 1500–1676* (Cambridge, MA: Harvard University Press, 2001), 84, 93–95; Woolf, *Idea of History in Early Stuart England*; Kevin Sharpe, "The foundation of the Chairs of History at Oxford and Cambridge: an episode in Jacobean politics," in *Politics and Ideas in Early Stuart England: Essays and Studies* (London: Pinter, 1989); Worden, *The Sound of Virtue*, 258; Brian P. Levack, *The Civil Lawyers in England, 1603–1641: A Political Study* (Oxford: Oxford University Press, 1973), 91–95; and Arthur Ferguson, *Utter Antiquity: Perceptions of Prehistory in Renaissance England* (Durham: Durham University Press, 1993), chap. 5.

34. Nathanael Carpenter, *Geography Delineated*, (London, 1625), 281–282; Stuart Piggott, *Ancient Britons and the Antiquarian Imagination: Ideas from the Renaissance to the Regency* (London: Thames and Hudson, 1989), chap. 3; Joan-Pau Rubiés, "Hugo Grotius's Dissertation on the Origin of the American Peoples and the Use of Comparative Methods," *Journal of the History of Ideas*, LII (1991): 221–244, esp. 231.

35. Marc Lescarbot, *The Conversion of the Savages Who Were Baptized in New France during this year, 1610* in *The Jesuit Relations and Allied Documents*, ed. Reuben Gold Thwaites, 73 vols. (Cleveland, Ohio: A. H. Clark, 1896–1901), I, 83–85.

36. R. C. Bald has supplied probable dates of composition in his editions of Fletcher's *Bonduca* (Oxford, 1951) and of Middleton's *Hengist* (New York, 1938), xiii. I thank Gary Taylor for bringing these plays to my attention.

37. Cornelius Tacitus, *The Description of Germanie: and Customes of the People*, trans. Richard Grenewey (London, 1598); Speed, *The History of Great Britaine Under the Conquests of the Romans, Saxons, Danes and Normans*, 287–289. The characterization of the witenagamot is from Camden, *Britaine*, 177.

38. On Saye and the issues of the relation between parliament and monarch, see Richard Tuck, *Philosophy and Government, 1572–1651* (Cambridge: Cambridge University Press, 1993), 74–75, chapter 6.

39. Thomas Jefferson to Edmund Pendleton, Aug. 13 1776, Julian P. Boyd et al., eds., *The Papers of Thomas Jefferson*, 28 vols. (Princeton: Princeton University Press, 1950–2000), I, 492; John Adams to Abigail Adams, Aug. 14 1776, in *Adams Family Correspondence*, 6 vols. ed. L. H. Butterfield et al. eds. (Cambridge, M A: Harvard University Press, 1963–1993), II, 96–97. Somewhat later, Jefferson remembered his suggestion differently; see Boyd et al., eds., *Papers of Thomas Jefferson*, ibid., 494–495. On Jefferson see Peter Thompson, " 'Judicious Neology': Thomas Jefferson and the Anglo-Saxon Language," paper delivered to the Columbia Seminar in Early American History, September 14, 2001.

40. David Armitage, *The Ideological Origins of the British Empire* (Cambridge, 2000), 37–46.

41. Thomas Morton, *New English Canaan*, 1637, in Peter Force, comp., *Tracts and Other Papers, Relating Principally to the Origin, Settlement, and Progress of the Colonies in North America*, 4 vols. (1844; rept. Gloucester, M A: Peter Smith, 1963): II, 15–18.

42. Gary Taylor, personal communication.

43. Colin Kidd, *British Identities Before Nationalism: Ethnicity and Nationhood in the Atlantic World, 1600–1800* (Cambridge: Cambridge University Press, 1999), chaps. 3–5, and 190–198. On the political meaning of the notion that the British derived from the Trojan Brutus, see Roger A. Mason, "Scotching the Brut: Politics, History and National Myth in Sixteenth-Century Britain," in *Scotland and England, 1286–1815*, ed. Mason (Edinburgh: John Donald, 1987), 60–84; Sidney Anglo, "The *British History* in Early Tudor Propaganda," *Bulletin of the John Rylands Library*, 44 (1961): 17–48; and Richard T. Vann, "The Free Anglo-Saxons: A Historical Myth," *Journal of the History of Ideas*, XIX, (1958), 259–272. On denunciation of the Trojan myth see J. H. M. Salmon, "Precept, Example, and Truth: Degory Wheare and the *Ars Historica*," in *Historical Imagination in Early Modern Britain*, ed. Kelley and Sacks, 28–29. For parallel developments in Scotland see Arthur H. Williamson, "Scots, Indians and Empire: The Scottish Politics of Civilization, 1519–1609," *Past and Present*, 150 (1966): 46–83.

44. I thank Gary Taylor for bringing this play to my attention.
45. Harriot, "Notes" to woodcuts of John White's paintings published by Theodor De Bry and printed in *The Roanoke Voyages, 1584–1590*, ed. David Beers Quinn, 2 vols (London, 1955), I, 430, 438. On Ben Jonson's use of the masque form to urge restraint in ostentation, as well as in eating and drinking on the Stuart court, see Martin Butler, "Ben Jonson and the Limits of Courtly Panegyric," in *Culture and Politics in Early Stuart England*, ed. Kevin Sharpe and Peter Lake (Stanford, 1993), 91–115. See also Joan Thirsk, *Economic Policy and Projects: The Development of a Consumer Society in Early Modern* England (Oxford: Clarendon Press, 1978).
46. Morton, *New English Canaan*, in Force, comp., *Tracts*, II, 39.
47. Jane H. Ohlmeyer, " 'Civilizing of those Rude Partes': Colonization within Britain and Ireland, 1580s–1640s," in *The Origins of Empire: British Overseas Enterprise to the Close of the Seventeenth Century*, ed. Nicholas Canny, vol. I of *The Oxford History of the British Empire*, gen. ed. William Roger Louis (Oxford: Oxford University Press, 1998), 141–143.
48. "Observations of State, and millitary affaires for the most parte collected out of Cornelius Tacitus," 1612, M S Huntington Lib. EL 6857, 13.
49. Tacitus, *Life of Julius Agricola*, trans. Savile, 188.
50. See Karen Ordahl Kupperman, *Providence Island, 1630–1641: The Other Puritan Colony* (Cambridge: Cambridge University Press, 1993) and Tuck, *Philosophy and Government*, 110–118.
51. This thesis is developed in my book, *Indians and English: Facing Off in Early America* (Ithaca, NY: Cornell University Press, 2000).
52. William Robertson, *The Progress of Society in Europe: A Historical Outline from the Subversion of the Roman Empire to the Beginning of the Sixteenth Century*, ed. Felix Gilbert (Chicago: University of Chicago Press, 1972), 149–154; "On the Institutions and Customs of the Barbarian Invaders of the Roman Empire." This work was the first part of Robertson's *History of the Reign of the Emperor Charles V* (1769).
53. Strachey, *Historie of Travell*, ed. Wright and Freund, 23–24;
54. Anthony Grafton posits Tacitus as "the intellectual great-grandfather of the concept of the Noble Savage," *New Worlds, Ancient Texts*, 43. See also Gordon Sayre, *Les Sauvages Américains: Representations of Native Americans in French and English Colonial Literature* (Chapel Hill: University of North Carolina Press, 1997), 124.
55. On Neostoicism see Salmon, "Stoicism and Roman Example: Seneca and Tacitus in Jacobean England," *Journal of the History of Ideas*, 50 (1989): 199–225 and Tuck, *Philosophy and Government*. On commentary on contemporary life see Schama, *Landscape and Memory*, 75–100; Patrick Cullen, *Spenser, Marvell, and Renaissance Pastoral* (Cambridge, MA: Harvard University Press, 1970), Introduction, esp. pp. 1, 6, 10; Peter Lindenbaum, *Changing Landscapes: Anti-Pastoral Sentiment in the*

English Renaissance (Athens, GA: University of Georgia Press, 1986). On the georgic tradition see Shuger, "Irishmen, Aristocrats, and Other White Barbarians," *Renaissance Quarterly*, 50 (1997): 507–522; Anthony Low, *The Georgic Revolution* (Princeton: Princeton University Press, 1985) and Alastair Fowler, "Georgic and Pastoral: Laws of Genre in the Seventeenth Century," in *Culture and Cultivation in Early Modern England: Writing and the Land*, ed. Michael Leslie and Timothy Raylor (Leicester: Leicester University Press, 1992), 81–88. On contemporary concerns about the danger of empire to England see Armitage, *Ideological Origins of the British Empire* and "John Milton: Poet against Empire," *Milton and Republicanism*, ed. David Armitage, Armany Himy, and Quentin Skinner (Cambridge: Cambridge University Press, 1995), 206–225.

56. Beverly, *History and Present State of Virginia*, ed. Wright, 233.

3

PREHISTORIC DIASPORAS: COLONIAL THEORIES OF THE ORIGINS OF NATIVE AMERICAN PEOPLES

Gordon M. Sayre

PROLOGUE: KENNEWICK MAN AND THE LEGACY OF COLONIAL THEORIES[1]

The cultural and political importance of the issue of Native American origins has been emphasized by the recent controversy over Kennewick Man. Kennewick Man is a skeleton that was first found by spectators at a powerboat race along the banks of the Columbia River near Kennewick, Washington in July 1996. Radiocarbon dating established that the bones are roughly 9,000 years old, making it a major archaeological discovery, since only thirty-two human remains that old have been found in North America, and this skeleton is among the most complete. A local anthropologist named James Chatters collected the bones and touched off a media sensation when he was quoted saying that features of the skull resembled "caucasoid" peoples more than modern Native Americans. Chatters later asked an artist friend to make a reconstruction of the flesh on Kennewick Man's head. When photos of the bald clay model appeared in newspapers and magazines across the country, many news stories repeated Chatters's suggestion, that Kennewick Man resembled the actor Patrick Stewart. Many also confused the paleontological term "caucasoid" with "caucasian," and concluded that Kennewick Man was white. However, under the terms of the Native American Grave Protection and Repatriation Act, a 1990 federal law known as NAGPRA for short, the U.S. Army Corps of Engineers, owner of the land where the bones were found, determined that they were the property of local Indian tribes. There ensued of course a lawsuit, filed by a group of eight physical anthropologists eager to study Kennewick Man in hope of building support for their theories about human migrations into North America at the end of the Ice Ages, ten to fifteen thousand years ago. In 2001, Judge Jelderks of Federal District Court in Portland, Oregon finally issued a ruling in favor of the plaintiffs, who apparently succeeded in portraying the Indian tribes as obscurantist foes of science, and as fearful that their claims might be nullified if examination of the bones was allowed to proceed.[2]

Kennewick Man reveals the huge stakes behind the question of the origins of Native American peoples. The basic question of "Who was here first?" carries enormous cultural, political, and legal weight, because it implies symbolic claims to sovereignty over the continent. And if answers can come from Kennewick Man, they will be built upon arguments that are as much racial as archeological. The measurement of his skull, and its classification according to a resemblance to Asian, European, or paleo-Indian skulls, may carry the authority of science, but the ways in which such classifications are perceived is deeply racialized, and bound up with colonial claims to North America established during the sixteenth to eighteenth centuries.[3] The public response to the controversy has followed a pattern established over the last five hundred years, as Euro-Americans have sought to assert sovereignty and "nativity" over the Americas. Twentieth-century science has done surprisingly little to change the terms of the debate about American Indian origins, the leading theories proposed, or even the types of evidence considered. An awareness of the history behind the question is necessary to a critical understanding of the colonialist patterns of this debate.

In the lawsuit over Kennewick Man, the plaintiffs asserted that NAGPRA did not apply because there was no evidence to meet the statutory requirement of a "cultural affiliation" linking the bones to any local Indian tribe. Paleontologists thus attempted to force the Corps of Engineers to prove that this man, 9,000 years ago, called himself Umatilla or Yakima, as his descendants do today. But can any culture, anywhere in the world, prove that its language, its material culture, and its name for itself have not changed in 9,000 years? The influence of dominant groups over prehistory lies in asserting affiliations with ancient cultures, in spite of changes that have occurred over thousands of years. One may claim to be descended from the Gauls, the Celts, the Romans, or the Anglo-Saxons, but will also identify oneself as Irish, English, French, or Italian. There are winners and losers, majorities and minorities among these European ethnicities, but a history of invasions and migrations is always involved, a history often elided or manipulated by European nationalist and essentialist ideologies such as the Nazi "Aryan race." Euro-Americans who call themselves "Caucasian," even if they can't place the Caucasus on a map, are eager to assert kinship to Kennewick Man, I believe, because such an affiliation supports myths of European sovereignty in North America, and marginalizes the sovereignty of American Indians. Among the plaintiffs was the Asatru fellowship, a New Age pagan group eager to support their theory of ancient Norse migrations to America. The news media gave as much attention to the Asatru as to the Native tribes' beliefs about their own ancient presence in the region.[4] What's more, the attempt to classify Kennewick Man according to a modern racial identity is simply ludicrous. Racial labels used in the U.S. today have little relevance in settings hundreds of years ago, much less thousands. And because the diversity within populations labelled as races is actually much greater than the differences between them, and there is only one Kennewick Man to measure, there is little rigor behind claims that he belonged to a population of ancient Asians, Europeans, or Caucasoids. Kennewick Man may have looked similar to his lost compatriots, or he might have appeared unusual beside them.

INTRODUCTION: COLONIAL THEORIES OF MIGRATION AND DIASPORA

Like other contributors to *Writing Race Across the Atlantic World*, I aim to compare our contemporary racial ideologies with those of early modern Europe, and to examine the intersection of scientific and literary discourses. The diasporas of interest here, however, cross not only the Atlantic but the Pacific, and extend back to the earliest of early modernities, the beginning of the Holocene era some ten thousand years ago. For just as beliefs about racial identity frequently depend upon notions of primitive or unconscious urges and essential or originary roots, popular and scientific beliefs about early man are shot through with racial thinking, and have been for hundreds of years. As news of the discovery of America spread in the fifteenth century, Europeans faced the challenge of accounting for American Indian peoples in the context of biblical and classical Mediterranean history. The biblical Genesis was axiomatic for most Europeans, and nearly all agreed that American peoples were part of that creation, but many also built a more specific cultural bias into their stories of Native American origins, so as to assert an affinity with or authority over indigenous Americans whose lives and land were being seized by colonists. The recent claim that Kennewick Man demonstrates an ancient migration of Europeans to North America repeats arguments advanced by Renaissance Europeans who constructed "anthropological" support for colonial claims over this continent.

There was an enormous and complex body of European and Euro-American writing from the sixteenth and the nineteenth centuries on the origins of the Native Americans; dozens of pamphlets and treatises on the question were published in England, Holland, Germany, France, and Spain, in all those national languages plus of course Latin. In addition, hundreds of colonial histories and exploration texts included brief chapters or longer dissertations devoted to the issue. Most of this literature is little known today. Some anthropologists have acknowledged its significance, for example David Hurst Thomas's *Skull Wars: Kennewick Man, Archaeology, and the Battle for Native American Identity* (New York, 2000) includes a brief discussion of these issues. But aside from Lee Huddleston's *Origins of the American Indians: European Concepts, 1492–1729* (Austin, 1967), which emphasizes Spanish colonial material, I have found no monographs about the early modern literature on the topic. Such a study would be difficult to write. As the eminent historian of colonial Mexico Jacques Lafaye wrote in addressing the theme, "To summarize here, one by one, the different positions, would be to compose a boring catalog."[5] Reading these texts is frustrating for several reasons: First, few of the writers who weighed in on the question had any new, first-hand ethnological evidence to present. Many of those known for the most provocative theories, such as Isaac la Peyrère, Johannes de Laet, Hugo Grotius, and Menasseh Ben Israel, four who shaped a fierce debate during the latter half of the seventeenth century, never went to America and wrote toward larger scholarly arguments for which the origin of the American Indians was merely incidental.[6] Second, as the author of another brief survey points out, many of those who wrote on the controversy did so as "a pretext for showing their great erudition, knowledge of classical texts, and pedantry."[7] With a few exceptions, such as Jose de Acosta and Joseph-François Lafitau, those who had been to America and gathered information directly from Native Americans were usually not learned enough to do battle with the pedants in Europe, and others who did have knowledge worth sharing often obscured it by repeating the theories propounded by others.[8] Thirdly, many theorists, like Gregorio Garcia, author of the 1607 *Origen de los indios de el nuevo mundo* or "Origins of the Indians of the New World," declined to come out in favor of any single origin theory or migration route, instead reviewing and endorsing several. The nineteenth-century Cherokee writer John Rollin Ridge concluded sardonically that American Indians were "descended from all the branches of the Old World stock at one and the same time."[9] Fourthly, the line between serious scientific conclusions and marginal speculations about Native American origins has never been easy to draw. As Stephen Williams has documented in *Fantastic Archaeology: The Wild Side of North American Prehistory* (Philadelphia, 1991), hoaxes and crackpot theories concerning prehistoric Americans have proliferated since the time of P. T. Barnum and include hundreds, even thousands of books. This essay cannot hope to touch upon this literature. I shall instead concentrate on sources prior to 1850, and rather than attempting the summary that Lafaye insisted would be boring, I will emphasize that many Early Modern theories are quite similar to those embraced today by anthropologists. The idea of migration across an Asia–America land bridge, for example, was widely circulated in the late 1500s, when Acosta argued for it. A critical judgment about how colonialist motives affect the scientific and popular debate about Native American origins will be possible only in light of the history of research and speculation on the issue. What follows is an introductory attempt at such a history, organized around five types of evidence that were and are used in debates about Native American origins, and then five major types of theories built upon that evidence.

Craniometry

Measurements of the skull of Kennewick Man provided initial support for the argument that he was "caucasoid" even though subsequent analysis supposedly documented closer similarities to the Ainu people indigenous to northern Japan. Although most try to avoid anachronistic or racial labels, archeologists today still classify ancient skulls as eighteenth-century theorists did in building racist theories of a progression from ape to a Grecian sculptural ideal. Such speculation found its most successful American practitioner in Samuel G. Morton, author of *Crania Americana* (1839) and proud owner of a collection of over a thousand skulls.[10] Earlier researchers had studied variations in skull shape for support of a theory of polygenesis, of races as separate species of mankind. Morton also endorsed polygenesis, but he was ambivalent about phrenology, the study of the shape of the skull, and sought to bring scientific rigor to craniometry by measuring the volume of the brain cavity. In his laboratory Morton would seal off the openings in a skull and fill it with lead shot, then empty and weigh the contents to determine its volume. Stephen Jay Gould in *The Mismeasure of Man* has exposed the unconscious bias in Morton's methodology, and other recent critics have used Morton as a leading example of nineteenth-century American scientific racism. Morton did assert that human races were products of separate creations, and that the white European species was superior, but he also admitted that his craniometric data did not fully support his racist ideas.[11] Like many earlier theorists, he believed in separate origins for two separate groups of Native Americans. He distinguished the "demi-civilized" Toltecans of central and South America, including both the Aztecs and Incas, from the totally uncivilized natives of North America. However, his measurements showed that the Inca skulls had the smallest volume of any in his collection. This did not support his hypothesis that the more advanced "races" had larger skulls, and he was honest enough to admit it.

The most alarming thing about *Crania Americana* is not its conclusions, but its method, which depended upon acquiring skulls by graverobbing. Most of the "Caucasian" skulls in Morton's collection were those of lunatics, idiots, and notorious criminals, collected in the hope of discerning some cause of their antisocial behavior. During the nineteenth century, when so-called resurrectionists supplied medical schools with cadavers, it was a mark of class status to be able to preserve one's body undamaged in its grave. Native Americans held the lowest status of all, for their bones were sought by entrepreneurs, amateur collectors, and scientists. As anthropologist Franz Boas wrote in his diary: "It is most unpleasant work to steal bones from a grave, but what is the use, someone has to do it."[12] The conflict over Kennnewick man suggests that the bones of Native Americans are still the objects of a fetishistic value, and that science indirectly contributes to this fetish, while denying Native Americans a contribution to the conclusions derived from their bones. Only in the past twenty years or so have Native American archeologists begun to contribute to the discourses that have defined their racial and cultural status.[13]

Pyramids of Egypt and the Yucatan

A second type of evidence used in the origins debate is what we now call "material culture" found in association with bones; the tools, structures, and art of human societies. For Early Modern Europeans, who had not yet developed archeology as a discipline, but who were deeply impressed by classical Greece and Rome, stone buildings were the *sine qua non* of civilization. This is the primary reason why the Aztecs and Incas (and, after the publications of John Lloyd Stephens, the Maya as well) were considered to be distinct from other Native Americans.[14] Their stone temples, plazas, and pyramids were the only stone structures found in America that matched the grandeur of the ancient Mediterranean world. Augustus le Plongeon and other nineteenth-century archeologists came up with a theory that the Mayan pyramids and the iconography of carvings on them demonstrated a common origin with the ancient Egyptians.[15] The seventeenth-century Mexican intellectual Carlos Siguenza y Gongora had made a similar assertion of Egyptian origin for the Aztecs, adding that both cultures also wrote in hieroglyphs.[16] These men had no proof that the Egyptian pyramids and writing actually predated the American developments, yet they did not entertain the notion that the Olmecs of ancient America might have colonized Egypt. Modern dating techniques have of course established that human presence in Eurasia and Africa preceded that in the Americas, and that the Egyptian pyramids are older than the Mayan, but these findings have been used to reinforce a notion that cultural progress diffused in one direction only, from the Old World to the New, even though any migration could have taken people out of America as well as into it. For another example, some specialists in the styles of stone projectile points assert that the spearheads of the Clovis culture of ancient America resemble those of the paleolithic Solutreans of Western Europe, and use this evidence to support theories of a pre-Columbian transatlantic migration.[17] Such diffusionist arguments generally rest upon a conviction that the independent invention of similar cultural materials is much less likely than a single invention followed by their diffusion, even diffusion to great distances.[18] Critics of diffusion insist that similarities in the style of projectile points or the architecture of temples could easily be the result of independent solutions to similar problems.

Atlantis and Mediterranean Myth

For European Renaissance humanists, even after Francis Bacon, the authority of classical texts often outweighed empirical data. It was very difficult for these scholars to accept that the Americas were a truly "New World" of which no mention could be found in Plato, Aristotle, or the Bible. Plato's *Timaeus* and *Critias* both mention a great lost land out in the western sea, the source of the myth of

Atlantis, which of course gave its name to the Atlantic Ocean, and has frequently been identified as America. Francisco Lopez de Gomara, the Spanish historian and biographer of Cortés, offered as confirmation the fact that the Nahua (Aztec) word for water was "atl."[19] But a more specific and influential myth arose out of Aristotle and Diodorus Siculus; both told a tale of Phonecian Carthaginians who sailed through the pillars of Hercules and settled an uninhabited land. The authorities in Carthage feared either that too much of their population would emigrate, or that an enemy power would seize the colony, so they put to death the discoverers, and forbade any further voyages. Gonzalo Fernandez de Oviedo y Valdez, author of the *Historia General y Natural de las Indias* of 1535, proposed this as a possible origin of the American Indians, and many others have revived the idea. While the seafaring prowess of the Phoenicians and Carthaginians was certainly adequate for crossing the Atlantic, the fact that no strong archeological evidence of their landfall has ever been found leaves the literary sources as the only support for the theory. It is quite possible, of course, that the Atlantis of Plato, Aristotle, or Diodorus derives from a voyage to the Canaries or Cape Verde islands, or even to a small island later destroyed by a volcanic explosion. But the relevance to the origin question is that the identity of Atlantis with America is only possible because "America" was a signifier with no referent. It has been the prerogative of Europeans to constitute "America" and its peoples within historical discourse. Hence the myth of Atlantis has been taken seriously as evidence for a pre-Columbian migration, whereas American Indian myths, even if no more fantastic, are not considered historically valid.[20]

Word Games

Thomas Jefferson declared, in pondering the "great question...from whence came those aboriginal inhabitants of America?" that "a knowledge of their several languages would be the most certain evidence of their derivation which could be produced."[21] But in his manuscript for *Notes on the State of Virginia* he here added an additional sentence: "so long as a passion for forcing a resemblance between two languages doesn't lead us to those irrational distortions of both which have involved this species of testimony in some degree of ridicule."[22] Indeed, the propensity for European writers about Native America to present homophonic words as evidence of cultural origins deserves plenty of ridicule. Gomara's "atl" and "atlantis" is a typical absurdity, and one could add many others. The few colonial and missionary writers who learned an American language fluently were less likely to make such claims. By Jefferson's time, however, linguistic methods had become more rigorous with the work of his contemporary Sir William Jones, who mastered twenty-eight languages and laid the groundwork for the idea of a common origin for all the Indo-European tongues. If German, French, and English had evolved from an Indo-European root in common with Sanskrit, might not the languages of Native America also be traced to a common root, and might this root also be in Asia? Jefferson was excited at the prospect, but recognized the challenge posed by the phenomenal diversity of languages in Native North America—at least three hundred separate tongues. For Jefferson this multitude of languages in America "proves them of greater antiquity than those of Asia," and this fit his general goal in *Notes on the State of Virginia* of refuting European prejudices against America as an immature, infertile, or unhealthy place.[23] Modern linguists, on the other hand, have not all accepted the idea that the great diversity of languages in the Americas is proof of humans' antiquity here. Joseph H. Greenberg of Stanford University has devoted his career to developing a unified theory of a single root for all human languages. To do so, he has reduced the hundreds of distinct languages of Native America into two basic types, defying colleagues who insist that there are as many as 100 independent root languages. His method is really not so different from his eighteenth-century precursors—examining words in different languages and the phonemic similarities among them. Since Greenberg cannot of course learn all of these languages himself, or even interview their native speakers, he is dependent upon the transcriptions of hundreds of collectors, whose ears for oral language and methods of transcription cannot all have been equally accurate. Greenberg also assumes a fairly constant rate of change in the evolution of human languages, a method of "glottochronology" that is highly uncertain. Compounding the difficulty is the fact that many of these languages are now lost. Jefferson was at once cognizant of this problem, and complicit in it. He wrote: "it is to be lamented... that we have suffered so many of the Indian tribes already to extinguish, without our having previously collected and deposted in the records of literature, the general rudiments at least of the langugages they spoke."[24] Jefferson and Greenberg reduce the oral cultures of native America to dead letters, transcriptions that "preserve" native cultures only by imprisoning them in an archive. And inquiries into the origins of American Indians have consistently rejected evidence from the oral traditions of these peoples today, relying instead on vague resemblances of words, of stones, or of bones.

Genetic and Continental Drift

The development of human genomics and of supercomputers has recently made available one entirely new form of evidence concerning the origins of Native Americans, the study of genetic markers. Research began with blood types, when it was observed that nearly all American Indians had type O blood, a few Canadian tribes had a high incidence of type A, and virtually none had type B. Luigi Luca Cavalli-Sforza pioneered this work in the 1950s and then moved on to the study of DNA, measuring the relative frequency of dozens of genes in samples taken from peoples residing in Europe and around the world. Cavalli-Sforza and his colleagues attempt to measure the diasporas of human history on the largest scale, such as the spread of agricultural peoples out of Africa and the Middle East, and their gradual displacement of and mixture with local hunter gatherers. His results for the Neolithic period in Western Europe have been quite compelling, but he admits that "the selection of markers used in research to date has mostly involved variables identified among populations of European origin.... New markers that take account of the variations in non-European populations need to be found."[25] Moreover, given the history of colonial genocide in the Americas, the speedy diffusion of European immigrants across the continents, and the variable degree of their intermarriage with indigenous peoples, this genetic evidence may prove to be of limited value in establishing a reliable history of prehistoric migration and diaspora in the Americas.

Acosta and the Land Bridge Migration

Anthropologists today generally believe that the Americas had no human inhabitants until the end of the Pleistocene about twelve to fifteen thousand years ago, when migrants crossed from Asia to Alaska on land exposed by the lower sea levels of the ice ages. Renaissance geographers had no conception of an ice age, but because the North Pacific was among the last coastal areas of the world to be explored by Europeans, such a land bridge was envisioned. In his 1590 *Natural and Moral History of the Indies,* Acosta rejected the myths of Atlantis and of a Carthaginian discovery, insisting that without the compass early mariners would not have succeeded in crossing the oceans. Observing also that the New World abounded in animal species which humans would not have chosen to transport on their ships, Acosta concluded "that the one and the other world are joyned and continued one with another in some part, or at the least are very neere," and that humans and animals gradually migrated to the new world from Asia. "Some peopling the lands they found, and others seeking for newe, in time they came to inhabit and people the Indies, with so many nations, people, and tongues as we see."[26] Acosta did ask some Natives of Peru how they came to inhabit that land, but he did not accept their answer: "I have found them so farre unable to give any reason thereof, as they beleeve confidently, that they were created at their first beginning at this new world, where they now dwell. But we have freed them of this error by our faith, which teacheth us that all men came from the first man."[27] Acosta's account of Native American origins is in outline the consensus view of today's anthropologists, and some have credited him with the first modern or scientific study of the origin question.[28] Yet because the geography of the North Pacific was still unknown, Acosta's thesis was still speculative. His theory was prescient not only for the land bridge migration theory, but also for its outright rejection of Native Americans' own account of their origins. Acosta may have guessed right, but the coincidence demonstrates how slowly the consensus has changed. Acosta of course stayed within the Biblical chronology, and modern anthropologists were also very slow to question it. Until the excavation of the Folsom and Clovis sites in New Mexico in the 1920s and 1930s, the dogmatic authority of Ales Hrdlicka of the Smithsonian Institution insisted that no humans had been in America for more than 4000 years, a date that preserved the Biblical creation even in the post-Darwin era.[29] Since then the date of migration has been pushed back to 12,000 years, and new findings may extend it even earlier.[30]

The Lost Tribes of Israel

From the most "modern" theory let us shift to what appears as the most obsolete, the notorious "Lost Tribes." The key primary source for this is the Fourth Book of Esdras in the Apocrypha, which, as Acosta quoted in rejecting the theory, tells how ten of the twelve tribes, after their captivity in Babylon, "tooke this counsell to themselves to leave the multitude of the heathen, and go forth into a farther countrie, where never mankind dwelt." They went eastward to a region called Azareth, where they will live until "the latter time."[31] Since the Esdras text has the tribes departing eastward across Asia, this story is easily reconciled with the land bridge theory, although the style and motives behind each are very different. Because the ten lost tribes theory derives from the Bible, some have assumed that it was widely held in the sixteenth and seventeenth centuries, but it was not.

Mexican historians Juan Tovar and Diego Duran endorsed it in the 1580s, but their texts were not published until the nineteenth century.[32] And although the lost tribes thesis fit with the millenarian beliefs of Franciscans in the sixteenth century, Protestants have championed the theory since then, including seventeenth-century New England missionaries John Eliot and Roger Williams, and their English contemporary Thomas Thorowgood. The theory's most colorful exposition in this era was in *The Hope of Israel* (1650) by Menasseh Ben Israel, a Spanish Jew exiled to Holland.[33] As Benjamin Braude has shown in his work on Menasseh, his translations of the account of a discovery of Jewish people living in the jungles of South America were tailored on the one hand to Hebrew readers pondering a Second Coming foretold by the spread of Jews to the ends of the earth, and on the other to Englishmen who might be inspired to lift the ban on Jewish immigration to England.[34] Thus the theory was closely tied to political and religious issues in seventeenth-century Europe.

It was in the nineteenth century that the Lost Tribes theory reached its widest influence. James Adair's *History of the American Indians* (1775), based on his residence among the Cherokee and building upon earlier ethnographers, documented for hundreds of pages apparent parallels between Indian languages and Hebrew, and customs such as taboos against menstruating women. Missionary official Elias Boudinot's *A Star in the West* (1816) was another popular book that updated the millenarian program. *The Book of Mormon*, supposedly based on ancient plates unearthed in New York state in 1827, laid out a comprehensive history of multiple pre-Columbian migrations by Israelite tribes, accounting for all the major civilizations of Meso-America. In response to this, Ojibway historian Peter Jones wrote that the Book of Mormon was actually written by the Matchi-Manitou, the evil spirit of Algonquian mythology.[35] James Fenimore Cooper even parodied the theory through his character Parson Amen in *The Oak Openings* (1848).

Madoc, St. Thomas, and Prester John

The route and the conveyance for pre-columbian migrations to America is really a separate issue from the ethnic identity of the migrants. And Israelites of whatever tribe offered only one possible ethnic origin. I won't even try to list all the other peoples of the Renaissance and ancient world who were proposed as probable migrants and ancestors of the Native Americans. Virtually all were candidates. Instead, as the third type of theory I want to point out a pattern whereby colonizers attempted to justify their dispossession of Native American peoples by claiming that these peoples originated from, or had already acknowledged the authority of, earlier European migrants.

English colonists in the seventeenth century were eager to catch up with the Spanish and to legitimate their imperial efforts by contrast with the Catholic conquistadors, and they developed several myths for this purpose. When Protestant publisher Theodore deBry printed the narrative of Thomas Hariot and engraved the paintings of John White from the Roanoke colony, he included an appendix showing the Picts, whose bodies were adorned with elaborate designs in "pictage" or tattoos. The Picts had been natives of Northern Britain, and foes of colonizing Romans. Hence by analogy the English colony at Roanoke could be seen as repeating the imperial project that had brought civilization to the British Isles. Because Britain had seen violent colonial conflicts in Roman times and more recently in Ireland, Wales, and Scotland, colonial theories could identify Native Americans either with the colonized, as White implied, or with the colonizers.[36] Thomas Morton in *New English Canaan* (1637) rejected the theory that the Natives had come from Tartary over a frozen sea, for he claimed that they spoke vestiges of Latin. "[I]t may perhaps be granted that the Natives of this Country might originally come of the scattered Trojans," descendants of Brutus, great-grandson of Aeneas, who left Latium and was cast away at sea.[37] Other versions of this legend, which Morton must have known, had Brutus himself landing in England.[38] Morton's theory, built upon the *Aeneid* and its classical and pagan associations, rebutted the evangelical beliefs of New England Puritans, and of Roger Williams, who saw the Indians as actual or potential Israelites.

The most enduring English colonial myth came out of medieval history. Richard Hakluyt's *Principall Navigations* of 1589, the chief propaganda organ for Elizabethan imperialism, promoted the legend of the Welsh king Madoc, who supposedly had discovered a land across the western sea in the twelfth century, then returned and collected ten ships to start a colony there. Hakluyt supported this story with claims of Welsh words in Indian languages, derived from a text by David Ingram that I believe is fictional. He then embellished it with allusions to the Aztec legends published by Gomara, and with Queen Elizabeth's claims of a Welsh ancestry, to come up with a justification for English rule in North America parallel to the recent annexation of Wales. The legend endured well enough that later explorers on the western plains, including George Catlin, claimed to have found tribes that spoke the Welsh language.[39]

These English efforts recapitulated those of the Spaniards earlier in the sixteenth century, when the historian of the conquest Gonzalo Fernández de Oviedo y Valdés had proposed that the Americas were the Isles of the Hesperides discovered by the legendary Spanish king Hesper, and hence that the conquest was really a reconquest of former Spanish subjects.[40] This far-fetched notion did not win many converts. The myth of Quetzalcoatl was much more successful. Instead of imagining adventurous Europeans settling a vacant Eden like Atlantis, the Quetzalcoatl story grounds the pre-Columbian connection in native Aztec mythology. This Aztec god or culture-hero was in human form a king among the Toltecs, the highly cultured people whom the Aztecs conquered and appropriated (much as the Romans did the Greeks). His image was bearded and fair-skinned, and he had departed across the sea to the east in ancient times, leaving a promise to return and claim sovereignty over his people. Cortez had the happy coincidence to land in Veracruz on One Reed of the Aztec calendar, the very year prophesized, and in confronting Montezuma he cultivated the impression that he was the returning Quetzalcoatl. The myth still commands popular assent and is part of the foundation of Mexican nationalism. However, a few scholars, such as Gesa Mackenthun, Susan Gillespie, and Jacques Lafaye, have questioned its authenticity, pointing out that all Spanish accounts of it can be traced back to a single source, Sahagun's *General History of the Things of New Spain*, the work of Aztec informants in the 1580s, who would have been aware of the myth's importance among their Spanish masters, and may have concocted it through a kind of mimicry.[41]

There were also legends of apostolic visits to the New World, a missionary variation upon the myths of the third type. The first such story arose from Columbus's conviction that he had sailed to India, which in medieval writings and maps was often identified as the site of Eden or Paradise, and as a land with Christian churches begun during an ancient visit by the apostle St. Thomas.[42] The presence of Christians in the Far East had evolved in medieval times out of the story of Prester John in Mandeville's *Travels*. Long after Columbus's confusion had been cleared up, the myth persisted as part of a millennial worldview, not just among the zealous Franciscans in Mexico, who saw themselves as typological embodiments of the twelve apostles, but also among Jesuits like Antonio Ruiz de Montoya in Paraguay, who imagined that St. Thomas had visited much of South

America, and planted among the natives a dormant potential for conversion.[43] Others saw Quetzalcoatl himself as the manifestation of St. Thomas, or even, say some Mormons, of Christ.[44] Northern Europeans writing in the seventeenth century did not share in this myth arising out of the travels of St. Thomas to India, and drew instead upon a tenth-century story that the Irish St. Brendan had crossed the Atlantic, accompanied, according to Breton patriots, by St. Malo, whose city was home to several early explorers including Jacques Cartier.[45] These myths of the third type do not necessarily explain the origins of the Native Americans, but they do try to legitimate European colonial rule over their societies. Whether the land King Madoc discovered was already inhabited or not, whether St. Thomas had actually converted all the Indians or just preached to them, these myths offered historical types or analogues supporting the European colonial conquest.

Prehistoric Diasporas

Most Renaissance treatises on the origin problem did not endorse one migration route to the exclusion of all others. Many articulated a fourth type—"multiple migration" theories that sought to explain why a few Native American cultures, such as the Aztecs, Incas, Natchez, or even the ancient Moundbuilders, appeared to be more sophisticated than the mass of others. Benjamin Smith Barton, one of the leading American scientists of the Early Republic, linked the Moundbuilders of the Ohio Valley to Danish or Welsh migrations across the Atlantic, and distinguished these people from the less civilized Indians who had come to that region from the West.[46] In this Barton echoed Hugo Grotius and his *De Origine Gentium Americanum* (1642), which claimed that the North American Natives were descended from Scandinavians who had arrived via Greenland, the Maya of the Yucatan from the Ethiopians, and the Incas from the Chinese.[47] Such theories influenced those who had first-hand ethnographic information. Antoine-Simon Le Page du Pratz, based on eight years living alongside the Natchez Indians in colonial Louisiana, wrote that although the majority of American "naturels" (as he called them) migrated from Northeast Asia, the Mexicans were from China and the Natchez descended from trans-Atlantic migrants, either Carthaginians or Phoenicians. Although presented in the words of a Natchez informant, this origin story follows in part the theories of Grotius and more specifically of an unpublished 1718 manuscript by a missionary to Louisiana, Le Maire.[48] Thus the Carthaginian migration legend persisted, and was used to grant a Mediterranean origin to Natives for whom Le Page du Pratz had particular respect.

These theories inspired my title, "Prehistoric Diasporas"; for to imagine multiple migrations from other nations, (or even several passages across the land bridge, as many archeologists propose) is to imagine confrontations and intermarriage among these distinct populations. Much as Cavalli-Sforza's measurements of genetic drift document the ancient confrontations between hunter-gatherers and agriculturalists in Europe, similar encounters may have occurred in America. Multiple migrations across a Bering Straits land bridge may have created distinct groups. Or, if Phoenician sailors did arrive two to three thousand years ago, they might have become a diasporic population, preserving their identity amidst a primitive "gentile" majority. Today "diffusionist" theories attract scorn from many anthropologists, but "diaspora" carries great prestige. The theories of American Indian origins should invite us to contrast and reexamine the dynamics of diffusion and diaspora. The real motive of Barton, Le Page du Pratz, and others, I believe, was to grant a European or classical Mediterranean origin to a select group of Indians, the Moundbuilders or the Natchez, as part of an elegaic narrative about their demise. The Natchez were attacked and dispersed by French attacks, while the Moundbuilder cultures, Adena, Hopewell, and Mississippian as they are called by anthropologists, declined for unknown reasons a thousand years ago or more. A popular nineteenth-century story, told in William Cullen Bryant's poem "The Prairies," held that they were killed off by invasions of the Indians who lived in the West at that time.[49] Early modern Northern Europeans admired the grandeur of classical Rome, mused upon the causes for its fall, and wavered between identifying themselves with Rome or with the barbarous tribes who sacked it. In the Americas, a similar process has occurred with the Moundbuilders, or, more recently, with the Anasazi who built the impressive cliff dwellings in the Southwest before their culture declined around the twelfth century. In a pattern similar to the Kennewick Man controversy, Euro-Americans have appropriated the mantle of a vanished people, denied the continuity between that culture and modern Native Americans, and sometimes even blamed the latter for destroying the former. These speculative visions of prehistoric diaspora establish the elite status of the vanished culture, Aztec, Natchez, or Moundbuilder, by giving them Eurasian origins.[50]

The debate over American Indian origins is shaped not only by race, but by region. Argentine anthropologist Augusto Cardich, who has excavated several sites in South America that show evidence of human habitation 9,000 years ago or longer, advocates a theory of a pre-Columbian migration from Australia to South America.[51] Because the Bering Straits land bridge theory makes South American civilizations even "younger" than North American, the appeal of such a migration route to South America is obvious.[52] Uruguayan cultural critic Enrique Dussel has drawn upon this theory for his provocative attempt to "unmask Hegel's vision of history" and propose an east-ward rather than westward course for human civilization, beginning in Mesopotamia and moving through India, China, and across the Pacific to Meso-America and the Andes. Dussel critiques the "myth of modernity" as an unfortunate anomaly in world history, and prob-ably would also rebuke the paradigm of "the Atlantic world," which has emerged in history and cultural studies since the 1990s, and inspired this symposium. Yet Dussel still endorses the myth of Quetzalcoatl, Montezuma's abdication to Cortes, and a quasi-Aztec millenarianism.[53] Latin American culture has appropriated the mantle of its Native civilizations to a much greater degree than in Anglo-America, and hence the regional pride associated with Inca or Aztec histories offers a perspective on the more obscure patterns of such appropriation in North America.

The Autochthony of Native Americans

Finally, let us turn to the most radical, that is, most rooted and most controversial type of theory, which grants an autochthony and auton-omy to Native American peoples. For most seventeenth-century Europeans the idea of an autochthonous American population was a novel heresy, but a few in America began to recognize the power of the idea for asserting the importance of the American colonies. Antonio Leon Pinelo, an official bibliographer and historiographer of the Indies who had lived eighteen years of his youth in Peru, wrote *El Paraison en el Nuevo Mundo* or "Paradise in the New World" in 1650. For creoles, or *criollos* (those born in the New World of European parents), locating the biblical Eden in America was a strong political statement, one that could bolster the chronic discrimination these colonials felt they received from Spanish *peninsulares*.[54] Yet such a "creole compromise" on the origin question did little to challenge the hegemony of Judeo-Christian colonialism over Native Americans. If, as nineteenth-century anthologist Josiah Priest claimed, "America was peopled before the flood...it was the country of Noah, and the place where the ark was erected" then the colonization of America by Judeo-Christians to Americas could be legitimated as a sort of homecoming.[55] The scale of time was greater, but the effect was similar to the Hesperides and Madoc legends, or Morton and the polygenecists. The genesis, mono- or poly-, remained a biblical one. Monogenesis seems today like the humanistic, scientific, and antiracist position, but in practice it has served to support the privileged position of western science and Judeo-christian cosmogyny. To unsettle it, we should read Native American origin stories and consider the idea that nearly every culture is ethnocentric, and sees itself as the product of a special creation.

My students, whiggish historians as they generally are, have sometimes assumed that the notion of polygenesis, of human races as separate species, was pervasive in the Age of Discovery because the conquistadors treated the Indians as beasts. In fact, polygenesis rose to prominence as an article of nineteenth-century "scientific racism" and was rare before then. Its most prominent Early Modern advocate was Isaac La Peyrère, author of *Prae-Adamitae*, subtitled in its English translation *A Theological Systeme upon that Presupposition that Men were before Adam* (1656). This treatise understandably turned La Peyrere into a celebrated heretic, and many pious writers set out to rebut him. The issue of American Indian origins was one of La Peyrère's primary pieces of evidence, but it was not what attracted most attention to the text. La Peyrère had already published a *Relation of Greenland*, and pointed out that since the Norse voyagers had encountered native Eskimos when they reached North America, the Native Americans could hardly be their descendants, as Hugo Grotius had claimed. Today a challenge to the Adamic Genesis is no longer a heresy, but the idea that human beings arose in the New World rather than migrating from the Old does place one beyond the pale of scientific respectability.

How can Euro-Americans disabuse ourselves of the Eurocentrism that for five hundred years has prevented recognition of American Indian autochthony and sovereignty? An Iroquois acquaintance of mine told an anecdote about his brother, who was employed as a tour guide. Some Japanese tourists commented on the resemblance of his facial features to their own, and he replied that this was because the Japanese were descendants of his people. The tourists were nonplussed, too polite to argue. But let us think critically about this anecdote. If Kennewick Man is most closely related to the Ainu people indigenous to Japan's northern isle of Hokkaido, as some anthropologists have claimed, and also the ancestor of the Umatilla and Yakima Indians of the Columbia River valley, then are not the

Ainu the offspring of a Yakima just as much as the Yakima of an Ainu?[56] We are misled, I think, by our habits of confusing racial terms with geographic ones. By using geographical terms as ethnic labels, and then using these ethnic labels as surrogates for race, as with "African-American" or "Causasian," we allow the characteristics of Kennewick Man, or of Native Americans generally, to support imperialistic claims that Native American sovereignty is invalid, and Native American identity somehow inauthentic.

CONCLUSION

The critical study of the question of Native American origins demands that we reflect upon how "race" has been constucted not only historically, but also prehistorically. Ethnocentric contradictions and biases have infected the popular discussions of human prehistory because we extend our names and notions for human races and cultures of the past few hundred years to the archeological vestiges of peoples as old as ten thousand years. In effect, our historiography has still not responded to the consequences of the shift from a shallow biblical time frame to a deeper geological and paleontological scale. Such an extreme application of anthropological "upstreaming" as deciding whether Kennewick Man is Umatilla or not may be compelled by the legal demands of NAGPRA, but when critically considered it only reveals the absurdity of popular notions of race and ethnicity. A thousand years is long enough to utterly transform cultures, languages, and races. Yet we too easily collapse temporal gaps and pretend to determine the "race" of a Kennewick Man, pretend that the landing of Phonecians in America two thousand years ago would make a difference in the racial identity of Native Americans today.

A critical recognition of how the deeply ingrained assumptions of Judeo-Christian cosmology and European colonialism have influenced the construction of Paleoindian cultures in the Americas should help Anglo-Americans appreciate the perspective of Native American cosmologies, even if such oral histories are not given the same weight as archaeological evidence.[57] In teaching about race and ethnicity in our courses, the perspectives offered by American pre-history and Native American myth and literature can be extremely valuable, precisely because most students' ignorance of this material leaves them open to enlightening perspectives, if the material is presented properly. When I teach the Mayan creation story *Popol Vuh* I try to deflect the inevitable comparisons to the creation story in Genesis by asking students to articulate the Judeo-Christian myth in the context and vocabulary of the Mayan, rather than the other way around. Ask not how "they are like us" but how "we are like them." Rather than impose an Old World origin upon New World peoples, try to imagine a New World influence upon Europe and Asia.

NOTES

1. My thanks to Gary Taylor and Phil Beidler, organizers of the conference in Tuscaloosa, and especially to Madonna Moss of the Department of Anthropology, University of Oregon, for her help in revising this essay. Assistance such as hers makes this sort of inter-disciplinary work possible.

2. For a fine study of Kennewick Man and the controversy, see Roger Downey, *Riddle of the Bones: Politics, Science, Race, and the Story of Kennewick Man* (New York: Copernicus, 2000). Although the case has aroused extensive press coverage for more than five years, it is important to recognize that conflicts between Native peoples and archeologists need not be so contentious. The excavation of remains of similar age in Idaho and Southeast Alaska proceeded much more smoothly, with the cooperation of local Native peoples. See Terence E. Fifield, "Human Remains Found in Alaska Reported to be 9,730 Years Old," Society for American Archaeology *Bulletin*, 14:5 at www.saa.org, and Susanne J. Miller et al., "The Buhl Burial: A Paleoindian Woman from Southern Idaho," *American Antiquity*, 63:3 (1998): 437–456. The latter paper is my source for the figure of thirty-two similar finds.

3. While my critique aims to expose the racial character of research in this field, at least one anthropologist has attacked the gender bias in this insular field dominated by men: "Paleoindian studies stands out as particularly circumscribed within a closely interactive group of scholars contained by boundaries of specialized journals dedicated solely to Paleoindian research (for example, the *Mammoth Trumpet*)." Joan Gero, "The Social World of Prehistoric Facts: Gender and Power in Paleoindian Research," *Women in Archaeology: A Feminist Critique*, ed. Hilary du Cros and Laurajane Smith (Canberra, Australia: Prehistory Press, 1993), 33.

4. See for example "Expert Panel Recasts Origin of Fossil Man in Northwest" by Timothy Egan, The *New York Times* October 16, 1999, which has photos of the skull and the reconstruction; "Find this man's origins: Congress should approve scientific study" editorial, *The Register-Guard*, Eugene, Oregon, November 23, 1997.

5. Lafaye, *Quetzalcoatl and Guadalupe: The Formation of Mexican National Consciousness, 1531–1813* (Chicago: University of Chicago Press, 1976), 39.

6. On this debate see Francois-Xavier de Charlevoix, *Journal d'un voyage fait par ordre du roi dans l'Amérique septentrionale*, ed. Pierre Berthiaume (Montreal: Les Presses Universitaires de Montreal, 1994),

116–135, and Richard Popkin, *Isaac La Peyrère: His Life, Work and Influence* (Leiden: E. J. Brill, 1987).

7. "[U]n pretexte a montrer beaucoup d'erudition, une connaissance des oeuvres classiques et du pedantisme." John R. Carpenter, *Histoire de la Littérature Française sur la Louisiane de 1673 à 1766* (Paris: Nizet, 1966), 261.

8. Joseph-François Lafitau, *Mœurs des Sauvages américains comparées aux mœurs des premiers temps* (Paris, 1724); English edition: *Customs of the American Indians Compared with the Customs of Primitive Times*, trans. and ed. William Fenton and Elizabeth Moore (Toronto: Champlain Society, 1974); on Acosta, see below.

9. Ridge, "The North American Indians, part 1," *The Hesperian*, 8:1 (March 1862) qtd. in Scott Michaelsen, *The Limits of Multiculturalism: Interrogating the Origins of American Anthropology* (Minneapolis: University of Minnesota Press, 1999), 142.

10. Morton, *Crania Americana: or, A Comparative View of the Skulls of Various Aboriginal Nations of North and South America: To Which is Prefixed an Essay on the Varieties of the Human Species* (Philadelphia: J. Dobson, 1839); see also Paul Semonin, "'Nature's Nation': Natural History as Nationalism in the New Republic," *Northwest Review*, 30:2 (1992): 6–41.

11. Gould, *The Mismeasure of Man* (New York: Norton, 1981), 50–68. See also Michaelsen, *The Limits of Multiculturalism*, 143–146, who treats Morton much more kindly.

12. Qtd. in Robert Bieder, *Science Encounters the Indian, 1820–1880* (Norman: University of Oklahoma Press, 1986), 67.

13. See Dorothy Lippert, "In Front of the Mirror: Native Americans and Academic Archaeology" and other essays in *Native Americans and Archaeologists: Stepping Stones to Common Ground*, ed. Nina Swidler et al. (Walnut Creek, C A: Altimira Press, 1997).

14. John Lloyd Stephens, *Incidents of Travel in Yucatán* (Norman: University of OK Press, 1962).

15. Le Plongeon, *Queen Moo and the Egyptian Sphinx* (Paris, 1878). See Robert Wauchope, *Lost Tribes and Sunken Continents: Myth and Method in the Study of American Indians* (Chicago: University of Chicago Press, 1962), 7–21; and Lawrence G. Desmond, "Augustus Le Plongeon: A Fall from Archaeological Grace," in *Assembling the Past: Studies in the Professionalization of Archeology* (Albuquerque: University of New Mexico Press, 1999), 81–90.

16. See David A. Brading, *The First America: The Spanish Monarchy, Creole Patriots, and the Liberal State, 1492–1867* (Cambridge: Cambridge University Press, 1991), 365.

17. James M. Chandler, "Immigrants from the Other Side," *Mammoth Trumpet*, 17:1 (December 2001): 11–16; Thomas D. Dillehay, *The Settlement of the Americas: A New Prehistory* (New York: Basic Books,

2000), 68. For a rebuttal to this theory, promoted by Dennis Stanford of the Smithsonian Institution, see Lawrence G. Straus, "Solutrean Settlement of North America? A review of reality," *American Antiquity*, 65:2(2000): 219–226.

18. Stephen C. Jett, "Diffusion versus Independent Development: The Bases of Controversy," *Man Across the Sea: Problems of Pre-Columbian Contacts*, ed. Riley et al. (Austin: University of Texas Press, 1971), 5–53.

19. Francisco Lopez de Gomara, *Historia generale de las Indias* (Madrid: Espasa-Calpe, 1941), II: 248–249; qtd. in Lee Huddleston, *Origins of the American Indians: European Concepts, 1492–1729* (Austin: University of Texas Press, Institute for Latin American Studies, 1967), 25.

20. On the Atlantis myth see Williams, *Fantastic Archeology*, 130–155, and Wauchope, *Lost Tribes and Sunken Continents*; both discuss some of the dozens of popular books on the subject. On Phoenician-Carthaginian migration, see Michael Frank Doran, "A Time Perspective for Study of the Trans-Atlantic Phoenician Problem," M.A. Thesis, University of Oregon, 1971.

21. Thomas Jefferson, *Notes on the State of Virginia*, ed. Frank Shuffleton, (Harmondsworth: Penguin, 1998), 107.

22. Ibid., 316.

23. Ibid., 108.

24. Ibid., 107.

25. Luigi Luca and Francesco Cavalli-Sforza, *The Great Human Diasporas: The History of Diversity and Evolution* (Reading, MA: Addison-Wesley, 1995),120–121. Related research using mitochondrial DNA has resulted in the theory of an "African Eve" origin of paleo-humans in Africa, some 150,000–200,000 years ago. See R. M. Cann, Stoneking and A. Wilson "Mitochondrial DNA and human evolution," *Nature*, 325 (1987): 31–36.

26. Jose de Acosta, *Historia natural y moral de las Indias* (1590). English edn. *Natural and Moral History of the Indies*, trans. Edward Grimston (1604, rpnt. Hakluyt Society, 1880), I: 60, 61.

27. Ibid., I: 72.

28. Williams, *Fantastic Archaeology*, 32.

29. Ibid., 126, 284.

30. Dillehay, *The Settlement of the Americas*, 168–180. Dillehay is the principal investigator of the Monte Verde site in Chile, dated at more than 12,000 years ago. This finding on the west coast of South America would imply a much earlier presence of humans in North America, or possibly a trans-Pacific migration.

31. Acosta, *History of the Indies*, I: 67.

32. Diego Duran, *The History of the Indies of New Spain,* trans. Doris Heyden (Norman: University of Oklahoma Press, 1994), 4–5.

33. Williams, *A Key into the Language of America* (London, 1645); Menasseh Ben Israel, *The hope of Israel/Menasseh ben Israel; the English translation by Moses Wall, 1652,* ed. Henry Méchoulan and Gérard Nahon (Oxford: Oxford University Press, 1987).

34. Braude, Benjamin, "Les contes persans de Menasseh Ben Israël: Polémique, apologétique et dissimulation à Amsterdam au xviie siècle," *Annales, Histoire, Sciences Sociales*, 49 (1994): 1107–1138.

35. Jones, *History of the Ojibway Indians* (1861), rprt. Toronto: Canadiana House, 1973; qtd. in Michaelsen, *The Limits of Multiculturalism*, 132.

36. The ideological links between English colonialism in North American and in Ireland are numerous, and several scholars have studied similaries in the representations of the two peoples as "savages." See for example Francis Jennings, *The Invasion of America: Indians, Colonialism, and the Cant of Conquest* (New York: Norton, 1976); and, for a much later period, Astrid Wind, "Irish Legislative Independence and the Politics of Staging American Indians in the 1790s," *Symbiosis: A Journal of Anglo-American Literary Relations*, 5:1 (April 2001), 1–16.

37. Morton, *New English Canaan or New Canaan* (New York: Arno Press, 1972), 20.

38. See Djelal Kadir, *Columbus and the Ends of the Earth: Europe's Prophetic Rhetoric as Conquering Ideology* (Berkeley: University of Califonia Press, 1992), 184–188. Karen Kupperman's paper in this volume is also relevant to the issue.

39. For a discussion of the Madoc myth, see Mackenthun, *Metaphors of Dispossession*, 29–30; and Gywn Williams, *Madoc: The Making of a Myth* (London: Methuen, 1979). For later claims, see Robert Silverberg, *Mound Builders of Ancient America: The Archaeology of a Myth* (Greenwich, CT: New York Graphic Society, 1968), 85.

40. Oviedo, *Historia general y natural de las Indias* (1535–1550, rpnt. Madrid, 1959), I: 17–18; see also Brading, *The First America*, 36.

41. Gillespie, *The Aztec Kings: The Construction of Rulership in Mexican History* (Tucson: University of Arizona Press, 1989), xli; Lafaye, *Quetzalcoatl and Guadalupe*, chap. 9; Bernardino de Sahagun, *Historia general de las cosas de Nueva España*, English edition *Florentine Codex: The General History of the Things of New Spain* (Santa Fe: School for American Research, 1951–55); Mackenthun, *Metaphors of Dispossession*, 89–140.

42. See John Moffitt and Santiago Sebastian, *O Brave New People: The European Invention of the Amerrican Indian* (Albuquerque: University of New Mexico Press, 1996), 31–43.

43. Brading, *The First America*, 173.

44. Wauchope, *Lost Tribes and Sunken Continents*, 61.

45. Moffitt and Sebastian, *O Brave New People*, 243,

46. Barton, *Observations on some parts of Natural History, to which is prefixed an account of several remarkable vestiges of an ancient date, which have been discovered in different parts of North America* (London: for the author, 1787).

47. On Grotius see Huddleston, *Origins of the American Indians*, 118–121; Charlevoix, *Journal d'un Voyage*, 121–130.

48. Le Page du Pratz, Antoine-Simon, *Histoire de la Louisiane* (Paris: De Bure, Veuve Delaguette, et Lambert, 1758), III, 61–86. For an English

translation, see my website at <http://www.darkwing.uoregon.edu/
~gsayre/LPDP>. For the Le Maire manuscript, see Jean Delanglez,
"M. Le Maire on Louisiana," *Mid-America*, 19:2 (1937): 124–154.

49. See my "The Mound Builders and the Imagination of American
Antiquity in Jefferson, Bartram, and Chateaubriand," *Early American
Literature*, 33:3 (Fall 1998): 225–249.

50. The politics of this dynamic are complicated by the existence of Native
oral histories that provide some support for these scenarios. The Aztec
legend of Aztlan, the Lenapes' *Walam Olum*, and the migration of the
Sauk from the St. Lawrence to the Mississippi all bear witness to the
dynamic movements of Native American populations. And given two or
three thousand years, Native American cultures and populations could
have changed so dramatically as to absorb and transform many groups of
trans-oceanic migrants without leaving a trace. While much current
interest in Atlantic history and diaspora as paradigms for the study of race
is driven by work on the Black Atlantic, a Native American diasporic history may offer quite different paradigms rotating around the Pacific, and
involving thousands rather than hundreds of years.

51. Interview with Augusto Cardich, "The Southern Route: not Beringia,
but Tierra del Fuego," *Mammoth Trumpet*, 16:2 (March 2001), 4–6.
Also, there has been research into the diffusion of the sweet potato and
certain squash species from South America to Polynesia or vice versa. See
Man Across the Sea, 328–375.

52. Because evidence of human presence on Pacific islands dates back only
2000 or 3000 years at most, the anthropological consensus is strongly
against Cardich's theory. On the intellectual history of the immaturity
and inferiority of the Americas, see Antonello Gerbi's classic *The Dispute
of the New World*, trans. Jeremy Moyle (Pittsburgh: University of
Pittsburgh Press, 1973).

53. Enrique Dussel, *The Invention of the Americas: Eclipse of the Other and
the Myth of Modernity*, trans. Michael D. Barber (New York: Continuum,
1995), 74, 75–90.

54. Leon Pinelo, *El Paradiso en el Nuevo Mundo* (Lima, 1943); for a discussion of this work, see David A. Brading, *The First America*, 200–204.

55. Priest, *American Antiquities and discoveries in the West : being an exhibi-
tion of the evidence that an ancient population of partially civilized nations
differing entirely from those of the present Indians peopled America many
centuries before its discovery by Columbus, and inquiries into their origins,
with a copious description of many of their stupendous works, now in ruins,
with conjectures concerning what may have become of them; compiled from
travels, authentic sources, and the researches of antiquarian societies*
(Albany, NY: Hoffman and White, 1835), preface, n.p.

56. The Ainu have been discriminated against by ethnic Japanese, who
nurture a myth of their own primal sovereignty over the islands in defi-
ance of evidence of their ancient migration from mainland Asia. But my

point here is that the changed residence of Native Americans should not alter how we trace their ancestry to Northeast Asia, if this is the conclusion supported by genetic and archeological evidence.

57. For one example of the debate over the value of oral histories of events thousands of years old, see Thomas, *Skull Wars*, 239–253; and Vine Deloria, Jr., *Red Earth, White Lies: Native Americans and the Myth of Scientific Fact* (Golden, CO: Fulcrum, 1997), 161–209.

2

SLAVERY AND RACE

4

MICHELANGELO AND THE CURSE OF HAM: FROM A TYPOLOGY OF JEW-HATRED TO A GENEALOGY OF RACISM

Benjamin Braude

Michelangelo's *Nakedness of Noah* signaled a turning point in a myth, foundational for nearly half a millennium in the Euro-American construction of race and ethnicity, the myth of Noah and his Sons. With this image, the theology of Noah as a first Christ contracted and the anthropology of Noah as a second Adam expanded. With this image, the story of Noah and his Sons started to shift from a vehicle for Jew-hatred to a vehicle for Black-hatred. It was only after this image was painted and its implications diffused that the Curse of Ham, the most widespread justification for the enslavement of Africans, dominated biblical exegesis. However the role of Michelangelo in this transformation, please note, is not causative, but rather indicative.

To persuade you of this claim we must go backward and forward from 1509 when Michelangelo painted Noah in Rome, but first we must briefly examine it on its own terms. Most now misname it the *Drunkenness of Noah,* the first or last (depending on perspective) fresco in the Sistine Chapel Bible cycle. It depicts a story from the book of Genesis, chapter nine. Noah gets off the ark, makes wine, and gets drunk and exposed. Son Ham sees his nakedness and rushes out to tell brothers Shem and Japhet. They come in and cover up father Noah. Later when he recovers, he knows what his little son has done to him. He then curses Ham's son Canaan with slavery and blesses the other two brothers with mastery over him.

Within the bimillennial history of the iconography of Noah there are two remarkable aspects that distinguish Michelangelo's work. It is the last major public painting or sculpture of Noah's nakedness that exposes his genitals. And it is the only image of Noah's nakedness that exposes practically everyone else's as well. One indication of the scandalous quality of Michelangelo's interpretation is the afterlife of the right third of this fresco that depicts two naked brothers embracing in a way that suggests anal intercourse. When the great authority on prints, Adam Bartsch, catalogued its engraving in 1811, he evinced no indication of the subject other than to suggest, struck by its nudity, that this was "an artist's fancy." Correctly he noted its accepted attribution to Marcantonio Raimondi, the founding genius of Italian print craft, otherwise notorious for his depiction of *heterosexual* intercourse. But Bartsch failed to state that this image of homosexual contact claimed a biblical source and originated in the Pope's private chapel.

Quite apart from the significance of what Michelangelo himself was up to—a subject to be explored presently—there is the broader question of how the story of Noah and his sons has been visually imagined, before and after the Sistine Chapel. An image dating from about 1220–1230 (Osterreichische Nationalbibliothek, Codex Vindobonensis 2554, folio 3v) from a so-called moralized Bible executed in the royal atelier in Paris presents one interpretation. By contrast a very different representation appeared in Albany, New York in 1843, published by a contemporary in both time and place of the Mormon prophet Joseph Smith.[2] Paradoxically, although the thirteenth century image was a model for hundreds and probably thousands of copies diffused in a variety of genres throughout Europe during the Middle Ages and the Renaissance, today its meaning is almost completely forgotten. On the other hand, although the 1843 image is today almost completely unknown, its meaning was familiar to most Americans and Europeans over much of the past three hundred years. The thirteenth century depiction of Ham makes him a Jew. The nineteenth century depiction of Ham makes him a Black.

Further details of that thirteenth-century manuscript will make the first point clear. First Noah drinks the wine. Then the sons respectively cover and uncover their father—Ham's actual uncovering of Noah is a significant departure from the early patristic description of this scene but is consistent with the medieval verbal and visual reconstruction of what happened. The Ham figure on the far left is depicted with a distinctive beard. The significance of that beard is manifest in the next two images, the underlying New Testament perspective through which this story is retold. We see the torment and crucifixion of Christ, the Noah-like figure. We further observe the figures, the instruments of the suffering of Jesus Christ, the figures similarly bearded and placed in this bottom frame. To make the identity of these Ham-like figures crystal clear most are given Jew's caps, in addition to the telltale beards. The two Christians by contrast modestly either cover eyes or avert their glance, like the good sons of Noah, Shem and Japhet, depicted above. The purpose of these images is expressed in the manuscript's moralizing caption; hence the name moralized Bible, "That one of the brothers [i.e. Ham] uncovered him and the others covered him signifies the Jews who uncovered the shame of Jesus Christ and the Christians who covered him."[3]

The propagation of these images is even more significant, for while they originated in a genre fit only for kings and the wealthiest aristocrats they soon trickled down into multiple manuscripts and print genres diffused throughout Europe and today to be found in practically every major library on the continent. From lavish comic books or tele-novellas for the rich they were transformed into the simpler *Speculum Humanae Salvationis*. Eventually the images spread to the so-called *Bible of the Poor, Armenbibel, Biblia Pauperum* that took an even cruder block-printed form and became a staple of the early modern print trade. Three examples illustrate this transformation: first, a far more primitive Vatican manuscript, the second and third, both printed; now housed respectively in the Topkapi Palace Museum (Istanbul) and the British Library.[4]

What is the basis for each of these different interpretations, Ham as Jew and Ham as Black? Neither is self-evident from the scriptural passage itself. Though one essential and permanent element is there. In all interpretations, Ham was the archetypal Other. Whatever the phobia of a moment, Ham was it. He was the featured offering in the Other of the Month Club. In the course of his long history Ham was Egyptian, heretic, sinner, satyr, sodomite, Jew, Muslim, Mongol, Black, Asian, and African. He was also both master of empire and slave, a paradoxical synthesis that Hegel could love and appreciate.

But what about the two cases before us, for these were arguably the most influential interpretations in his long history? What made him a Jew in the thirteenth century and a black in the nineteenth? Ham, the Jew, can be traced back to the *City of God,* the roughly early-fifth-century work of Augustine, Bishop of Hippo.[5] Ham, the Black, starts to come to the fore in the sixteenth century, though anticipations of it can be traced back to ambiguous Christian and Jewish sources, as early, in some cases, as the third century, as well as to clearer ninth century Muslim texts.[6] The particular Christian hermeneutic that allowed the Black Ham to emerge in Euro-America however only gained strength much later during the era of print, reformations, exploration, and exploitation.

A brief digression about scriptural hermeneutics and its role in the story would be helpful. The classic Christian approach to the so-called Old Testament, or as I prefer to call it, the First Bible was to read it through the perspective of the Christian appendix, the Second Bible, that is the New Testament. Everything in the First Bible antic-ipated everything in the Second, the so-called typological reading. Thus Noah adumbrated Christ. Ham adumbrated the Jews. Ham's derisive treatment of Noah anticipated the Jews' derisive treatment of Christ. The very different hermeneutic that emerged in the early modern world preferred literal to allegorical readings. Since the scriptural genealogies of Ham did not tie him to Abraham, Isaac, and Jacob, it became increasingly difficult to connect him to the Jews. On the other hand, it did tie Ham to Kush, one of his four sons, often misleadingly translated Ethiopia. Kush itself had originally des-ignated what today would roughly be southern Egypt, northern Sudan.

Ancient Aithiopia itself should not be confused with the modern state of Ethiopia since the former could extend from the Atlantic to the Indian Ocean, across Africa and Asia. Although muted this ancient transcontinental legacy survived at least into the nineteenth cen-tury.[7] In medieval iconography Ham was never depicted as black. Kush and Africa were rarely so depicted. A late-fifteenth-century English royal genealogical table portrayed the line of Ham, Kush, and his son Nimrod in proper Tudor regalia and skin color.[8] Another English manuscript, about a century earlier, ignored Kush altogether, but depicted his son, Nimrod, as a Black in one frame and as White in another, the latter being the norm in Christian iconography. How seriously to take this artistic inconsistency is not at all clear since the same manuscript also depicted the Old Testament figure Enoch, never otherwise identified with sub-Saharan Africa, as a white-skinned figure with so-called Negroid facial features and curly-kinky-hair.[9] Such hair has by itself merited the inclusion of a depiction of Kush, to be found in a genealogy of Christ originating in a small German church around 1230, in the magnificently illustrated *Image of the Black in Western Art*.[10] However not only do these German Kushites have the same white skin as all the others in the scroll, they also have pinkish-red cheeks, a detail only visible if you examine the original to be found today in Berlin. Furthermore the adjoining Nimrodites—all white in this image—in contrast to their paternal ancestor have wavy hair like all the other non-Kushites. Africa well into the mid-fifteenth century was often white in the European imagination, as demonstrated by a Burgundian map of Noah's sons established on their respective thirds of the world. Note that Ham's African realm included Athens, a metropolis similarly located by a German chronicle a few decades earlier.[11]

More than a century later such images began to be displaced by a new world-view embodied in a popular artistic theme, the allegory of the four continents. From the seventeenth century on it flooded the entrance halls of merchant houses from Antwerp to Evora, inspired artists such as Rubens, and decorated frontispieces of the new omnipresent genre of cosmography. The frontispiece from the book of that name by Peter Heylyn, first printed in London in 1652 can stand for hundreds of similar images from Basle, Paris, Rome, Turin, and Madrid displayed and distributed throughout Europe.[12] The contrast between the Burgundian illumination in 1455 and the English engraving two hundred years later demonstrates how radical was the shift. The Albany Black Ham of 1843 marked a culmination of this transformation. For the first time in the history of Jewish, Christian, and Muslim iconography Ham was depicted with a distinctive color.[13] By the mid-nineteenth century this new interpretation became so confidently established that the following commentary on Genesis, popular on both sides of the Atlantic, could be written by a leader of the Church of Scotland:

> "Cursed be Canaan"—this doom has been fulfilled in—the slavery of the Africans, the descendants of Ham—'God shall enlarge Japheth'— 'he shall dwell in the tents of Shem'—a prophecy being fulfilled at the present day, as in India British Government is established, and the Anglo-Saxons being ascendant from Europe to India, from India over the American continent.
>   What a wonderful prophecy in a few verses![14]

Now you know the range of the pre- and post-Sistine images of the story, but what about the signal role I have assigned Michelangelo's *Nakedness of Noah* in this story? What was Michelangelo up to? Another image helps answer that question, one found in an early fourteenth-century Haggadah from Catalonia, the ritual reenactment of the Passover *seder* meal.[15] The scene unfolds like a triptych from the center, first to the right and then to the left. In the center Noah is cutting the fruit of the vine. The sharp blade is poised about to clip the genital-like cluster of grapes. On the right, he has drunk himself silly. On the left, his two good sons cover him, but the damage has already been done. He is reaching down between his legs to figure out where the rest of him is. More than Ham is missing from the scene. However far-fetched we might find the images of Jew and Black assigned to this story, the notions of castration might seem even more remote. But in fact castration is one part of a well-established tradition of interpretation, what might be called a polemic of sexual abuse, which culminates in Michelangelo's images in the Sistine Chapel.

The story is ancient, the evidence complex. What I give here are the conclusions. The Bible understood that somehow or other Ham sexually abused his father in the tent, probably through rape. Around the third century, rabbinical interpretation added castration to the crimes. Ham had both raped and castrated Noah. This addition was part of a controversy over celibacy particularly heated after the destruction of the Temple in the year 70 C.E. As I reconstruct it, extreme Jewish ascetics argued that the Temple's destruction demanded communal penance, including mass celibacy. The dominant rabbinic position argued this would violate God's commandment to Noah and his sons: "be fruitful and multiply." The ascetics responded, but Noah had no more children after that commandment so it did not represent a procreative imperative. The rabbis responded, true Noah had no more children, but that was simply because he could not. He was a eunuch. Ham became the hook—actually one of several—upon which this interpretation could hang.[16]

With the rise of Christianity's belief in incarnation this Jewish interpretation acquired a new anti-Christian polemical edge. Noah, remember, was Christ. Christ was Noah spiritual, according to Origen, the great third-century Church Father from Alexandria.[17] Therefore Noah was Christ physical. Christ's physicality was one cornerstone of the central mystery of Christianity that God had been made perfect and complete human flesh. However if Jews and others were arguing that Noah was a eunuch, in effect they were claiming that Christ was one too. And if Christ was a eunuch, could he be full and complete human flesh? While there were disputes on that point, the dominant approach, certainly by the Middle Ages was that Christ was fully equipped. The issue of castration was particularly sensitive for early Christians since some—perhaps even the famous eunuch Origen himself—had interpreted Christ's statement in Matthew 19:12, praising "eunuchs for the sake of the kingdom of heaven" as justification for preferring the literal deed to the metaphor of celibacy.[18] To display Noah as genitally intact was one proof positive against the heretic cult of castration. As a consequence from at least the sixth century in the famous illuminated Greek Bible produced in Syria, now known as the Vienna Genesis, through the very late eleventh century in the towering frescoes of St. Savin sur Gartempe in western France, into the magnificent thirteenth-century mosaics of San Marco in Venice, and more, throughout Latin Christendom, Christian artists were given license to expose Noah's most private parts. This display anticipated the Renaissance display of Christ's genitals intended to reinforce the complete incarnation of Christ, as Leo Steinberg has demonstrated.[19]

Around 1278 a Catalan scholar (re?)discovered and circulated the Jewish interpretation of Ham's behavior, as evidence of Jewish perversity, of the rabbis' dirty minds. Ramon Marti's revelation appeared in his *Pugio Fidei (The Dagger of Faith)*, one of the most thorough works of Christian polemic against Judaism ever composed.[20] Its only rival is the eighteenth-century German work *Entdektes Judenthum* by Johann Andreas Eisenmenger, which later became the Bible of Nazi anti-Semitism.[21] What Marti's research disseminated to the polemicists of Christendom was not merely evidence of dirty minds, but of something even worse, given the tradition of the Christian typological reading of the Bible. If Jews claimed that Ham had buggered and cut off Noah and if Christians read and viewed their omnipresent moralized Bibles, their Bibles of the Poor, to believe that Ham was the Jew and Noah was the Christ, then in effect the Jews were admitting that they had buggered and cut off Christ as well. The deicide and the crucifixion were a genteel tea party compared to what really happened.

Starting in the fifteenth century awareness of this interpretation began to enter the iconography of Christian altarpiece paintings. There are three extant, two from Ferrara, that by Ercole de' Roberti and that by Cosme Tura known as the Roveralla altarpiece, and a third, by the so-called Master of the Life of the Virgin, possibly Bavarian, from the same period, roughly the 1470s.[22] Two of the three compare the nakedness of Noah to the circumcision and presentation of the Christ child in the Temple, reinforcing for the faithful at the moment of communion the connection between Christ and Noah, as well as the connection articulated by the moralized Bibles between Ham and the Jew. The two Ferrara pieces slyly expose the secret language of the Jews. Each merits detailed attention. The altarpiece by Ercole de' Roberti is framed on the top by David and Moses, their names spelled out in clear Hebrew letters, as if to proclaim that Hebrew knowledge is to be opened to the viewer. In the middle is the prone sleeping Christ child and just below him is the prone drunken Noah. The two linked together in exposed repose. Perhaps the circumcision to which Christ has just been subjected parallels the castration to which Noah has been subjected. The Rovarella altarpiece also prominently displays its Hebrew learning, through the Hebrew version of the Ten Commandments that frames the Virgin Mary's throne. Here again the Christ child lies in exposed repose, but unlike the Roberti piece, the support below is not Noah, but the Christ child himself, seeking to escape the circumcising blade. These two Ferrara pieces together link the circumcision of Christ with the exposure of Noah, and perhaps through the flaunting of Hebrew the assertion that their secrets, including the teachings about Noah that *The Dagger of Faith* had exposed two centuries earlier, are hidden no longer. The last image by a German artist, known as the Master of the Life of the Virgin, reinforces the Roberti linkage of the exposed (and perhaps just sexually abused Noah) with the just-circumcised Christ. The retable or altar backdrop displays on its far right in a pose parallel to the Christ child, the exposed Noah.

Accordingly it should be no surprise that in these very areas, northern Italy, southern Germany, at this very time, the charge of the blood-libel, that Jews murdered and mutilated Christ-like young boys, assumed a frenzied frequency and came to be expressed in an iconography that repeated the images of the altarpieces. Compare the image of the circumcision of Christ in the altarpiece of the Liebfrauenkirche in Nuremberg to a broadside depiction of the most famous blood libel of the age, Simon of Trent: ominously goggle-eyed Jews abusing the genitals of innocent children, Christ and Simon.[23] A second image of the Simon story comes from the famous *Schedel Chronicle,* that was first designed and printed in Nuremberg, 1493, just a few minutes walk from that same church, the Liebfrauenkirche in the town's market center.

All of which brings us back to Michelangelo and the sexual display with which we started this essay. The theme of sexual exposure, excess, and frenzy to the point of anal penetration that greets the lay visitor upon entering the Chapel is repeated as the last image just over the priestly entrance to the Chapel, the last corner of the Last Judgment. The so-called Minos figure, the commendatore of the underworld, on whom simultaneously both fellatio and castration are performed by a snake is placed right over that route to the sacristy.[24] These acts are similar to what the rabbis had said Ham had performed on Noah. Michelangelo then incorporated into his art the iconography of sexual abuse that had surfaced in late-fifteenth-century Italy. He also did something else. He realized in these images an interpretation

of the story that had been published in Rome to
well-respected scholar, who uncovered new do͟
world of ancient Greek literature, written in surp.
Renaissance Latin. That scholar was subsequently appoin͟
influential position in charge of vetting the orthodoxy ot
sermon preached before the Pope. If the Pope's own theologɪa
published an ancient account that Ham had raped and castrated his
father—only centuries later recognized as a fraud—why should
Michelangelo try to hide it.[25]

But Michelangelo went too far. Words on the printed page were
not images in open sacred space. They were over the top and artists
and theologians pulled back from their implications. After the Sistine
Chapel no artist ever painted or sculpted Noah's genitals again and
the ones who tried quickly found their work censored, covered up,
defaced, ignored, or suppressed. With the visualization of sexual
excess abandoned, the story of Noah and Ham became a blank slate.
Gradually a new way for Christians to read Noah evolved. Previously
he had been read to prefigure Christ. Now the focus shifted back to
Adam. Increasingly the stories of Noah and his family were read to
recall this founder of humanity in all its disturbing and newly discovered diversity. In the Sistine Chapel Genesis cycle Michelangelo's central Adam in fact anticipates, in youthful pose and physique, the aged
Noah. The curse of slavery, which previously could be interpreted
allegorically as a sign of heresy and infidelity, was increasingly interpreted literally as the mandate for a specific social and economic institution. These new readings drew upon and recast tales that previous
generations had ignored or cast into the shadows. As Noah's genitals
receded into the dark background, dark stories of the past intruded
into the foreground. In an age of exploration and exploitation those
stories shaped the Curse of Ham.

The late—only in the nineteenth century—visualization of Ham
the Black Man suggests how entrenched the earlier identification of
the story with Jewish tormenters and sexual abuse had become. It
took a very long time for these new images to emerge. However in
print if not in image, this new interpretation had arisen centuries earlier in response to the needs of an age of expansion. The Curse entered
English letters through George Best in 1578. Although long known,
the highly significant context of his introduction has been ignored.[26]
Surprisingly, it appeared in an account of Martin Frobisher's quest for
the Northwest Passage. That in turn was excerpted and reprinted in
the second installment of Richard Hakluyt's paean to exploration and
expansion, *Principal Navigations*.[27] The motive behind Best's inclusion

ᴛhe Curse of Africans in a book about Arctic waters lies buried in ᴛe middle of a typically endless title page, . . . *also, there are annexed certayne reasons, to proue all partes of the worlde habitable.* . . . Hakluyt's own title for Best's work reiterates it, "Experiences and reasons of the Sphere to prooue all parts of the worlde habitable, and thereby to confute the position of the fiue Zones." Best and Hakluyt were committed to English expansion worldwide. They wished to dispel the frightening rumors that horrible consequences attended voyages to the north or the south. Would travelers return frozen? Would travelers "be burned as black as a cole, as the Indians or Black Moores"? The source of such fears was "the persuasions of certaine Philosophers," who believed that the "Sphere" was divided into "five Zones," only some of which can support human life.[28] According to the most extreme versions of climate theory, those who lived in the antipodes might be monsters, not humans, and, perhaps, those from other regions who stayed there might become like them as well.[29] Before the advent of global explorations and schemes for transoceanic colonization, such concerns had rarely arisen, but now they were becoming real. After such a voyage what guarantee did the Englishman have that a return to England would quickly return him to normality, even if he were willing to run the risk of temporary monstrosity? The urgent desire to refute the Philosophers in order to set the stage for English expansion demanded not only that Best disprove the climate theory of human diversity, but also provide a convincing alternative. The Curse of Ham was constructed out of ancient shards in the sixteenth century to provide it. A hoary biblical Curse, however problematic its original meaning, might displace climate as the cause for color. Even before the Curse of Ham became a justification for enslaving Africans, it became a means of constructing them. The Curse of Ham not only created African identity; it was also essential to the fixing of white identity. Just as Africans made it possible for Europeans to master and tame the wild reaches of the lands beyond the western ocean, so a theory of African origins allowed Europeans to tame the fear that they themselves might become as wild as the lands they sought to conquer. Europeans dared to master the Western Hemisphere first on the skin of Africans and only then on their muscle.

NOTES

Acknowledgments: Earlier versions of this paper were given at various forums that stimulated my thinking and improved my argument. I thank Dr. Vera

Lind and Prof. Helmut Keil, of the German Historical Institute, Washington DC and American Studies Institute, University of Leipzig respectively, Prof. David Brion Davis and Dr. Robert Forbes of the the Gilder Lehrman Center for the Study of Slavery, Resistance and Abolition, Yale University, Prof. Michael Fishbane and the Programs in Jewish Studies, Race and the Reproduction of Racial Ideologies, and African Studies and the Divinity School of the University of Chicago, Prof. Maurice Kriegel of the Ecole des Hautes Etudes en Sciences Sociales, Paris as well as Prof. John Brady of the Liberal Arts Luncheon Lecture, Smith College. This article is a summary without the iconographic evidence, of what will appear as Part One, "The Nakedness of Noah" in my *Sex, Slavery, and Racism: The Secret History of Noah and His Sons,* to be published by Alfred J. Knopf.

1. "Les deux hommes nuds debout," Adam Bartsch, *Le Peintre Graveur* (Vienna: J. V. Degen, 1811), no. 464, 13:345–346.

2. Josiah Priest, *Slavery, as it relates to the Negro, or African race, examined in the light of circumstances, history and the Holy Scriptures; with an account of the origin of the black man's color, causes of his* state *of servitude and* traces *of his character* as *well in ancient* as *in modern times: with strictures on abolitionism* (Albany: C. Van Benthuysen, 1843), 152.

3. Gerald B. Guest, ed., *Bible Moralisee, Codex Vindobonensis 2554, Vienna Osterreichische Nationalbibliothek* (London: Harvey Miller Publishers, 1995), 57. For a recent discussion of this genre and its role in fostering Jew-hatred see Sara Lipton, *Images of Intolerance: the Representation of Jews and Judaism in the Bible Moralisee* (Berkeley: University of California, 1999).

4. Vatican ms. Codex Palatinus Latinus 871, *Biblia Pauperum, Armenbibel,* ed. Christoph Wetzel and Heike Drechsler (Stuttgart: Belser Verlag, 1995), folio 12 verso; *Die Armenbibel des Serai: Rotulus Seragliensis Nr. 52,* ed. Adolf Deissmann and Hans Wegener (Berlin: W. de Gruyter, 1934), plate 21; *Biblia pauperum,* ed. Avril Henry (Ithaca: Cornell University Press, 1987), folio c.

5. Augustine, *The City of God,* tr. Marcus Dods (New York: The Modern Library, 1950), Book 16:2, p. 523; CCSL XLVIII, *De Civitate Dei* (Turnholt: Brepols, 1955), 500.

6. This argument is fully developed in Part Three, "The Blackening of Ham," in my *Sex, Slavery and Racism.* See also my "Cham et Noë. Race, esclavage, et exegese entre Islam, Judaisme, et Christianisme," in the theme issue devoted to L'Exercice de la comparaison: Comparer au plus proche/comparer au pluriel in *Annales: Histoire, Sciences Sociales,* March 2002.

7. See *Pall Mall Gazette,* April. 28, 1865, where the king of Ethiopia is an "Asiatic monarch." Cf. my "Palgrave and His Critics, the Origins and Implications of a Controversy: Part I, the Nineteenth Century—the Abyssinian Imbroglio," *Arabian Studies,* 7 (1985): 97–139.

8. British Library, Department of Western Manuscripts, King's 395, Folio 3 recto. The porosity of a distinction between Kush (Ethiopia) and the other

Noahides in pre-modern culture was not limited to iconography, but appears repeatedly as a variant in the most popular secular literary corpus of the Renaissance, the hundreds of manuscripts and printed editions of the mid-fourteenth century *Mandeville's Travels*. See my "The Sons of Noah and the Construction of Ethnic and Geographical Identities in the Medieval and Early Modern Periods," *William and Mary Quarterly*, 3rd series, 54 (1997): 103–142.

9. British Library, Department of Western Manuscripts, Egerton 1395: folio 5 recto, Nimrod and fire; folio 4 verso, Ham's descendants including Nimrod; folio 2 recto, Enoch among others.

10. Berlin, Staatsbibliothek Preussischer Kulturbesitz, Haus 2, Ms lat. f. 141, Rotullus of the Genealogy of Christ, c. 1230. See the multivolume, multiauthored collection *The Image of the Black in Western Art:* vol. 2, pt. 1, Jean Devisse, *From the Early Christian Era to the "Age of Discovery": From the Demonic Threat to the Incarnation of Sainthood,* tr. William G. Ryan, (New York: William Morrow, 1979), 142–144.

11. Brussels, Bibliotheque royale Albert 1ᵉᶠ, *La fleurdes histoires,* 281v–282r. *Ulrichs von Richental Chronik des constanzer Concils 1414 bis 1418,* ed. Michael Buck (1882, reprint Hildesheim: Olm Verlag, 1962), pp. 158, 171, 203, and 206. The English translation must be dismissed as unreliable, Louise Ropes Loomis, tr., *The Council of Constance: The Unification of the Church,* ed. John Hine Mundy and Kennerly M. Woody (New York: Columbia University Press, 1961). The editors of this posthumously published work did note that "occasional repetitious material has been cut," but the numerous references to Africa were cut even before they could be repeated.

12. Peter Heylyn, *Cosmographie in foure Bookes* (London: Henry Seile, 1652).

13. My argument for this late date is confirmed, *inter alia,* by the magisterial and prodigiously illustrated collection, *The Image of the Black in Western Art,* gen. ed. Ladislas Bugner (New York and Cambridge: William Morrow and Harvard University Press, 1976). Even more thorough is the source on which these volumes are based, the Image of the Black in Western Art, Research Project and Photo Archive, Harvard University, whose collection is ten-fold larger than what has been published. I thank its director, Dr. Karen Dalton, and her assistant, Dr. Sheldon Cheek, for allowing me to consult their records. Despite the absence of a pre-nineteenth century iconography of the Black Ham, Jean Devisse persisted in taking his black servitude for granted, rather than problematizing its origins, e.g. see., Devisse, *From the early Christian Era,* vol. 2, part 1, p. 55–56. Werner Sollors, *Neither Black nor White Yet Both, Thematic Explorations of Interracial Literature* (New York: Oxford University Press, 1997), p. 99, was the first to call attention to the originality of Priest's illustration.

14. Rev. Robert Jamieson, *Old Testament Genesis-Esther,* vol. I of *A Commentary Critical and Explanatory on the Old and New Testaments*

(first edition Edinburgh, 1861–65 reprinted Hartford and Philadelphia, 1871), p. 23.

15. British Library, Oriental and India Office, Manuscripts Or. 2884, Sister Haggadah, folio 3 recto.

16. The sodomy is evident through comparing Leviticus 18 to Genesis 9, which tie Canaan son of Ham with the violation of sexual taboos, most notably incest against a parent. See also the second-century bishop, Theophilus of Antioch, *Ad Autolycum*, tr. R. M. Grant (Oxford: Oxford University Press, 1970), 124–125, book 3:19 and the debate attributed to the third-centuries rabbis, Rab and Samuel, *Babylonian Talmud, Sanhedrin*, 70a.

17. Louis Doutrelau, S. J., ed. and tr., *Origene, Homelies sur la* Genese, new edition (Paris: Editions du Cerf, 1976), pp. 76–114.

18. Gary Taylor, *Castration, an Abbreviated History of Western Manhood* (New York: Routledge, 2000), pp. 185–209; Mathew Kuefler, *The Manly Eunuch, Masculinity, Gender Ambiguity, and Christian Ideology in Late Antiquity* (Chicago: University of Chicago Press, 2001), pp. 245–254.

19. *The Sexuality of Christ in Renaissance Art and in Modern Oblivion*, second edition, revised and expanded (Chicago: University of Chicago Press, 1996).

20. Jeremy Cohen, *The Friars and the Jews: the Evolution of Medieval Anti-Judaism* (Ithaca: Cornell Univerity Press, 1982), p. 129.

21. See my, "The Myth of the Sefardi Economic Superman," in Jeremy Adelman and Stephen Aron, ed., *Trading Cultures, the Worlds of Western Merchants, Essays on Authority, Objectivity, and Evidence* (Turnhout: Brepols Publishers, 2001), 165–194.

22. I thank Catherine Turrill, Keith Christiansen, and Leo Steinberg, respectively, for calling these works to my attention. Stephen John Campbell, *Cosme Tura of Ferrara : Style, Politics, and the Renaissance City, 1450–1495* (New Haven: Yale University Press, 1998), plate 99, p. 124, plate 87, p. 108, plate 102, p. 102. Michael Levey, *National Gallery Catalogues: The German School* (London: National Gallery Publications, 1959), 84.

23. Heinz Schrenkenberg, *The Jews in Christian Art: An Illustrated History* (New York: Continuum Publishers, 1996), 145, 280, and 278.

24. The fullest discussion of this image is Leo Steinberg, "A Corner of the Last Judgment," *Daedalus*, 109 (1980), 207–274.

25. Giovanni Nanni of Viterbo, *Commentaria super opera diversorum auctorum de antiquitatibus loquentium* (Commentaries on the Works of Various Authors who Spoke of Antique Matters), Rome, 1492.

26. Winthrop Jordan, *White over Black, American Attitudes toward the Negro, 1550–1812* (Chapel Hill: University of North Carolina Press, 1968), 17, 40 mischaracterizes Best's argument as a diversion; Alden Vaughan and Virginia Mason Vaughan, "Before *Othello*: Elizabethan Representations of Sub-Saharan Africans," *William & Mary Quarterly*, 3d Series, 54 (1997): 27.

27. (London, 1598–1600), vol. 3, 48–69.

28. Best *A True Discourse of the Late Voyages* (1578), 18, 19–20, 28–32.

29. In general, see Valerie I. J. Flint, "Monsters and the Antipodes in the Early Middle Ages and Enlightenment," *Viator, Medieval and Renaissance Studies*, 15 (1984), 65–80; Susan Scott Parrish, "Poisoned Knowledge and the Curious Body in America," Paper for the Early Modern Colloquium Panel, "Rethinking the History of Science: Race, Climate Theory, and Physiology, England and America," November 17, 2000; Jim Egan, *Authorizing Experience: Refigurations of the Body Politic in Seventeenth-Century New England Writing* (Princeton: Princeton University Press, 1999), 15–16; Karen Ordahl Kupperman, "Fear of Hot Climates in the Anglo-American Colonial Experience," *William & Mary Quarterly*, third Series, 41 (1984): 213–240, and "The Puzzle of the American Climate," *American Historical Review*, 87 (1982): 1262–1289. I thank Prof. Parrish for allowing me to consult her unpublished work.

5

"EXTRAVAGANT VICIOUSNESS": SLAVERY AND GLUTTONY IN THE WORKS OF THOMAS TRYON

Kim F. Hall

PROLOGUE: SEINFELD

George: I just heard that salsa is now the most popular condiment in this country.

Jerry: Do you know why? –because people like to say Salsa.

This moment from the television series "Seinfeld" springs from the media announcement of an important culinary event: the arrival of salsa, a "foreign" food, as the most widely consumed condiment in 1991 (presumably taking the place of the good old-fashioned "American" product ketchup). The setting, the ubiquitous "Mom's/Tom's diner," evokes the all-American diner that has been revived and celebrated in the past decades through national chains and suggests the possibility of community (albeit limited) in the large city.

The success of salsa marked in this conversation has global implications: many companies, particularly Pillsbury, are developing Americanized Mexican foods to sell to a worldwide market.[1] Adapted for the palate of one country, this "gringo food" is marketed to people who want to experience authentic Mexican taste (while in Latin American countries it is sold as "Mexican American food."). "Hispanic" becomes one of a number of "ethnic flavor profiles" developed by food conglomerates to satisfy the American appetite for novelty.[2] At the very moment that salsa becomes an "American" food—through homogenization of production and mass marketing to "mainstream" U.S. tastes—Seinfeld reminds us of its difference—his exaggerated pronunciation suggests that we like it for its "otherness"—its strangeness and novelty—as well as for its taste.

The oscillation between sameness and difference in this culinary phenomenon fits Robert Young's definition of hybridity:

> Hybridity thus makes difference into sameness, and sameness into difference, but in a way that makes the same no longer the same, the different no longer simply different. In that sense it operates according to the form of logic that Derrida isolates in the term "brisure," a breaking and joining at the same time, in the same place: difference and sameness in an apparently impossible simultaneity.[3]

Salsa—in commercials and in media coverage of its place in the U.S. economy—is simultaneously domestic and foreign. So too Seinfeld's continued play on "salsa/seltzer" continues this oscillation, joining salsa with another regionally marked "food"—seltzer—and offering another mark of ethnicity.

Young begins his study of hybridity by noting, "If language preserves one major product of contact, a second, less usual model ... is equally literal and more physical: sex."[4] Young's view is not singular. With the exception of anthropology, in postcolonial, colonial, and race studies, language and sex are the two points of contact focused on when thinking through hybridity: many in postcolonial theory investigate the ways in which Creole, patois, and other languages bear the weight of colonial encounters and a key question for early natural philosophers was whether the offspring of inter-racial couplings would be fertile. While language and sex/desire do produce intimate points of convergence that allow us to open up discussions of hybridity, food is in literary studies a less theorized way that societies mark cross-cultural encounters and articulate changing notions of difference. Eating is physical; it involves incorporation of substances that potentially alter the body. It also draws one into a system of exchange that connects the consumer with the many—farmers, laborers, cooks, and the like—who produce food. When I speak of "food" in this essay I refer to a variety of phenomena: the actual consumption of spices, drinks, and other substances, the production of cooked dishes from their raw ingredients, the production of agricultural products from the land, the exchange of edible commodities, and the use of food imagery in representation. In other words, the mechanisms that come into play in sugar's movement from nature to material culture.

The U.S. media conversations around salsa interest me because they demonstrate how food may function as an index of cultural identity, particularly how it queries the boundaries of the nation in the face of global movement of commodities as well as adoptions/colonizations of the "foreign" (or, in early modern terms, the "strange"). The widespread assumption of the media in covering this story is that the nation is constituted by what it consumes. The idea that ketchup and salsa are somehow substitutes for each other since they are both red sauces made with tomatoes allowed the media to use a statistic about salsa sales to work through the meanings of diversity in the United States as well as to assess the cultural influence of peoples ordinarily at the margins, particularly the implications of Latinos as the fastest-growing ethnic group.[5] Foods mark local, regional, and national boundaries even when they are through global exchange readily available (and even produced) miles from their point of origin. Salsa itself originates in a borderland of Texas/Mexico whose boundaries are still contested, porous, and uneasy.

Food as a point of contact between cultures thus helps us query, among other things, identity, economic relations, and aesthetics. The acceptance of new products identified as edible and desirable produces hybridity: to be understandable as food, the plant/substance must be perceived as somehow familiar. This is usually accomplished in food discourse by analogy and simile. However, the desire for novelty that can be a product of colonial exchange hinges on a perception of the food's newness and difference.

*   *   *

I began with salsa because it seems a readily accessible framework for thinking about the numerous culinary incursions produced by the expansion of the European world in the seventeenth century and accompanying questions of hybridity: tomatoes, tea, and chocolate were among the entirely new tastes introduced to European palates while other substances—sugar is the one I am concerned with here—become more accessible to a broader range of society.[6] "The seventeenth century was the century in which sugar changed in Britain from luxury and medicine to necessity and food."[7] Richard Sheridan estimates that sugar use quadrupled in the last four decades of the seventeenth century and then tripled again during the first four decades of the eighteenth.[8] I am positing that the entry of any "foreign" substance into a cuisine has a moment of hybridity.

Simultaneously familiar and strange, domestic and foreign, the varied meanings of this food become available to writers as registers of a wide array of social, political, and economic issues. While all eating is "culturally symbolic and partakes in the social flow of commodities,"[9] the consumption of sugar is particularly overdetermined since it is for England linked to the institutionalization of a new method of production (as capitalist as it was agricultural),[10] and the growth of differently configured economic arrangements including relations between a (successful) colony and the metropole, transnational migration of goods and labor, more elaborate systems of credit, and the increased use of forced labor. In its earliest stages of Atlantic production, sugar brings together Europe, Africa, and America, owners of labor and producers of labor, into a new intimacy that would have profound implications for the modern world.

Concerns about the "foreign" nature of now common substances and the proper balance of trade animates much of the discourse on food in the early modern period. The rest of this essay focuses on two works by Thomas Tryon who, because of his interest in diet and colonial affairs in the seventeenth century, is a pivotal figure for discussions of food, sugar, and consumption. Tryon was a prominent figure in the reemergence of vegetarianism in late seventeenth- and eighteenth-century Britain (Guerrini 34).[11] He began his youth as a shepherd, became a hatter, and, after a religious awakening when he became a follower of mystic Jacob Boehme,[12] turned to writing treatises on diet and health with the intention "to recommend to the world temperance, cleanness and innocency of living" (*Some Memoirs*). A late-blooming, but prolific author, Tryon's treatises, specifically *The Way to Health* (1682/1691), *The Good housewife made doctor* (1682) and *Friendly Advice to the Gentlemen-Planters of the East and West Indies* (1684), are characterized by an almost obsessive concern with imported foods and overindulgence. These diverse ideas had currency on both sides of the Atlantic. Aphra Behn wrote a poem to the author of *The Way to Health*, and Benjamin Franklin became a "Tryonist" for a short while after reading the same work.

Tryon's views are based on a vision of national bodies with discrete boundaries that are linked to their geographic origin. He is a dedicated nativist who strongly recommends not only a vegetarian diet but also abstinence from tobacco, alcohol, and all luxuries as the way to achieve long life, prosperity, and closer communion with God: "They ought to observe the Rules of Temperance, Sobriety, and Cleanness; both in Meats, Drinks, Exercises and Communications, which renders man fit and capable of all Noble Functions of the Body and Mind; observing and Practicing of these Rules, they shall find an inward and outward serenity, and walk in a happy Calm, through all the Thunders and Lightenings of a Tempestuous World."[13] A vocabulary of heterogeneity and excess is at the center of a constellation of issues: food's potential to change the individual body or to preserve a "national" body, the affects of labor conditions on consumers and the transplantation of bodies from one climate to another.

As I discuss later, his views on the preservation of the natural bodies of Englishmen (and therefore the national body) through avoidance of unhealthy combinations of food are formative for his specific arguments against the behaviors of planters and their treatment of slaves. For example, his *Friendly Advice to the Gentlemen-Planters* begins as a domestic manual of sorts—outlining the edible plants on the island and recommending which to eat and which to avoid—and ends as a discourse on slavery, two sections that are blackface "performances" in which Tryon uses the voices of enslaved black men to speak out against the evils of Caribbean slavery and living conditions.[14] His focus on "dangerous mixture" reverberates powerfully within an Anglo-Caribbean context, in a region whose early modern beginnings were conceived in the heterogeneous early modern traffic of people and goods.

The most striking part of Tryon's doctrine is his insistence on "purity" in diet. He argues that a healthy English diet must include foods grown in England served as close to their natural state as possible—raw or simply prepared. His texts rely on the idea that there is a specifically English body that has been corrupted by current food practices. For him, the way to restore/preserve the body is to stick with homegrown, simple, English foods. For example, in *The Good Housewife Made Doctor*, he advises, "all that have any regard to their Healths, to refrain from all such hurtful things, and content themselves (as their innocent lusty Fore Fathers did) with the Growth of our own Country, which will abundantly furnish our Tables, and contribute whatever is needfull for the maintenance of health and strength."[15] Although Tryon's work is motivated by religious concerns, his theories that the avoidance of improper mixture and heterogeneity in diet can produce stronger bodies and spiritual grace produce a fictive English purity that is both past and prologue; it is masculine English history as edenic past and a Promised Land to be achieved through the discipline of diet.

His views are largely rooted in humoral theory, a view of human physiology that insists that bodies (and character) are shaped by imbalances in the four essences/humors–blood, phlegm, black bile, and yellow bile.[16] As Mary Floyd Wilson notes, "early seventeenth century natural philosophy also suggests that varying degrees of a body's internal liquidity and temperature determine what modern readers would classify as 'racial' charactertistics. Renaissance climate theory avers that a region's atmospheric temperature, moisture level, soil, and topography help fix an inhabitant's humoral complexion, coloration, and temperament."[17] The humors link the body with character and spirit; the theory assumes climate's decisive affect on the body in a taxonomic way that prefigures (or is drawn upon by) later racial ideologies.[18] One can see this in *The Good Housewife Made Doctor*, where Tryon's articulation of the differences between food and its affects spills over into views on the absolute difference between peoples:

> What agreement or affinity is there between our *Fruits, Grains, Herbs* and *Seeds*, and those that come from the *East* and *West* Indies? not so much as that between the complexion of a Fat-nosed Lubber-lip'd Blackamore, or swarthy Bantamen, with a head like a Sugar loaf, and our most *Florid Beauties*. In particular, what likeness or correspondence is there between *Cloves, Mace, Nutmegs, Cinnamon, Ginger* or *Pomento*, and the Flower of Wheat, or any other Grain, with *Apples, Milk, Butter, Herbs* or *Flesh*? Verily, there is no simile between them, and the foolish Painter, that to a *Mans Head* added a *Stags Neck* and a *Fishes Body*, did not Limn a more deformed Monster, than those prepare a monstrous unwholsom Diet for either the well or sick, who jumble together Ingredients so heterogenious, and as it were diametrically opposite. The compounding of these Foreign Ingredients with our Domestick Productions, that chiefly destroys the Health of our People, and not so much the Compositions of our own Growth, though there are too often very improper Mixtures of them also ... (103–104)

His positing of the absolute incompatibility of foods produced in tropical regions with those produced in Northern Europe slides into an affirmation of absolute difference in color: racial difference itself and the mixture of foreign and domestic produce monstrosity that sickens the English body. His list of differences ends with the "deformed Monster," drawn from the opening of Horace's *Ars Poetica*, "a *Mans Head* added a *Stags Neck* and a *Fishes Body*."[19] This image of literally monstrous cross-species mixture—in Horace a figure of derision— here signifies a more dangerous hybridity.

Tryon's use of the word "heterogenious" here and elsewhere similarly marks the mixing of differences as dangerous. It is a relatively recent addition to the language; the *OED* lists a first use in 1624 and defines it in part as: "Diverse in kind or nature, of completely different characters; incongruous, foreign."[20] Thus it suggests an incompatibility that verges on an abnormal otherness or strangeness. Jennifer deVere Brody reminds us that "hybridity and purity are related terms that must be thought of as mutually constitutive representations."[21] The use of hybrid (or heterogeneous) "only confirms a strategic taxonomy that constructs purity as a prior (fictive) ground."[22] In this case, Tryon's recommended regimen rests on the spectral presence of an uncorrupted English body.

The rhetorical commodification of laborers is overwhelming in this passage. "Bantamen" are here made monstrous/hybrid through simile; "head like a Sugar loaf" resonates with the bodily substitution suggested later (the painting of a man's body with a "stag's neck") but here the head is equated with a commodity—sugarloaves were both exchanged as gifts and used as currency at this time.[23] The passage goes on to align colored labor with expensive, foreign, commodities— "Bantaman" or "Blackamore" is to Florid Beauty as exotic spice is to "native" foods. I would also argue that he indirectly draws on a common trope of woman as unnatural artist.[24] Women are painters who usurp nature's design and create monsters. The type of cooking valued in contemporary "receipt" or cookbooks is a kind of false art that makes domestic work potentially fatal to the nation's health.

Tryon consistently indicts English women for their role in "contaminating" the English diet. In a move familiar to readers of early modern works on clothing, we see Tryon not only blaming women for their failure to put truly nourishing food on the English table ("their unskillful ways of Preparation"), but also for an excessive appetite for variety:

> But our English have such an itching desire after Novelties, and every Joan is so proud to be of my Lady Fiddle-Faddles Humour, and long for things Far-Fetcht and Dear-bought, that if we had ten times as many more brought over as we have, there be those amongst us would cry up the excellent Vertues of them...(*Good Housewife* 102)

Although he begins with a blanket indictment of the English, the focus quickly turns to women who are here targeted as the main consumers of increasingly available exotic goods: women are the ones whose allegedly out-of-control desire for prominence and novelties potentially destroys the nation.

In many ways, Tryon's addresses to women are a response to the domestic manuals produced for women throughout the seventeenth century. Most of these earlier works claim cooking as a particularly female form of creativity and the production of sugar goods—cordials, preserves, confections, sweetmeats, and so on—comes to be touted as a specifically English talent.[25] Tryon argues that women and children are the "chief eaters" of sugar; he too identifies confectionary-making as part of female culture, but condemns its effects on the household:

> . . . how many Pounds do some Women trifle away in a year upon these harmful Vanities and Superfluities? yea, and some think themselves rare Housewives too, for this Prodigality, and are at pains or Cost to bring up their Daughters to these Baneful Mysteries of Preserving, Conserving &c. All which, besides a most impenitent Waste of their Husbands Money and spoil of Gods good Creatures, tend likewise to the detriment of their own Health and that of their Children. (106)

What is for cookbook author Hannah Wooley the "Accomplisht Ladys Delight" becomes Tryon's "harmful vanities" and "Baneful Mysteries."

I have argued elsewhere that English domestic manuals traffic in nostalgia: many harken back to a past of noble good housekeeping—of elaborate feasts composed of excessive amounts and extraordinary "devices."[26] Some even include bills of fare and descriptions of actual feasts supposedly held at court or in noble houses. Tryon both opposes and exceeds this move by positing a primal moment in English history before the incorporation of the "foreign":

> But these things are seldom consulted either by the Learned or by the good House-Wives, but they go on in the Road, and every day create hurtful Extravagances, perswading themselves that the more cost they bestow, the more rich things they jumble together, the better and more nourishing their Food must be; and more nourishing indeed it is, but of Diseases and evil Juices; whereas plain, course, cheap, simple Foods are much more friendly to Nature, and consequently more strengthening and restorative. And therefore in former Ages, when Sugar, *Spanish* Fruits, Spices, Sweet-Meats, and the like, were not known in these Northern Climates, People were not only healthier, but stronger, larger, and bigger bon'd than of late Years, since the frequent eating and mixing those foreign Ingredients with our more natural Food, which have and do daily prove of fatal consequence to the Healths of many that immoderately use them. (*Good Housewife* 86–87)

Unlike other manuals, *The Good Housewife Made Doctor* does not revere a specific feast or moment in England's past; it sees such events as evidence of English degeneration. Tryon instead generates an unlocatable space—"former Ages"—inhabited by a large, healthy, and pure English populace. Seventeenth-century women are the agents of degeneration; opening the doors of their homes to foreign goods and compelling exotic tastes, they disrupt the proper alignment of climate, region, and simple diet that is Tryon's passion.

If women's labor in the kitchen has an unsalutary affect on the English constitution because of their misguided practices, the labor of foreigners and slaves has a negative and immediate impact on the English body. Perhaps the most striking part of Tryon's rhetoric is his insistence that the conditions of labor directly and physically affect the consumer. He seems to assume that English goods are always produced under ideal conditions (or that, since they are mostly harvested by Englishmen, the circumstances are still "pure"); conversely, foreign goods are seemingly always tainted in production. For example, in discouraging English housewives from including currants in their foods, he argues that currants are not only bad because processed in a foreign clime ("Currants are much more injurious to the Health of English Constitutions than Raisins"), but also because the act of eating currants forces the English to consume the unhealthy bodies of foreign workers. He argues strenuously that currants should be substituted with hawthornes or elderberries:

> ...nay, these [Hawthorn or Elderberries] by a little custom would be much more proper for our Healths to be eaten by themselves, or mixed with other things, than Currants, which are of such an untoward Nature, that those Natives that work amongst them, and strew and pack them into Casks, have their *Feet, Legs* and *Hands* made *Leporous* and *Scabby* thereby, which proceeds from their hot, venomous Qualities, and with these *loathsome, Leporous Feet* and *Legs* they tread them into the Casks, and then *you eat them for dainties.* And though when eaten here these evil Qualities, are mitigated by being mixed with our moderate and more friendly *Grains* and *Fruits;* yet still, whatever they are put into, does thereby become the worse, and the more unwholsom. (*Good Housewife* 97)

Tryon argues that the very process of harvesting disintegrates the workers' bodies ("have their Feet, legs and Hands made Lebrous and Scabby thereby") and that this putrefaction in turn pollutes the food. His oddly cryptic syntax suggests the directness of the connection: "with these loathsome Lebrous Feet and Legs they tread them into the Casks and you eat them for dainties": "them" is indeterminate—you are eating both the worker and the currant as "dainties."[27] In making valued foods unpalatable, Tryon relies on a kind of rhetorical defamiliarization. He attempts to make accepted foods foreign again by negatively reminding us of climate and conditions of production. At the moment that would be the ultimate performance of aristocratic (or aspiring aristocratic) identity—the eating of dainties or sweetmeats—the eater is made the opposite, a cannibal.

This strategy of suggesting that the corrupted laboring body poisons the consuming body is a significant weapon in his attack on Caribbean slavery. His views on English food consumption and English slavery are thoroughly intertwined in *His Friendly Advice to the Gentleman Planters* where he is a vocal opponent of the Caribbean system of slavery (if not of slavery itself). *Friendly Advice* appears in three sections: The first, "A Brief Treatise of the most principal Fruits and Herbs/Directions for the preservation of Health and Life in those hot Climates" follows Tryon's theories of diet, specifically identifying which native foods are best to maintain health in foreign climates and arguing for temperance in eat and drink. The final two sections, "Complaints of the Negro-Slaves against the hard Usages and barbarous Cruelties inflicted upon them" and "A dialogue between an Ethiopian or Negro-Slave and a Christian that was his Master in America" specifically create black personae to speak out against the harsh conditions of Carribean slavery. Tryon oscillates between arguing that Planters overconsume the labor of slaves and hinting that they consume the slaves themselves. In "the Negros' Complaint," the slave bemoans the de-valuation of his life: "Do not your Plantations which have drank up our innocent and unrevenged Blood, call unto the Lord, the righteous Judge of Heaven and Earth, for Justice and Retaliation? For divers of our Country-men have been Butcher'd this way, and little more notice taken of it than if we were Fleas or Gnats, or Wolves or Bears" (110). He suggests that, in the planter's mind, the only difference between himself and a dog is the value of slave labor. Here and elsewhere, however, that labor is equated with blood; the plantation and the home consume the body as well as the labor.

Tryon also paints a picture of slave bodies as commodities, as food in themselves, "cooked" by their inhumane working conditions:

> ...there we are in the hottest of Summer, and under that scorching Climate without any of the sweet Influences of the Air, or briezing Gale to refresh us, suffocated, stewed and par-boyled altogether in a Crowd, till we almost rot each other and our selves. (82)

Using the language of cookery, Tryon vividly depicts the natural process of becoming overheated as a man-made, unnatural process of exhaustion. "Stewing" and "par-boiling" hint that the dismal working conditions are a deliberate kind of "bad husbandry" on the part of planters. While in earlier Caribbean narratives culinary terms are used to suggest the desirability of colonial life and the availability of islands for consumption, Tryon hints that the planters have poisoned this idyll. They drink the blood of slaves and contaminate the land with fluids drained from overworked bodies. His rhetoric anticipates the more directly and graphically rendered denaturalization of sugar consumption in abolitionist discourse of the late eighteenth century. As Charlotte Sussman argues: "While supporters of the West Indian sugar trade imagined a British constitution that could expand to incorporate any product of the colonial arena, abolitionists imagined a domestic body in constant danger from a poisonous world; in order to make their moral point, they mobilized fears of bodily pollution."[28]

Tryon's images of consumption resonate within a compelling focus on Caribbean food practices in colonial narratives and also show to the modern readers the ways in which foodways were used to mark often racialized status differences. While the precise terms Sussman outlines respond to later interests and thus were not available to him, Tryon is similarly concerned with bodily/national boundaries as he inveighs against all kinds of dietary and geographic mixture: he abhors foods from different climates used in the same dish as well as eating of foods foreign to the climate the body inhabits. Climate, geography and diet are intimately related and must be carefully balanced to preserve the body's integrity. However, while the body is constituted by its climate, it is ultimately adaptable to changes in place; this supposition is key to Tryon's advice to colonial planters and to general concerns about maintaining English health in a foreign land. Tryon argues that planters suffer more from the tropical climate than they should because of their reliance on English luxury goods and refusal to adopt a diet suited to place: "…and that the Meat and Drinks we so much desire are not proper for our Bodies in such Climates, where not our own irregular Fancies, but the usages of the Natives of each Country ought to be our Guides and examples" (*Friendly Advice* D2r). While he is relatively mild in giving dietary advice and admonitions to temperance early in the text, the slaves whom he makes speak in the succeeding sections continually reference the planter's extravagant eating habits in relation to their dismal servitude.

In taking on the diets of wealthy planters and condemning their seemingly excessive consumption of food and drink, Tryon undermines a symbolically crucial facet of planter life. While it is impossible to know fully the eating habits of the Caribbean planter,[29] lavish gestures of hospitality and liberality are continually marked in early modern texts on the Caribbean in a way that suggests that they are significant indices to the culture and codes of England's early sugar colonies. Tryon's advice to "go native" in eating obscures the social reasons behind the planter's appetites for English food—reasons that have to do with establishing national identity and social status in a foreign land. West Indian planters, particularly those in Barbados, were legendary for their feasts. As Richard Dunn has noted, one of the most "striking feature[s] of the island life-style is the wide contrast in living habits between rich and poor," a disparity that, at least on record, appeared greater than that between rich and poor in England.[30] Dunn, suggesting that Caribbean eating habits are so remarked upon because the excess displayed was available beyond the social scale in England, reveals: "Having plenty of easy money to spend, they freely indulged in conspicuous consumption, living in a much more showy fashion than persons of their station would do in England."[31] Feasts showed the ability to maintain—and exceed—English standards of hospitality in a foreign land and thus the triumph and desirability of West Indian colonization. More important, feasts allowed planters to maintain social distinction and accounts of meals dramatize the differences between master, servant, and slave.

As I have discussed elsewhere, the first Anglo-Caribbean narrative, Richard Ligon's *A True and Exact History of Barbados* (1657), carefully notes the differences in diet between social classes and a much later text, John Oldmixon's *The British Empire in America* (1708), suggests that diet solidifies the boundary between indentured servitude and slavery: "Their [servants'] Diet is not so good, as those who have been us'd to rich Farmers Tables in England would desire, because they cannot be fed every Day with Beef and Mutton; however, they cannot complain of any Want; and the Planters distinguish them from the Negroes, by providing them Bisket from England."[32] Planters use imported English biscuits to remind servants of their connection with England in spite of different working conditions and, significantly, to make them not the "Negroes" (although perhaps not entirely "white") who are chiefly fed plantains and other locally produced starches.[33]

For Tryon, the plenty of masters must be measured against the dearth in the diets of indentured servants and enslaved Africans. Pleas for culinary temperance and more humane servitude overlap in the problem of excessive high living. Tryon's slaves' commentary on Caribbean feasts and drinking runs throughout the texts. Feasts are sites of license and excess; self-indulgence creates the conditions for English barbarity:

> O you brave and swaggering Christians! who exercise this strange and severe mastership over us, who sport your selves in all manner of superfluity and wantonness, and grow fat with our Blood and Sweat, gourmandizing with the fruits procured by our Slavery and sore Labour; set by your Rum-Pots, your Punch Bowls, your Brandy Bottles, and the rest of your intoxicating Enchantments for a while...(*Friendly Advice* 96)

Tryon's slave dwells at length on the disparity between the eating habits of slave and master in a way that reminds us of the special meaning of food and feasting for the Caribbean planter. Excessive luxury and poor treatment of slaves are both for Tryon acts that violate Christianity and Tryon's slave bases a great part of his complaint on the unchristian nature of plantation life: "But why, O ye Christians! do you thus violate the Commands of our Creator, and withstand, and walk contrary to the pure innocent Laws of Nature, and by your Intemperances and Oppressions contemn the Great Law of Love, and doing unto all their fellow Creatures as they would be done unto..." (126). "Intemperance and Oppression" are twinned evils as the labor of enslaved peoples creates luxurious excess. Indeed, their conspicuous consumption is a kind of idolatry:

> They wantonly consume the Encrease and Product of our heavy Pains in Riot and Voluptuousness, in Superfluity, and all kinds of Extravagant Vitiousness; their chief *Study* and *Philosophy* being to gratifie their liqourish Palates, and insatiate Paunches, and to enslave us with many intollerable Burthens; so that their Lamps are ready to be extinguished by their Superfluity and Excess of Oyl, whilst they make frequent and Solemn feasts, (that is, offer Sacrifices, and celebrate Festivals to their Idol *Belly God-Paunch*, the Divinity which they chiefly adore). (*Friendly Advice* 123–124)

The insistence on superfluity becomes for Tryon a reversal: the supposed Christians have become idolators and the "heathen" slave is the clearest proponent of Christianity. This focus on diet suggests that there is an intimate balance between planters' and slaves' lives captured in his phrase "extravagant viciousness": the excess and luxury in one produces the damage to and meagerness in the other. Tryon's focus on excess may in fact be key to a critique of the capitalist nature of plantation slavery. In order to achieve the wealth to live in luxury, the planter must create "the Encrease and Product of our heavy Pains" by extracting from his worker the most labor with the least input of capital.

Adamant in *The Way to Health* on the differences between food and the differences foodways create in human bodies, Tryon ultimately builds his critique of slavery on the insistence that bodies are essentially the same. Historian Hillary MacD. Beckles reminds us that "chattel slavery was more than just a labor system, it was part of a political campaign to differentiate the European culturally from the rest of humanity and to establish representations of a self-serving ethnic pecking order for the enforcement of 'otherness' upon colonized peoples."[34] In attacking a system that was as ideological as economic, Tryon's slave approaches the problem of race from a number of angles, drawing from the wide range of early modern discourses of race that increasingly constrict to an equation of blackness with slavery in the race for profit from Atlantic sugar. In each instance he argues that there are very few natural differences, "setting aside Custom and Education" (120); blackness is a climate-based difference, but not an essential or fundamental one:

> As for the blackness of our Skins, we find no reason to be ashamed of it, 'tis the *Livery* which our great Lord and Maker hath though fit we should wear; Do not you amongst Furs, prize pure Sables as much as Ermins? Is Jett or Ebony despised for its Colour? Can we help it, if the Sun by too close and fervent Kisses, and the nature of the Climate and Soil where we were Born, hath tinctur'd us with a dark Complexion? (*Friendly Advice* 115)

Using the language of aesthetics, black for Tryon becomes a removable veil that obscures the essential sameness of man from eyes narrowed by greed. It is capital, what Tryon calls "the false conceit" of interest that creates the absolute difference between black slave and white master.

The "Negro" attempts to undermine race-based slavery by reminding the reader that color is but one of many physical differences and suggesting the arbitrariness of color-based slavery:

> Have not you a variety of Complexions amongst your selves: some very White and Fair, other Brown, many Swarthy, and several Coal-black? And would it be reasonable that each sort of these should quarrel with the other, and a man be made a Slave forever, merely because his Beard is Red, or his Eyebrows Black? In a word, if our Hue be the only difference, since White is so contrary to Black, as Black is to white, there

is as much reason that you should be our Slaves, as we yours. (*Friendly Advice* 115–116)

Elsewhere, he relies on monogenist ideas of race as descent (the belief that "men started off the same and had become different because of climate and their different response to environmental opportunities"[35]) which, in the crucible of Atlantic slavery becomes replaced by race as type: "...are we not of as good Parentage, as ancient a Family, as noble a Descent as the best of you? Ought you not then to love us as your Brethren, descended from the same common Father? Or at least respect us as your Kinsmen, and of the same Lineage" (114). Under this racial formulation, African and European are of the same "race" in the now lost sense of lineage or family.

Interestingly, Tryon's religious enthusiasm almost anticipates the later debates of natural philosophy. The plantation system produces its own unnatural mixture of man and beast that makes some men masters and others beasts of burden. Tryon's response is to insist that master and slave are both of the same "species": a word that resonates eerily against a later history that would debate whether black and white did indeed belong within that same classification:

> If all, or any of these thing, I say, have any weight with you, then speedily leave off your Severities, and let your usage be such as is fit for *Men*, to practice toward *Men*, let us see the excellency of the Christian Religion, by the goodness of your *Lives* that profess it, by your Meekness, and Charity, and Benignity, and Compassion towards your fellow Creatures, especially those of the same Species with your selves, and who have no less rational and *immortal Souls* than the best of you.... (*Friendly Advice* 219–220)

Friendly Advice offers a dual critique of capitalist practices and modern notions of racial difference, both of which were constitutive features of Atlantic slavery. Although there is some debate over how firm the link was between blackness and slavery at the time, I would argue that Tryon certainly sees the two as inextricably linked in planter ideology. His attention to these elements suggests that they were already a substantial part of the discourse of Caribbean slavery. He counteracts this newly charged ideology with older notions of race that are less strictly insistent on absolute, irrevocable distance. In *Friendly Advice*, his sense of difference becomes more complicated and at times contradictory. The mutability of the body, so dangerous for individual health, becomes essential in changing the diseased culture of slavery that so appalls Tryon.

Tryon's images of pollution, putrefaction, and bodily excess make the reader consider more thoroughly the nature of the food s/he eats. Targeting the home and women's culinary practices as the first line of defense in *The Way to Health*, he insists that the boundaries of the body—and by extension the nation—are alarmingly porous and susceptible to foreign encroachment: the nature of food production and food commerce thus become legible as a site of protest. The idea that food and its production has the ability to change individuals and cultures speaks from the early modern period to our own. Early French legal moves to bar British beef, recent Japanese concerns with the same problem, popular protests against bioengineered foods, "eat local" movements, and more recently, emerging calls to boycott companies that use cacao produced by child slaves in the Sudan—all suggest the global circulation of food worries and solidify the boundaries that global trade claims to dispel. As sugar moves from the king's board to the workingman's table in the early modern period, it generates newly visible and vexed relationships—not simply slave to master but also (as Tryon shows) slave to consumer—that similarly worry the boundaries of the English national body.

NOTES

1. Glenn Collins, *New York Times*, "The Americanization of Salsa; With Mexican Food Tamed, Big Business looks abroad," January 9, 1997, D1. See also Molly O'Neill, *New York Times*, "New Mainstream: Hot Dogs, Apple Pie and Salsa," March 11, 1992. A later, more refined, study suggests that salsa's ascendancy is not so clear-cut. See Marcia Mogelonsky, "Salsa Plays Ketchup," *American Demographics*, 20:1 (January 1998): 36.
2. O'Neill, "New mainstream".
3. Robert J.C. Young, *Colonial Desire: Hybridity in Theory, Culture, and Race* (New York and London: Routledge, 1995), 26.
4. Young, *Colonial Desire*, 5.
5. This conflation of the two items has profound political and economic overtones. Based on the debacle over the Reagan administration attempt to count ketchup as a vegetable in public school lunches, many school systems in the U.S. West refuse to allow salsa to count even though freshly prepared salsa has no nutritional relationship to ketchup.
6. Sophie and Michael Coe's book, *The True History of Chocolate* (New York: Thames and Hudson, 1996), 110 ff., gives a precise account of colonial hybridization marked through food in the early history of the Iberian conquest of Meso-America. Rachel Laudan and Jeffrey M. Pilcher's study of Spanish, Creole, and Native American foodways offers a compelling critique of modern narratives that suggest the creation of an early mestizo cuisine that is also a cautionary tale of how cultures identify the national

and the hybrid. "Chiles, Chocolate, and Race in New Spain: Glancing Backward to Spain or Looking Forward to Mexico?" *Eighteenth Century Life*, 23:2 (1999): 59–70.

7. Sidney Mintz, "Time, Sugar, and Sweetness," in *Food and Culture: A Reader*, ed. Carole Counihan and Penny Van Esterik (Routledge: New York and London, 1997), 363.

8. Richard Sheridan, *Sugar and Slavery: An Economic History of the British West Indies, 1623-1775* (Baltimore: The Johns Hopkins University Press, 1974).

9. Timothy Morton. *Shelley and the Revolution in Taste: The Body and the Natural World* (Cambridge: Cambridge University Press, 1994), 13.

10. I am aware that there still seems to be some controversy over calling early modern sugar production capitalist, but I remain convinced of Eric Williams's early point that "sugar was and is essentially a capitalist undertaking": See *Capitalism and Slavery* (Chapel Hill and London: University of North Carolina Press, 1994), 25. Even the earliest sugar plantations contained the nascent features of capitalist labor: "Long before the common features of the industrialized West (imported foods, time-conscious work regimes, factory production, impersonal work relations, etc.) had spread through much of Europe, they were commonplace aspects of life for Caribbean slaves. Today, and even in the most exotic corners of the Caribbean, from the river rain villages of the Guianese rain forest to the rural hamlets of the mountainous Haitian interior, European and North American interests contribute steadily and massively to the shaping of everyday life" (Sidney W Mintz and Sally Price, *Carribean Contours* [Baltimore and London: The Johns Hopkins University Press, 1985], 9).

11. Anita Guerrini, "A Diet for the Sensitive Soul: Vegetarianism in Eighteenth Century Britain" *Eighteenth Century Life*, 23:2 (1999): 34. See also Nigel Smith. "Enthusiasm and Enlightenment: of food, filth and slavery," in *The Country and the City Revisited: England and the Politics of Culture, 1550–1850*, ed. Gerald Maclean, Donna Landry and Joseph P. Ward (Cambridge: Cambridge University Press, 1999), 106–118. There is no modern account of Tryon's life and most of the information about him comes from the *Dictionary of National Biography*.

12. Smith, "Enthusiasm and Enlightenment," 107.

13. Thomas Tryon, *Friendly Advice to the Gentlemen-Planters of the East and West Indies* (London, 1684), 76. Subsequent notes appear in the text.

14. I investigate the adoption of this view extensively in an essay, "Strange and Severe Mastery: Understanding Slavery in Seventeenth Century Britain" in *Slavery: A Comparative Exploration*, ed. Rudolph Hock, Joseph Reidy and Ibrahim Sundiata (in circulation). Much of the discussion of Tryon's early life is duplicated in this essay.

15. Thomas Tryon, *Good house-wife made a doctor; or, Health's Choice and sure friend being a plain way of nature's own prescribing, to prevent and cure most diseases*...(London, 1692), 101. Subsequent notes appear in the text.

16. For a succinct description of the humors, see Merry Wiesner, *Women and Gender in Early Modern Europe and England* (Cambridge: Cambridge University Press, 2001), 32.

17. Mary Floyd-Wilson. "Transmigrations: Crossing Regional and Gender Boundaries in *Antony and Cleopatra*," in *Enacting Gender on the Renaissance Stage*, ed. Viviana Comensoli and Anne Russell (Urbana and Chicago: Illinois University Press, 1999), 73–74.

18. See for example, Immanuel Kant, "On the different Races of Man" in *Race and Enlightenment: A Reader*, ed. Emmanuel Chukwudi Eze (London: Blackwell Publishers, 1997): The olive-yellow of the Indian skin, the true gypsy color, which is at the base of the more or less dark brown of other eastern peoples, is just as characteristic and maintains itself as constantly as the black color of the Negroes; and it seems, along with the rest of the formation and the different temperament, to be as much the effect a dry heat as the other of a moist one. According to Ives, the common diseases of the Indians are congested gall-bladders and swollen livers; but their innate color is inclined to yellow anyway and seems to indicate a continuous excretion of the gall that has entered the blood and that in saponified form dissolves perhaps the thickened juices and dissipates them, and thereby cools blood at least in the external parts" (*Eze* 47); see also, Hume's disagreement with climate theory: "nor do I think, that men owe anything of their temper or genius to the air, food, or climate" (*Eze* 31).

19. I thank Moshe Gold for this reference. Horace's *Art of Poetry* becomes the basis for the later very popular satire on foodways, *The Art of Cookery in Imitation of Horace's Art of Poetry* (1709) by William King. See Timothy Morton, "Old Spice: William King, Culinary Antiquarianism, and National Boundaries," *Eighteenth Century Life*, 23:2 (1999): 97–101 and John Fuller, "Carving Trifles: William King's Imitation of Horace," *Proceedings of the British Academy*, 62 (1976): 3–25.

20. The most well known usage of the word is probably Defoe's evocation of "That Het'rogeneous Thing, *An Englishman*" in his "A True-Born Englishman: A Satyr." See Brody for a compelling discussion of hybridity in this poem.

21. Jennifer Brody, *Impossible Purities: Blackness, Femininity, and Victorian Culture* (Durham, N.C.: Duke University Press, 1998), 12.

22. Brody, *Impossible Purities*, 12.

23. See Horace, *Ars Poetica* "If a painter chose to set a human head on the neck and shoulders of a horse, to gather limbs from every animal and clothe them with feathers from every kind of bird, and make what was at the top a beautiful woman have ugly ending in a black fish's tail—when you were admitted to view this picture, should you refrain from laughing, my good friends?" in *Critical Theory since Plato*, ed. Hazard Adams (New York: Harcourt Brace Jovanovich, 1971), 68.

24. Frances E. Dolan, "Taking the Pencil Out of God's Hand: Art, Nature and the Face-Painting Debate in Early Modern England," *PMLA*, 108 (1993): 225.

25. Kim F. Hall, "Culinary Spaces, Colonial Spaces: The Gendering of Sugar in the Seventeenth Century," in *Feminist Readings of Early Modern Culture: Emerging Subjects*, ed. Valerie Traub, M. Lindsay Kaplan and Dympna Callaghan (Cambridge: Cambridge University Press, 1996), 175.

26. Kim F. Hall, *Things of Darkness: Economies of Race and Gender in Early Modern England* (New York and London: Cornell University Press, 1995), 188 n.27.

27. This is too complicated to go into here, but evidence suggests that currants were grown in England at this time, yet Tryon assumes that they are foreign. He doesn't, for example, argue that the English should eat only home-grown currants. This gap might be explained by the English habit of valuing imported goods over domestic. Foreign currants may have been more highly prized than English and thus a ready target for Tryon.

28. Charlotte Sussman. "Women and the Politics of Sugar, 1792," *Representations*, 48 (Fall 1994), 50.

29. Stephen Mennell ("On the Civilising of Appetite") offers the very useful reminder that literary depictions of banquets do not accurately reflect eating patterns and that "from the spectacular bills of fare it is difficult to work out precisely what each individual actually ate" (*Food and Culture*, 317).

30. In part because the intake of food of slaves can be regulated rather precisely whereas the food of English workers was controlled by their income and, as Joan Thirsk has demonstrated, their ability to use creatively edibles available wild in the countryside.

31. Richard Dunn, *Sugar and slaves; the rise of the planter class in the English West Indies, 1624–1713* (Chapel Hill: University of North Carolina Press, 1972), 264; James Walvin *Black Ivory: A History of British Slavery* (Washington, DC.: Howard University Press, 1994), 71–77, also comments extensively on the ostentatious life-style and the great gulf between master and slave on the plantation.

32. John Oldmixion, *The British Empire in America*. 1708., 116,

33. Beth Fowkes Tobin, " 'And there raise yams': Slaves' Gardens in the Writings of West Indian Plantocrats," *Eighteenth Century Life*, 23:2 (1999): 164–176 argues that enslaved Africans would also have eaten imported foods such as salt cod, but she it is not clear whether this refers to the earliest decades of the Barbados sugar trade or later in the eighteenth century when slaves were allowed (although with a great deal of hesitancy) to have kitchen gardens.

34. Hilary MacD. Beckles, "Capitalism, Slavery and Caribbean Modernity," *Callaloo*, 20:4 (1977): 779.

35. For more on race as descent, see Michael Banton, "The Idiom of Race," in *Theories of Race and Racism: A Reader*, ed. Les Back and John Solomos (New York and London: Routledge, 2000); for more on race as lineage, see Liu, "Race."

6

"WORKING LIKE A DOG": AFRICAN LABOR AND RACING THE HUMAN–ANIMAL DIVIDE IN EARLY MODERN ENGLAND

Francesca Royster

Jeanne Addison Roberts sees the function of animal imagery in early modern English culture as means to explore what can't be faced directly: "As agents of revelation, animals operate effectively because they operate to expose a duality in humanity, a haunting combination of the recognized and the strange. Because they are both familiar and mysterious, they can often serve as links between the known and the unknown. In literature and in art, animals often function as guides to previously unexplored psychic landscapes—regions hitherto unsuspected, ignored, or avoided."[1]

What can representational intersections between African and Animal in early modern drama tell us about the perceived subjectivity of black people during this period? In John Webster's drama, *The White Devil*, Zanche, the Moorish serving maid makes several dubious relationships in the play. Zanche's particular brand of criminality is one of betrayed alliances with her lovers and her social betters. Throughout the play, we see "proof" of the African's duplicity and also the fear of what can happen when one "goes native" by imitating blackness, allying with blackness, and desiring blackness. When Duke Francisco goes into blackface to win the trust of Zanche, he not only risks his status as white and noble; he risks his status as human. Her white lover, Flamineo, tells a friend that "I so love her just as a man holds a wolf by the ears; but for fear of turning upon me and pulling out my throat, I would let her go to the devil" (5.1.156–160).[2] The links between Zanche and wolfishness make her a dangerous ally.

Why begin with animals to talk about the theoretical and historical foundations of race in early modern England? It was an Elizabethan commonplace that humans had rationality, while animals did not and that animals are moved by appetite while human beings had the capacity to overcome their appetites—sometimes. These very same elements—rationality and control of appetite—were also used to distinguish white humans from Blacks as early as the fifteenth century. Of course, the ability to control appetite also separated many other humans from white ones, too: women, actors, sodomites, and criminals, just for starters.

This essay will frame Zanche's image of black female duplicity with early modern discourse about the ownership and domestication of animals—namely dogs. On the one hand, dogs are often presented as the protectors of the domestic space: the faithful servants, the guards of the margins of civilization and the outside (see Cerebus, three-headed guard dog of Hades, and the dogs that Columbus meets when landing in the New World, for example). These dogs symbolize an understood and trusted alliance between self and other, which is negotiated through a system of service and reward. We might connect this image of dogs to the increasing visibility of Moorish servants in the early seventeenth century. Like the dogs in Renaissance portraits and in plays, these servants are decorative, sometimes exotic, and most often seen but not heard.

On the other hand, as cousins to the wolf, dogs are still linked to the wild. Because humans have created a relationship of interdependence with dogs, they are even more dangerous than wolves because they have the potential to infiltrate intimate spaces, to create bonds of trust with their owners and then, like Zanche, to turn on their human allies. Dogs are the domesticated wolves, the sign of God's dominion over man reflected in miniature. Because the wolf has never been controlled, it presents an elsewhere, a dream state that could even turn into a man. Because they occupy a status in between wild and civilized, the dog has been the subject of a large body of writing about controlling and best utilizing their labor—especially their reproductive labor. For that reason, they make a timely link with the image of the black servant, who was just beginning to be conceived of as a long-term source of labor.

In the early seventeenth century, we see an explosion of imagery of black people as servants in well-to-do households. While we are not yet at the point when England was fully participating in the Transatlantic slave trade, which was then dominated by the Spanish and Portuguese, we are at a point when having black servants was a fashionable thing to do—a way of staging wealth and worldliness. Kim Hall has pointed out in her book, *Things of Darkness* that black people were treated as "objects among other objects" and we see these signs of blackness in many household items, especially luxury items like jewelry and paintings.[3] More often than not, in these paintings we see black servants engaged in public rather than private aspects of their masters' households, in entertainments for dignitaries, for example. Such a function requires that these servants continue to behave as objects: serving their masters, representing their master's wealth, being seen rather than heard. These representations of blackness present the servants as exotic, and unknown, but nonetheless contained by an objectifying eye.

Webster's *The White Devil* presents us with two contrasting images of the Moor servant: the Moor as a silent object and the Moor as a dangerous ally. Zanche is not the only Moor servant in the play. Webster also includes in his list of characters, "Little Jacques the Moor," a silent servant who accompanies Giovanni, the young son of Duke Brachiano and the heir apparent. Little Jacques is an example of the use of the Moor as a purely visual accessory—the sign of his young master's potential power. With Zanche, on the other hand, Webster considers what happens when we think of these objects as having eyes, voices, and appetites—what happens when alliances are made. These representations, I will argue, are symptoms of the tension around potential domestication of black people, which can be linked to emerging discussions of black peoples' capacity for humanity, rationality, and social control.

RACING THE ANIMAL/HUMAN DIVIDE

The anxieties produced by the increasing presence of black servants in London might be linked to an explosion of writings about the nature of humanity itself, including handbooks about domesticating and training animals from the early modern period, philosophical and theological writings on the differences between humans and animals, and representations of animals, especially dogs, as laborers.[4] Such documents might be considered in the context of political arguments for and against England's increased participation in the Trans-Atlantic slave trade.[5] Though beyond the scope of this paper, a full historicization of how black bodies become pure labor, and in turn how this notion of labor haunts black subjectivity is important both in understanding emerging theories of race, self, and other in the Early Modern period and is vitally relevant to the construction of the

African American subject in the here and now. Take for example, the mostly tabled discussions of reparations at the 2001 World Conference on Race, in Durban, South Africa, which, for better or for worse, asked us to take an account of the economic value of African slave labor and its impact on African American notions of agency in current life.

At the time of *The White Devil's* writing, in 1612, England had not yet invested in the full-grown drama of the auction block and certainly not in the technology of breeding sources of efficient labor that we see even seventy-five years later. But we may certainly consider the ways that Europe discusses its other not quite human laborers as a means of planting the seeds for the philosophy and science of racing the animal–human divide later. In the Enlightenment, for example, Immanuel Kant will derive a genus of racial division based on prior systems of animal taxonomies.[6] In "On the Different Races of Man," for example (1775), Kant argues that Africans differ in physicality, smell, intelligence, bravery, and capacity for pain from Northern Europeans—all of which make Africans more suitable for enslavement, he says.[7] Kant argues that Africans are "weak hearted" and therefore, must necessarily be led by Northern Europeans.[8] But this same intellectual, civic, and spiritual weakness described by Kant and others also makes Africans potentially dangerous allies. Confidence in the control of African slaves was never fully manifest and therefore required the rhetorical as well as material technologies of control. See for example, the entry for "Negro" provided in the first American Edition of the *Encyclopaedia Britannica* (1798):

> Vices the most notorious seem to be the portion of this unhappy race: idleness, treachery, revenge, cruelty, impudence, stealing, lying, profanity, debauchery, nastiness and intemperance, are said to have extinguished the principles of natural law, and to have silenced the reproofs of conscience. They are strangers to every sentiment of compassion, and are an awful example of the corruption of man when left to himself.[9]

Preceding the writings of Kant and the Enlightenment philosophers, in the early modern period, technologies of control like travel books and animal domestication handbooks provided an anatomy of animal types and their behavior that use similar taxonomic systems of control. In Fynes Moryson's *Itinerary* (1617), he discusses different dog breeds, the propensity of each breed for hunting and hawking, their ability to adapt to and even imitate human behavior, and their national identity.[10] For example, in the same way that Moryson argues that "the Nature of the English is very singular above other Nations in liberality and bounty,"[11] this "liberality" is reflected in the dogs that the English breed:

> England hath without comparison greater nomber and better dogs, then any other Nation, as Mastiues for keeping the howse, rough water dogs for the Duck, grayhounds for the hayre, diuers kyndes of hounds for all huntings, and Spanyels for hawking, and bloodhounds to track stolen Deere or other thinges, and litle dogs for wemens pleasure, and all these beautifull and good, and some most rare, as the sayd blood-houndes and Tumblers for Couyes, and setting doges to catch Patriges by the nett.[12]

Works like Moryson's *Itinerary*, which doubled as a travelogue, often shared on the same pages ways of documenting and under-standing national and racial difference at the same time that they also discussed the human–animal divide. Moryson, for example, uses the metaphor of the breeding of horses and other animals to discuss the danger of cultural and racial mixture for the English colonizing Ireland:

> But as horses, calves and sheepe transported out of England into Ireland, doe each race and breeding declyne worse and worse, till in fewe years they nothing differ from the races and breeds of the Irish horses and Cattle. So the posterities of the English planted in Ireland, doe each discent, growe more and more Irish, in nature manners and customes, so as wee founde in the last Rebellion divers of the most ancient English Familyes planted of old in Ireland, to be turned as rude and barbarous as any of the meere Irish lordes.[13]

Dogs and other domesticated animals are raced insofar as they become a language for separating national and racial others. As Steve Baker has argued, the human/animal (and with that, nature/culture and self/object) opposition—which can be traced as far back as Aristotle—can be understood as part of a process of self definition: that "sentiments about animals are typically projections of attitudes to humans; that the contrasting of humans and animals invariably serves as an analogy for the relation of those regarded by a particu-lar society either as insiders or as outsiders; and that some societies have arrogantly appropriated the name 'human' for themselves while giving neighboring groups derogatory animal names."[14] Thus we have Shakespeare's figuring of Turks as "circumcised dogs" at the point of Venice's heightened national and racial crisis in *Othello*

(5.2.360–365);[15] John Derricke's image of the Irish as "ravening hungry dogs" in *The Image of Irelande* (1581)[16] and Thomas Cavendish's descriptions of the Patagonians as "leaping and running like brute beasts, having vizards on their faces like dogs faces, or else their faces are dogs indeed."[17]

In Shakespeare's *Othello*, Arthur Little points out, Iago's references to the Othello and Desdemona courtship as "a Barbary horse" (1.1.108–9), "the beast with two backs" (1.1.114), and the "tupping" old black ram (1.1.85–6) references

> early modern Europe's belief in the bestial sexual practices of Africans and the suspicion that Africans are at least partly beast. The sixteenth century French political theorist Jean Bodin, for example, writes in his *Method for the Easy Comprehension of History* (first published in Latin in 1566): "Because self-control was difficult, particularly when plunging into lust, [Africans] gave themselves over to horrible excesses. Promiscuous coition of men and animals took place wherefore the regions of Africa produce for us so many monsters." In 1534 England made bestiality a capital crime, in part because "in popular estimation at least, man was not so distinct a species that he could not breed with beasts . . . [and] the separateness of the human race was thought so precarious."[18]

The human/animal divide was evoked both to order and understand others who were faraway, and, as in the case of the Moors and Turks in *Othello*, also as a means of patrolling the invading outsiders from within.

This system of sexual difference is evoked in contemporary popular culture as well—where the image of black people as lacking sexual control and as animalistic and duplicitous is exploited for its frission, even appropriated by the artists themselves. In contemporary U. S. culture, the meaning of "working like a dog," "dogging," being someone else's dog, or doing it "doggie style"—is easily transmogrified into sex—particularly masculine sex. Funk master George Clinton's chorus in his song "Atomic Dog," with its background of rhythmic panting aurally connects boasts of sexual conquest ("Why must I be like that? Why must I chase the cat? Nothing but the dog in me!") with the signifiers of labor and exertion: panting. To do it "Doggie Style" signifies getting down and dirty, pushing the limits of both physical strength (and/or flexibility) and propriety. Such imagery quickly descends to fears of moral impropriety and danger— and yet, when cathected onto the body of black men, for example, they produce occasions for admiration. Consider for example, the success of eleven-year-old rap ingenue Lil' Bow Wow, whose precocious sexuality is one of his main selling points. Death Row rapper Snoop Doggie-Dog uses a cartoon-dog in his videos and CD cover art to speak to the image of the gangster rapper as trickster. Like George Clinton's use of animated, anthropomorphized and thoroughly funky dogs in his video for "Atomic Dog," Snoop's use of the dog as icon makes full use of the association between black culture and animality alluded to in *Othello*, and particularly the association between dogs and perverse black sexual practices. These uses of dogs remind us of the ways that black people have been figured as not quite human and demand for us to reconsider the associations between dogs and "dogging" as work, dogging as "animalistic" sexuality, and ultimately, as signs of racial control through the surveillance of black male sexuality.

When we consider the associations between animality and female sexuality, whether in Early Modern Culture or now, the associations with perverse and outlaw sexuality become even stronger. Since its earliest uses in the Middle English period, the word "bitch" emphasizes the reproducing function of the female dog, or wolf . The earliest entries in the Oxford English Dictionary using the word "bitch" feature the spectacle of birth, feeding, or weaning; the body, displayed, open, demanding response. See, for example, this 1555 entry from Richard Eden's *Decades*: "The dogge tiger beynge thus kylled they came to the denne where the bytche remayned with her twoo younge suckynge whelpes." By the early modern period, "bitch" becomes associated with human women—especially lewd, malicious, or treacherous ones, and was frequently used in connection with prostitution. See for example, this entry from 1400: "Whom callest thou queine skabde biche?" or this 1575 entry from the play, *Gammer Gurton's Needle*: "Come out, thou hungry needy bitch" (2.2). Similarly, in Shakespeare's *King Lear*, Lear transforms his thankless daughters into three little barking dogs, Tray, Blanch, and Sweetheart (3.6.18–19).

The word "bitch" has contested meanings in contemporary popular subcultures like hip-hop, queer theory, feminism, and post-feminism. In some uses in hip-hop and rap culture, "bitch" is used derogatorily to connote a woman (or man) who is kept for sexual "use."(See Notorious BIG's "Me and My Bitch" or Dr. Dre's "Bitch Niggaz.") In even wider use is the function of "bitch" to connote the woman who makes demands—who interrupts the rituals of male bonding and escape from responsibility. (See, for example, Guns 'N Roses' "Back off, Bitch.") On the other hand, some women rappers have appropriated "bitch" to signify sexual transgression and economic and linguistic savvy (as in Lil' Kim's "Queen Bitch").[19] In the work of rappers like Lil' Kim, or white grunge rockers Courtney Love and Meredith Brooks, the iconic figure of the bitch-goddess has been reappropriated for critique, though not without complexity and even contradiction. (In Meredith Brook's song, "Bitch," she writes "I'm a Bitch, I'm a lover./I'm a child, I'm a mother./I'm a sinner, I'm a saint./I do not feel ashamed," while Lil' Kim calls herself a "Diamond cluster hustler" in her song "Queen Bitch.") The staging of sexual disobedience through the image of "the bitch" brings up some complex issues of subjectivity and objectification. Like the use of the "dog" in male rapper discourse, the use of "bitch" in some of these examples would seem to exploit the connection between women and black people with subhuman desires. Indeed, in its early modern representations, the "bitch" seems even more passive and abject as a description than "dog", perhaps because of its more explicit connection to breeding. But in some of its recent appropriations, "bitch" would seem to capitalize on the duplicitous and therefore dangerously unpredictable aspects of the dog figure that I've described throughout this essay.[20]

As we consider the repercussions of the racing of the animal/human divide in early modern England, we might consider further how dogs continue to be "raced." In the hands of recent visual artists, the image of the dog has been explicitly raced to think about race and sexuality, consumption, and geographical boundaries of cities. In his art piece, *Humanscape 141: Barrio Dog* (1987) Chicano artist Mel Casas uses the image of a black, red-eyed salivating dog to express the rage and territoriality brought up in the discourses around immigration policies, gentrification, and English-only policies in Los Angeles.

In her study of performative roles for animals in contemporary popular culture, Jennifer Donaghy points out that particular breeds of dogs have been made to have specific ideological uses for humans, in the ways that they mimic human behavior: "advertisements aimed at middle income, stability-seeking consumers often include dogs that make semiotic statements about family life, happiness, stability, childhood, loyalty and love. And not just any dog. Golden Retrievers, perhaps because they can be understood to smile and have submissively dropping ears and a patient temperament, best reflect such qualities. Golden Retrievers are frequently used in advertisements for homes and cars, neighborhoods and child raising. The dogs are shown to complement these images, completing them.

They are part of a lifestyle and play a large role in creating ideas of comfort, love, and daily routine."[21] One might also consider the specific racial codes of golden retrievers, blonde rather than black, in relation to this specific hypothesis. Golden, they are part of a mean, less dangerous, even capturing the light in the ways that Richard Dyer suggests blonde hair has been used in advertisements and cinemas to convey spirituality.[22]

William Wegman's *Lion King* (1999), *Bikini* (1999) and *Disguise* (1999), which feature light-colored Weimaraners sporting blonde Afros, and other wigs and toupees and posed in comely human poses, ask us to think about some of these projections of white human ideals of beauty onto animals that can be at once cute, uncanny, and disturbing. In Bikini, the dog subject peers through sunglasses and stiff blonde bangs over its shoulder at the onlooker, coyly catching her/his gaze. Here and elsewhere, Wegman plays with the illusion of his dogs' subjectivity, played up by his staging of style and flirtation via clothing and accessories. In Wegman's *Bikini*, the dog is both panderer and pandered. The body of the dog, its spine, and ribs poking through the textures of the bikini and fur, remind us of the ways that the bodies of the objectified other—here, our pets—are made accessible for our consumption, via the fiction of permission that is produced by the camera. Wegman's *Bikini* echoes the cartoon Coppertone suntan lotion ads of the early 1960s, where a young girl's bikini is pulled down to expose an untanned bottom by her accompanying spaniel. In the Coppertone advertisement, the dog is panderer to the pedophilic eye, allowing the viewer to sexualize the body of the white, blond girl via the illusion of spontaneity of the dog's bite. The dog acts out the desire that would be otherwise unseemly. Moreover, the dog becomes a way to frame whiteness, presented in the pure and idealized body of the young, innocent girl. Whether used to frame whiteness as in Wegman's work, or as a means to discuss nonwhite race relations, as in the work of Mel Casas, the dog remains a dangerous alliance, both familiar and never entirely within the viewer's control.

Too Close for Comfort: Anxieties of Alliance

We can find the roots of our contemporary images of animality in early modern discourse—especially in discourse around travel and taxonomies of the other. In Donna Haraway's work on race, gender, and animals, she figures discourse of the primate as a form of orientalism—a discourse that includes technologies of surveillance and control of the self as well as the other. Haraway writes that in primatology we find "primal stories, the origin and nature of "man" and...reformation stories, the reform and construction of human nature. Implicitly and explicitly, the story of the Garden of Eden emerges in the sciences of monkeys and apes, along with versions of the origin of society, marriage, and language."[23]

Haraway's work asks us to consider how the science of knowing animals is inherently connected to the discourse of colonization. For Linnaeus, the eighteenth-century founder of modern biological classification, "Nature was a theater, a stage for the playing out of natural and salvation history. The role of the one who renamed the animals was to ensure a true and faithful order of nature, to purify the eye and the word. The 'balance of nature' was maintained partly by the role of a new 'man' who could see clearly and name accurately, hardly a trivial identity in the face of eighteenth century European expansion. Indeed, this is the identity of the modern authorial subject, for whom inscribing the body of nature gives assurance of his mastery."[24] Haraway figures the co-emergence of a discourse of the European colonial self and these technologies of classification. We see this formulation at work, for example, in "The Country-Man's Companion: Or, A New Method of Ordering Horses and Sheep" by Philotheos Physiologus (London, 1684). The larger social function of this chain of being in action is "to remind that Insolent Creature [Man] (too apt to forget it) of his miserable degenerate state, and to awaken him to aspire to that real Dignity which he seems almost wholly to have forgot."[25] In this text, the care of horses and sheep is used as a metaphor for being a good servant to God and a good servant to the British colonies.

While Haraway's work on racing the human/animal divide concentrates on the full emergence of a discourse of science and technology, in full blossom by the turn of the twentieth century, discourse from the early modern period draws on some of these same elements, including the use of the story of the Garden of Eden to present man as the namer and master of elements. Arthur Little's powerful formulation of the early modern period's "Jungle Fever" further connects the use of images of beasts, domesticated and otherwise, to ongoing campaigns of nationalism and racism. The Early Modern jungle and its fever, with "its conjurations of pollution, wild terrain, national and imperial competitiveness, incivility, animalism, and racial boundary crossing, sacrificing and rape...—looming large in the English imagination—will literally and figuratively get mapped out in and across all the wild and potential wild places of Rome, Venice,

Egypt, Africa, and Ireland, these places variously figuring as the jungle of a nationally and imperially anxious England."[26]

Kim Hall has argued that as early as the seventeenth century, images of Africans and apes work to construct categories within Western imperialism, about wildness, "sexual lust and the unrestrained body."[27] But what different aspects of the body are brought to light when we look at animal/human hybrids that are closer to home? What I've discovered is two seemingly opposite patterns in the process of domestication of the dog and of black people: one is the construction of the dog and African subject as agent of alliance, and the other is the often pornographic interest in a loss of control, in wildness itself. These patterns are, in fact, interwoven, for as Wolciech Kalaga and Tadeuz Rachwal suggest in their volume, *The Wild and The Tame: Essays in Cultural Practice*, "Wildness, unlike other forms of otherness, preserves a trace of familiarity."[28]

In many ways, dogs are well-worn, well-known territories in terms of Early Modern culture. Unlike images of the wild, like snakes, lions, monkeys and apes, dogs have the resonance of familiarity and comfort. According to Jeanne Addison Roberts's 1991 study, *The Shakespearean Wild*, the dog is so common a symbol that "they pass through the consciousness of audience and probably author only as stereotyped allusion to popular wisdom. The great abundance of dog and ass comparisons are funny precisely because they fit into readily recognizable categories, eliciting stock responses which include only the faintest evocation of any authentic animal figures. To the Elizabethan they were everyday cliches, prefabricated and dependable terms of derogation."[29] A projection of the controlled male world, they are the other that is so very much a part of human culture that they become synonymous with acquiescence, pandering to human culture, and willingness to please. In *The White Devil*, we see this use of the dog as a sign of abjection and shameful servitude. In 5.3, when Lodovico and Gasparo murder Brachiano, the two threaten that the Duke shall "die like a poor rogue" and "stink like a dead fly-blown dog.... forgotten before thy funeral sermon" (5.4.167–169).

A positive version of the fantasy of man's dominion over nature through the dog is the image of the hunt. Hunting combines dogs' associations with property, where dogs are both owned and also used to mark out property. Though more often symbolic than for sustenance, in the ritual of the hunt the dog brings in food, sustenance for the owner, as well as sustenance for himself. At the same time, through the hunt, the dog insures pleasure and release. Note the abundance of literary sources that evoke the sound of the hunt as a source of pleasure, from Ovid to Shakespeare's Ovidian *Titus Andronicus*. The dog's barking is a form of communication beyond the range of the human, but within this ritual it is still civilized. Through the labor of the dog we see a demonstration of the parts of the noble household—Lord and huntsman, huntsman and dog, man and wife, all working together well.

At the same time that dogs could work as a sign of the mastery over nature, dogs could also be a sign to voice anxieties of disloyalty and duplicity. According to Joyce E. Salisbury, in the medieval animal fables of Marie of France and Odo of Chreiton, dogs and other domesticated animals, synonymous with servants, became a chance to talk about the potential for human disloyalty.[30] In only one of Marie's tales, dogs are portrayed as loyal: a dog refuses a bribe from a thief. In others, dogs were shown as "greedy, litigious and garrulous.... Canines were repeatedly vilified for greed, for it was said to drive them to return to eat their own vomit" (a characteristic that preoccupied medieval commentators).[31]

But even while there have been efforts to capture and contain what is potentially perverse about the dog, as with the human, these images still have a powerful theatrical resonance, both in the ways that they are contained and the ways that are displayed as supposedly losing control. It is the success of Snoop Doggie Dog's cartoon gangster-dog persona that most closely corresponds to the early modern practice of using animals in performances, who are trained not to mimic proper human actions or speech but to disobey. In these kinds of performances, what was being highlighted was the triumph of humankind over nature, but also the thrill of the spectacle of physical strength, including stamina, contortion, sexual violence, and brutality. As is well known, activities such as bear baitings in the medieval and renaissance period pitted cur against bear for the thrill of watching a death match. These activities were geographically located in the same areas as theaters, gambling houses, and brothels. This entertainment was codified enough as "theater" to have a Master of Revels-like position: and to be put in the same vicinity as theaters. Theater historian Matthew Bliss says that the Mastership of the Royal Game of Bears, Bulls and Mastiffs, was established under Henry VIII, to handle the care and feeding of the performing animals.[32] Rather than watching a display of animal's displays of gentility, like the dancing bear, "disobedient animal" acts fed audience's voyeuristic pleasure in watching outside acts, out-of-control hungers, to the point of death, while perhaps as well, watching the ultimate display of control of the masters (though the control of masters may or may not actually be explicit, or even consistent).

The disobedient animal act is by far the most common motif in animal acts throughout their history and in contemporary performance. Animal training takes time and patience and training an animal to "disobey" could be a subtle endeavor. But the disobedient-animal act has more to do with the audience's idea of animal/human relations than it does with training. The idea of building the act around downright disobedience plays on a most basic narrative. A performer who claims to have trained an animal and is then ignored by the animal in the demonstration is himself the butt of the joke. The very idea, indeed, of an animal daring to disobey, or of a trainer not fully controlling an animal, is disconcerting or, in a comic setting, radically funny. The act in which an animal is trained to "come over the chain" at one command and not another, shifts the focus from the skill of the animal to the references in the narrative . . . What is interesting in these early acts, both on and off the formal stage, is that these trainers had already discovered that spectators are not so interested in what an animal can do as they are in how an animal might think—or more importantly, that animals might think as we do.[33]

These performances are vital to our understanding of early modern interest in the dog not just as a keeper of peace and boundaries but also as an image of display of thrilling lack of control.

Animals on stage are never fully under human control—they can overpower and attack their masters, bark at the wrong time, or, like Crab in *Two Gentlemen of Verona*, upstage the humans and steal the show. And even while this disobedience puts to the test the very definition of what it means to be human, there is a kind of pleasure in the possibility of losing control that theater also exploits. This possibility of a loss of control is one of the pleasures of live theater. We can relate these potential moments of disobedience to other titilations of live performance: the possibility that an actor may miss or even deliberately change a line, that the supposedly staged sword fights might draw real blood, or that a staged death might draw real tears. It is my contention that the dangling of the possibility of losing control by a director or a ringmaster is also a form of power. Animals, because they are thought of as being irrational, are a culturally safe way of enjoying the spectacle of losing control. This pleasure might, in fact be compared with that staged in a roller coaster, where the audience pays to feel that their lives are in danger. At the same time, these staged moments of disobedience still confirm the animal as "other."

If Africans were considered less than human, as at least some of the travel and scientific discourse from the early modern period attest, then they too might provide a lucrative opportunity to watch both the staging and unraveling of control. Black villains like Zanche in *The White Devil*, Aaron the Moor in Shakespeare's *Titus Andronicus*, or even Othello toward the end of the play, might provide the audience with this pleasure. My interest in these representations of sensual appetite and loss of control as "black" is complicated by the fact that these were simulations of blackness. As Dympna Callaghan has pointed out, no African actors ever trod the Renaissance stage.[34] While there were "displays" and exhibitions of African bodies, mimetic performances like Othello or Aaron were only performed by white actors in blackface. We might see, then, a key reason that the performance of blackness on the early modern stage might be termed a *"staged* disobedience": the very convention of presenting blackness as an imitation or simulation is a means of containing the performance of racial difference. Like the animal trainer, the actor in blackface demonstrates a form of mastery that ultimately distances his "self"— his body that he skillfully manipulates and controls to form a new shape—from the out-of-control African image that he is bringing to life. At the same time, as these plays use language that equates the African with the animal, the same danger and ambiguous thrill of watching animals can be evoked.

STAGING DISOBEDIENCE IN *THE WHITE DEVIL*

In the final section of this paper, I'd like to return to the image of Zanche in The White Devil, to consider her performance as a form of "staged disobedience." This potential for disobedience, ambiguous as feigned or not, presents one of the ways that the African servant could present a problem of control for her owners, both on and off stage.

Many of *The White Devil*'s feminist critics link the play to masculine anxieties around female duplicity. Christina Luckyj, for example argues that "Like many early modern texts, *The White Devil* invests its anxieties about performance in women. "O ye dissembling men!" cries Vittoria, who is promptly corrected by Flamineo,: "We suck'd that, sister, From women's breasts, in our first infancy" (4.2.179–80). Women are "politic" (1.2.21) performers whose pretense to mask virtue masks a voracious sexual appetite and whose apparent tears are "but moonish shades of griefs or fears" (5.3.187).[35] Likewise Ania Loomba points out that "The splitting of feminine identity in patriarchal stereotypes is adequately summed up by Brachiano in *The White Devil*: 'Woman to man/Is either a god or a wolf'" (IV.ii.88–9). Such an oscillation between pit and pedestal is common in European feudal society which treated women as a curious mixture of 'saints in the Church, angels in the streets, devils in the kitchen and apes in bed.' "[36]

But while the power of women to dissemble is a central theme in *The White Devil*, most critics treat Zanche, marked by blackness, as completely transparent and readable. Anthony Gerard Barthelemy, for example argues that Zanche's overall untrustworthiness ultimately makes the world more predictable. The play uses blackness repeatedly to symbolize evil: "She makes visible the blackness that is only figuratively present in Brachiano, Vittoria, and Flamineo. The willingness of these three to trust the 'black Fury' declares them to be of the devil's part. When men finally come to end the reign of the lustful trio of Vittoria, Flamineo and Zanche, one of the murderers shouts: 'Kill the Moor first' (V.vi.215). Perhaps the murderer believes that with Zanche's death, satanic rule will cease or that Vittoria, without her black servant, can no longer be so vile and dangerous."[37]

Certainly the play uses the language of blackness to mark evil throughout, especially in reference to Zanche's strongest alliances, Vittoria and Flamineo. For example, during her arraignment, the lawyer describes Vittoria as "a debauched and diversivolent woman" who has created "a black concatenation/of mischief" (3.2.28–29).

But at the same time, if the language of blackness is used to mark evil, it is also used to describe alliances, whose repercussions are hard to predict. Blackness is evil but we don't really know yet how far its reach may go. For example, in 3.1, Monticelso says that Vittoria's "black lust" will "make her infamous/to all our neighboring kingdoms" (3.1.6–7). Vittoria's lust here will somehow infect not only her reputation but also the view of the court in the eyes of the neighboring territories. Her blackness has international consequences. In act 1, scene 2, Flamineo also uses the language of darkness to connote his own willingness to calculate to win what he wants. Blaming his mother for his lack of political and social power in the court, Flamineo refashions himself in the Machiavellian mold:

> And shall I,
> Having a path so open and so free
> To my perferment, still retain your milk
> In my pale forehead? No, this face of mine
> I'll arm, and fortify with lusty wine,
> 'Gainst shame and blushing. (1.2.333–338)

Whiteness is transposed by Flamineo here not as moral purity but instead as shamefulness, naivete, and the opposite of manliness. Flamineo must fortify his whiteness to succeed in this world of white devils. Blackness (and here, wine-flushed redness) is connected in the play not only with evil, but also with sexual and political savvy. Again, the outcome and direction of this evil is left to be revealed. Unlike the proverbial blush, its meanings are hard to decipher or predict.

The ontological problems that Zanche sets off might be connected to the numerous images of dogs and wolves that populate the play. The wolf is never fully known. The question of whether or not the wolf will reveal its true nature is one of the very first images to open the play. Lodovico, who has been banished from the court of Rome complains that the worst offenders—people who have committed vast murder—have gone unpunished. He (who is a voice of satire and criticism of the court, and who later becomes a spy) characterizes the court as wolfish in its predatory nature: "Your wolf no longer seems to be a wolf/Than when she's hungry" (1.1.8–9).

Unlike the wolf, the dog is associated in the play with servility. Flamineo's disingenuous advice to the cuckolded Camillo is to lock up Vittoria, keep her "out of the sight of revels" and "Let her not go to church, but like a hound/In Leon at your heels" (1.2.81–82)— that is, like a leashed dog. But the dog is also associated in the play with duplicity and with hidden motives. Later in the same scene, having convinced Vittoria to become the Duke of Brachiano's lover (and to betray her husband) for the price of diamonds, Flamineo tells her "Come sister; darkness hides your blush. Women are like curst dogs. Civility keeps them tied all daytime, But they are let loose at midnight; then they do most good, or most mischief" (1.2.206–208). Note that here as elsewhere, Vittoria, like Zanche, is connected to both dogs and darkness. When Vittoria and Zanche attempt to murder Flamineo, he describes this betrayal as "Killed with a couple of braches!" (5.6.135).

The language of dogs is not limited only to women. As the alliance between Flamineo and Brachiano shows its strain (Francisco sending Vittoria a love letter) Flamineo says "What, me, my lord, am I your dog?" Brachiano says: "A blood-hound" (4.2.48–49). Pandering is connected to hunting here, and the servitude of a dog is explicitly sexualized.

In the final scene of the play Zanche and Vittoria attempt to trick Flamineo into shooting himself. This is the moment when Flamineo's fantasy of Zanche as the wolf that must be "held by the ears" becomes true. Most critics read this Zanche as the frustrated lover who has first been rejected by a commitment-shy Flamineo and then fooled into confession with the erotic machinations of her supposed countryman,

Muly Mulinassar. Her whispered bedroom confession to Mulinassar would seem to support the idea that Zanche is motivated less by strategy and primarily by pleasure. But once she works together with Vittoria to kill Flamineo, we realize that she has strategies that go beyond the world of sexual satisfaction. This is a place of not quite knowing, where Zanche is truly a wolf. At this point, she is neither really serving Flamineo and (as is true throughout the play), she doesn't really serve Vittoria either. She works actually beyond the power and will of Vittoria, although "for" Vittoria.

But do we ever really know whom Zanche is working for? When Vittoria agrees to sleep with Brachiano, Zanche is already working behind the scenes, preparing the bed itself, spreading a carpet and cushions (1.2 after line 212). It is as though she knows that her mistress will be convinced by Flamineo even before Vittoria does. Zanche and Flamineo stand together, commenting on the seduction that they have worked together to produce. This is the first speech we get from her: "See, now they close" (1.2.224)—a comment on the completion of circuitry that she herself has produced.

We might compare Zanche's function here with Aaron's in Shakespeare's *Titus Andronicus.* Aaron is given no concrete social role or homeland. In the play, this means that he can move around, take advantage of his role as an observer, and accomplish villainies that must take place out of the public eye. Captured as a prisoner of war along with Tamora and her sons, Aaron's past is a mystery. Unlike Othello, he is not a soldier, though he exhibits the strengths of a warrior. As far as we know, he has not been a slave. Aaron is not a leader of his own kingdom, like Cleopatra or *The Battle of Alcazar*'s Muly Hamet. In fact, we are never told where Aaron is from exactly, though his black skin and kinky hair connect him to Africa.[38] Aaron skirts around the borders of the play, watching, taking in information, offering advice, and doing his most important actions behind the scenes. The homeless quality of blackness—the removal of his blackness from a specific geographic location—effects his function as a character.

The central question in my mind as we think about Zanche's function is to what extent is our knowledge of her and her function limited by the stereotype of the lascivious Moor. That stereotype assumes that first, her agenda is always readable, reducible to her physical being and her social station; second, that her most important actions are in pleasing herself, in sexual pleasure; and third, that sexual pleasure is a much stronger force than strategy for some other stake.

Zanche has a tremendous and in some ways unpredictable impact on the characters who form alliances with her. These alliances are with characters that are already on the edge of propriety. Vittoria Corombona is called bawd, prostitute, and murderer. Almost all of her stage appearances are shadowed by Zanche. And Zanche is privy to all of her plans. Flamineo, pimp to his own sister, is an impoverished, destitute hanger-on of court who confesses sexual feelings for Zanche.

Francisco, disguised as the Moor of Mulinassar, is the most ambiguous in terms of the effects of his black disguise on his view of blackness. In 5.3, Francisco improvises a dream to draw out Zanche, win her trust and her confession of her part in the murders of Isabella and Camillo. Zanche enters, crying, and tells Francisco that she has been dreaming of him. Francisco whispers to Lodovico, the courtier who has been witnessing the exchange, that "for fashion sake I'll dream with her" (5.3.226). As this flirtation heats up, Francisco improvises an erotic dream to match Zanche's:

> *Zanche:* Methought, sir, you came stealing to my bed.
> *Francisco:* Wilt thou believe me, sweeting? By this light,
> I was a-dreamt on thee too; for methought
> I saw thee naked.
> *Zanche:* Fie, sir! As I told you,
> Methought you lay down with me.
> *Francisco:* So dreamt I:
> And lest thou shouldst take cold, I covered thee
> With this Irish mantle.
> *Zanche:* Verily, I did dream
> You were somewhat bold with me; but come to't-

At this point, Lodovico, either horrified or stimulated or both, interjects, "How, how! I hope you will not go to't here" (5.3.235). The boundary between flirtation and foreplay has clearly been breached. Francisco continues, and from Zanche's reactions, he might well be acting out the dream as he speaks:

> *Francisco:* When I threw the mantle o'er thee, though didst laugh
> Exceedingly, methought.
>
> *Francisco:* And cried'st out,
> The hair did tickle thee.
> *Zanche:* That was a dream indeed! (5.3.228–234; 237–240)

Francisco matches and then tops Zanche's erotic boldness, made doubly scandalous by the fact that his performance of black sexuality takes place in public and is witnessed by an equal—a courtier who knows of his true identity. Though the eroticism of the play is produced in the name of snaring Zanche, and therefore, supposedly bringing some kind of justice to the court, we also see that Francisco goes above and beyond the call of duty. This trap, in its sensual details, takes on much more power for its listeners—and perhaps for Francisco himself—than he might be willing to admit. Moreover, we might consider this "dream" in light of the status of another central dream in the play—Vittoria's dream of the murder of her husband and her lover's wife in 1.2.239–262. Here, the epistemological status of the dream is ambiguous—we don't know if the dream is a subconscious desire—really a dream—or a command made by a fully awake Vittoria, couched in the language of dreams to be more acceptable as a command coming from a woman. If dreams in the play reveal strategies as well as subconscious desires, perhaps Francisco's dreaming strategy may also reveal a desire that is otherwise socially unacceptable.

At the close of the play, as Vittoria, Zanche, and Flamineo are murdered by Lodovico and Gasparo, Zanche is the first conspirator to die. Her corpse, dead and now silent, remains on the stage throughout the rest of the scene—another sign, somehow that the dark element of the play has been identified and purged. This message is confirmed by the moralistic use of the images of black evil throughout the rest of the scene. Vittoria, dying, tell us: "My soul, like to as ship in a black storm,/Is driven I know not whither" (5.6.247–248). Flamineo says "Tis well yet there's some goodness in my death,/My life was a black charnel" (5.6.270–271). These deathbed confessions of evil souls and lives misled might lend some immediate sense that the world of the court will be put to right. So, too, might Giovanni's righteous concluding warning: "Let guilty men remember, their black deeds/Do lean on crutches made of slender reeds" (5.6.302–303). And yet, despite these gestures, we are left with the overall suspicion that the real evil of the play lies elsewhere. As Kate Aughterson writes, "Despite the very visible conventional tragic punishments and arrival of a new political order, we recognize that nothing has fundamentally changed. The absence of Monticelso and Francisco at the close of the play leaves us with a sense that corruption is endemic to the political process."[39] Images of darkness and subterfuge haunt the closing of the play, ultimately confirming the overall ambiguity of justice and lack of closure and moral conclusion.

As the black "devil" against Vittoria's white, Zanche is corruption at its most manifest. Like the hierarchies of dogs that attempt to make clear and predictable which animals are evil and are best under which conditions, Zanche would seem to be under a similar control in the play, never able to get away with her corruption. And yet she also can't be fully read—her danger lies in her alliances, the ways that the "hunter gets captured by the game."

NOTES

1. Jeanne Addison Roberts, "Animals as Agents of Revelation: The Horizontalizing of the Chain of Being in Shakespeare's Comedies" in *New York Literary Forum*, vol. 5/6 (1980) 81.

2. All references to John Webster's *The White Devil* are from *The Drama of the English Renaissance. Vol. II: The Stuart Period*, ed. Russell A. Fraser and Norman Rabkin (New York: Macmillan Publishing Co., Inc., 1976), 431–474.

3. See Hall's *Things of Darkness* (Ithaca: Cornell University Press, 1995), especially pages 211–253.

4. Some early modern documents on the human/animal divide include Edward Topsell's *The History of Four-footed Beasts and Serpents* (London. 1607); Godfrey Goodman's *The Fall of Man or the Corruption of Nature* (London, 1616); Thomas Hodges's *The Creatures goodness, as they Came out of God's Hands* (London, 1675); and Thomas Robinson's *New Observations of the Natural History of this World of Matter and of this World of Life* (London, 1696). Treatises on the domestication of animals include *A Treatise of Oxen, Sheep, Hogs, and Dogs, With their Natures, Qualities and Uses* (London: Obadiah Balgrave, 1683); Thomas Tryon's *The Country-Man's Companion* (London: 1684); and *A Choice Collection of Several Strange and Wonderful Dogs* (1738).

5. The tensions between the black servant as exotic object and as source of slave labor explode with the seventeenth century. Seventeenth century documents discussing the pros and cons of English entry into the slave trade include Richard Jobson's *The Golden Trade* (1623); Nicolas Villaut's *A Relation of the Coasts of Africk called Guinee* (1670), Robert Lewes's *The Merchants Map of Commerce* (1671); Nathaniel Crouch's *A View of the English Acquisions in Guinea* (1686); and later, in the eighteenth century, *A Short Treatise on the Unfair purchase of Slaves* (1794).

6. Sir Thomas Browne uses comparative taxonomic language to discuss the nature of blackness even earlier in *Pseudodoxia Epidemica* (1646), ed. Robin Robbins (Oxford: Clarendon, 1981).

7. Immanuel Kant, "On the Different Races of Man" in *Race and the Enlightenment: A Reader*, ed. Emmanuel Chukwudi Eze (London: Blackwell Publishers, 1997), 38–48.

8. Immanuuel Kant, "On Natural Characteristics" in Eze, 64.

9. Quoted in Eze, *Race and Enlightenment*, 94.

10. Quotations from Fynes Moryson's *Itinerary* (1617) come from *Shakespeare's Europe: A Survey of the Condition of Europe at the end of the 16th century, being the unpublished chapters of Fynes Moryson's Itinerary (1617), with an introduction and an account of Fynes Moryson's career*, ed. Charles Hughes. 2nd edn. (London: 1903; Reissued New York: Benjamin Blom, 1967).

11. Moryson, *Itinerary*, 478.

12. Moryson, *Itinerary*, 477–478.

13. Moryson, *Itinerary*, 481.

14. Steve Baker, *Picturing the Beast: Animals, Identity and Representation* (Manchester and New York: Manchester University Press, 1993), 79.

15. All quotations from Shakespeare's plays will be from *The Norton Shakespeare, Based on the Oxford Edition* ed. Stephen Greenblatt, Walter Cohen, Jean E. Howard, and Katharine Eisaman Maus (New York: W. W. Norton & Company, 1997).

16. John Derricke, *The Image of Irelande with A Discoverie of Woodkarne* (1581), ed. David B. Quinn (r. Belfast, 1985), 200.

17. Richard Hakluyt, *Principle Navigation's, Voyages, Traffiques and Discoveries of the English Nation* (London 1907), vol. 8, 299.

18. Arthur Little, *Shakespeare Jungle Fever: National-Imperial Re-Visions of Race, Rape, and Sacrifice* (Stanford, CA: Stanford University Press, 2000), 83–84.

19. As Tricia Rose has written in her essay, " 'Two Inches or a Yard': Silencing Black Women's Sexual Expression," in *Talking Visions: Multicultural Feminism in a Transnational Age*, ed. Ella Shohat (Cambridge, MA: The MIT Press, 1998), the reappropriation of an image of black sexual agency and aggressiveness in the public sphere is especially vexed for black women performers because these appropriations must confront the view that female sexuality is itself vulgar. Moreover, such appropriation "displaces the white female sexual subject [and object] in a racist culture that reveres white female sexuality (as much as any female-narrated sexuality is openly revered) at the direct expense of public affirmation of black female sexuality" (320).

20. For more examples of reappropriations of the word "bitch" for feminist critique, see Elizabeth Wurtzel's *Bitch: In Praise of Difficult Women* (New York: Anchor Books, 1999).

21. Jennifer Donaghy, *An Exploration of Performative Roles for Animals in American Popular Culture* (New York: New York University Press, 1996), 106.

22. See Richard Dyer's book, *White* (New York: Routledge, 1995)— particularly his introduction, "The Matter of Whiteness" and chapter 3: "Technologies of Whiteness."

23. Donna Haraway, *Primate Visions: Gender, Race, and Nature in the World of Modern Science* (London: Routledge, 1989), 9.

24. Haraway, *Primate Visions*, 9.

25. "The Country-Man's Companion: Or, A New Method of Ordering Horses and Sheep" by Philotheos Physiologus (London, 1684) Preface, A2.

26. Little, *Shakespeare Jungle Fever,* 14–15.

27. Kim Hall, " 'Troubling Doubles': Apes, Africans, and Blackface in *Mr. Moore's Revels*" in *Race, Ethnicity, and Power in the Renaissance,* ed. Joyce Green McDonald (Madison: Farleigh Dickinson University Press, 1997), 122.

28. Wolciech Kalaga and Tadeusz Rachwal,*The Wild and The Tame: Essays in Cultural Practice* (Wydawnictwo Uniwersytetu Slaskiego, Katawice 1997), 2.

29. Jeanne Addison Roberts, *The Shakespearean Wild: Geographies, Genus and Gender* (Lincoln and London: The University of Nebraska Press, 1991), 56.

30. Joyce E. Salisbury, "Human Animals of Medieval Fables" in *Animals of the Middle Ages,* ed. Nona Flores (New York and London: Garland Publishing, Inc., 1996), 49–65.

31. Salisbury, *Human Animals of Medieval Fables,* 56.

32. Matthew Bliss, "Property or Performer?: Animals on the Elizabethan Stage" in *Theater Studies,* vol. 39 (1994): 45–59.

33. Donaghy, *An Exploration of Performative Roles,* 24–25.

34. Dympna Callaghan, " 'Othello was a White Man': Properties of Race on Shakespeare's Stage" in *Shakespeare Without Women: Representing Gender and Race on the Renaissance Stage* (New York: Routledge, 1999), 76.

35. Christina Luckyj, "Gender, Rhetoric and Performance in John Webster's *The White Devil,*" in *Enacting Gender on the English Renaissance Stage,* ed. Viviana Comensoli and Anne Russell (Urbana and Chicago: University of Illinois Press, 1999), 219.

36. Ania Loomba, *Gender, Race, Renaissance Drama* (Delhi: Oxford University Press, 1991), 73. Here, Loomba quotes Sheila Rowbowthan in *Women, Resistance and Revolution* (Middlesex, Penguin, 1972), 20.

37. Anthony Gerard Barthelemy, *Black Face, Maligned Race: The Representation of Blacks in English Drama from Shakespeare to Southerne* (Baton Rouge: Louisiana State University Press, 1987), 127.

38. In *Titus Andronicus'* criticism, the temptation has been to forego questioning Aaron's ethnic origins, to let the irredeemability of his evil displace him from place or history. Ania Loomba writes in *Gender, Race, Renaissance Drama*:

> Significantly, there has been no debate about the color or ethnic origins of Aaron the Moor, no effort to prove that Shakespeare had not seen Moors, or that racial hatred and miscegenation had not been invented in Elizabethan times, for, unlike Othello, Aaron is more easily reconciled to the stereotype of black wickedness, lust, and malignity (46).

39. Kate Aughterson, *Webster: The Tragedies* (New York: Palgrave 2001), 34.

3

RACE AND CULTURE

7

FRESH PRODUCE

Joseph Roach

The scene is unforgettable, at least to any devotee of movie musicals
of my generation. Beneath the severity of the Tuscan portico of Inigo
Jones's St. Paul's Church in London's Covent Garden, Rex Harrison
as Professor Henry Higgins, arguing on behalf of classical order in
building as well as in speaking, berates a copiously weeping Eliza
Doolittle, hydraulically enacted by Audrey Hepburn: "You squashed
cabbage leaf, you disgrace to the noble architecture of these columns,
you incarnate insult to the English language."[1] Jay Lerner's book for
My Fair Lady follows the dialogue of George Bernard Shaw's
Pygmalion closely, especially in the introduction of the flower girl
Eliza Doolittle as an example of human refuse. The flowers she has
been selling from her basket are purported to be fresh. She is not.
Only as "clean as she can afford to be," foul of odor and of speech,
she is but one inmate among many, a "pris'ner of the gutters" serving time in the streets of Edwardian London (*My Fair Lady*, 20, 27).
With his characteristically enthusiastic insensitivity, Shaw's Professor
Higgins waxes eloquent on the vividness of her abjection: "Oh it's a
fine life, the life of the gutter. It's real: it's warm: it's violent: you can
feel it through the thickest skin: you can taste it and smell it without
any training or any work."[2] As a merchant who sells to others the
opportunity to condescend to her condition, Eliza's pitch to the toffs
sheltering in the portico during a sudden shower after the opera has
let out—"buy a flower off a poor girl?"—is just barely a notch above
begging (*Pygmalion*, 200). She fears, not without reason, that she will
be (mis)taken for a prostitute: "Freddy," Shaw's name for the well-
born twit who bumps into her, knocking a day's wages worth of
unsold flowers into the muddy street, was a generic name for the
young men who cruised Covent Garden in search of tarts; "Captain,"

the title by which she carelessly addresses the upright (and uptight) Colonel Pickering, harkens perhaps all the way back to the whoremaster Macheath, a sybaritic fixture in nearby Drury Lane, from John Gay's *The Beggar's Opera* of 1728. Her use of such a dubious honorific threatens to mark her more than it does the object of her salutation, and she knows it: "Oh, sir," she implores (*"crying wildly"*) in fear that Higgins, who has been recording her speech stenographically, is a police informer, "dont let him charge me. You dunno what it means to me. Theyll take away my character and drive me on the streets for speaking to gentlemen" (*Pygmalion*, 201). She has taken Higgins for the law, someone who can make or mar her character in a stroke, and so he turns out to be, in his own realm and for his own purposes. Against the incriminating presuppositions leveled against her, unrebutted by her dirty face, Eliza's refrain is "I'm a good girl I am" (*Pygmalion*, 203, 217, 219). Chief among the circumstances that impugn her goodness is the locale—the situation of the scene in the Covent Garden market and theater district with all its historic but unsavory associations.

I want to evoke a particular place, a situation, which is also a place in time, a predicament that goes by the name of the modern. The predicament of the modern resides in its limited conception of time: linear, empty, abstract, and homogenous—a hollow chrysalis to contain the fiction of the constantly new, the perennially fresh. Call it "progress." As Walter Benjamin famously puts the issue in his thirteenth thesis on the philosophy of history: "The concept of the historical progress of mankind cannot be sundered from the concept of its progression through homogenous, empty time. A critique of the concept of such progression must be the basis of any criticism of the concept of progress itself."[3] What follows argues that time—the supreme cultural fiction no matter how it is narrated—is more often experienced as heterogenous and uneven, as cyclical rather linear, as asynchronous rather than synchronous. As Michel Serres and Bruno Latour succinctly put it, "time doesn't flow; it percolates."[4]

As a percolator of time, Covent Garden is an open space that has never been entirely empty. Laid out in the Italian style by Inigo Jones in 1638 for the Duke of Bedford on the spare ground that had been the site of the old "Convent Garden" from medieval times, the Covent Garden Piazza and the buildings that surrounded it became a principal locus of theatrical and other leisure pursuits in eighteenth-century London. Indeed, the commercialization of leisure as a component of the consumer revolution appeared powerfully and early on in this modern urban landmark, which was speculatively developed as commercial real estate between the two medieval cities of London and Westminster. It served simultaneously as a major fruit and vegetable market, a shopping mall of curious boutiques and coffee houses, a meeting point of beggars from every corner of the metropole and colonial margin, a scene of popular cultural performances from puppet acts to posture molls, a notorious place of assignation featuring sex workers of every specialty, and (not coincidentally) home to the legitimate playhouses of Drury Lane and Covent Garden, which, through many rebuildings, continue to operate on the same sites today. Their location on the urban grid gives me the opportunity to place them within a relatively recent trend of theater history. Under the influence of the notions of "social space" developed by Henri Lefebvre, the history of the physical theaters themselves has been expanded to include their situation as "places of performance" in their given urban contexts. Here the built environment and its social uses both occasion and are occasioned by the theatrical productions carried on within their purlieus.[5]

The Act One setting of *Pygmalion*, "Covent Garden at 11:15 p.m." (after the show has let out of the opera house), situates theater history, by association with a place of many kinds of performance, in the text of a canonical play and its popular spin-offs on the screen and musical stage. But that is not all it does. The first act of *Pygmalion* is a veritable compendium of the practices and quotidian performances that accumulate over time and in the fullness of time become second nature in a social space like Covent Garden. The very action of *Pygmalion* represents the intensely performative creation of an assumed persona from the supposed raw materials of life—the passing off of a "guttersnipe" as a duchess at the Embassy Ball. This audacious hypocrisy is the fundamental condition of theater and the source of many moralistic attacks against it, from Solon's rebuke of Thespis to such prurient reformist tracts as *The Night Walker: or Evening Rambles in Search of Lewd Women* of 1696, which inveighs against the false piety on display in little St. Paul's, later known as "The Actors' Church" (because so many Thespians worshipped and are buried there): "I Rambled to [Covent Garden] Church," the Night Walker writes, "Where I understood, that under the pretence of attending *Evening Prayers*, many loose Women made their *Assignations* with their Gallants."[6]

In such a place as Covent Garden, as in the theater itself, the agon of refinement and abjection never completely ends. However much Shaw may have believed that the difference between a flower girl and a duchess is not in how she behaves, but in how she is treated

(*Pygmalion*, 270), he sees to it that this flamboyantly successful Pygmalion treats his Galatea like garbage. Not only is Eliza Doolittle, like Covent Garden market itself, dirty, noisy, and smelly, as Higgins tells her to her face; she leaks. Eliza enters St. Paul's portico out of chaos ("torrents of heavy summer rain"), spouting glossolalic ejaculations, "Aaaooowah" and "Garn." On the cusp of utterance and secretion, the *gestus* of her role is that of a bathtub overflowing. She is repeatedly reproved for "boohooing," which the Professor equates with nothing less than blasphemy, a taboo, a pollution worthy of expulsion from a sacred place: "Woman: cease this detestable boohooing instantly; or else seek the shelter of some other place of worship" (*Pygmalion*, 205–206). Higgins's counter-*gestus* is to staunch the flow of her excretions with rags and to cleanse her, offering her his silk handkerchief, "To wipe your eyes. To wipe any part of your face that feels moist. Remember: thats your handkerchief; and thats your sleeve" (*Pygmalion*, 214). Her rite of passage into the Higgins household is celebrated by the burning of her clothes and the imposition of a scalding bath, overseen by the implacably postmenopausal Mrs. Pearce and her starchy housekeeping acolytes, who hold the screaming Eliza under all the way under to make her as clean as she can be.

In her unreconstructed state, Eliza strikes Higgins as promising if repulsive raw material, little more sensate than the block of stone in the mythological original of the sculptor who falls in love with his work, but irresistibly malleable as she quickens to his transformative and ultimately adoring touch. The medium here is no longer sculpted marble, but English speech, performed as Higgins insists that it be in the airy transhistorical community of Shakespeare and Milton. What a great story for the stage: by turning nature into culture before our very eyes, the action of *Pygmalion* recapitulates the act of performance itself. As synthetic experience, performance furnishes forth the products that invention wrests from the raw material of inchoate possibility. That is why the word *performance* has proven so powerfully descriptive of such a variety of practices, from dancing to cooking, any one of which will consist of a set of conscious adjustments called "art" in a preexisting structure of expectation that experience gives the name of "life." The theater is central to the study of performance in this sense, but it does not by any means stand alone or even supreme in the capacious category of synthetic behavior. Performance, like Galatea's animation, is never about a state of being, but always about a stage of becoming.

Increasingly, the condition of performance is a claim made in relation to other arts as well. Art historian Dian Kriz, for instance, is examining what she calls "the multi-valent *process* of refinement" in the circum-Atlantic world of the long eighteenth century. She links the refinement of visual culture (in natural history illustrations, graphic satire, landscape painting, and topographical prints) to the refinement of sugar, from the cane fields of West Indian slave plantations where it was grown to the London chocolate houses where it was consumed. Like the transformation of Galatea, this refinement is a process that ends in a finished product but at the cost of enormous waste, material and human. Waste is a by-product of refinement, the sign of its success but also a warning about its equivocal nature. For whom is refinement progress and at what cost? *Pygmalion* begins with a bouquet of flowers being cast into the mud, and it ends with the ominous possibility that Eliza will be similarly discharged after she has blossomed briefly and faded. In the world constituted by the play, she is left in the end without means of employment except to be sold into a brokered marriage, which she recognizes as a form of prostitution: "I sold flowers," she reminds Higgins after the Ball. "I didn't sell myself. Now you've made a lady of me I'm not fit to sell anything else" (*Pygmalion*, 257). She has been refined, and she has been wasted. In the world visualized in Kriz's "multi-valent process of refinement," such a performance is constituted on a scale no less imposing than that of a transoceanic system of chattel slavery, a staggering toll of human waste, which justified itself in the eyes of some of its apologists as part of a "civilizing" process.[7]

Moving along similarly transoceanic lines, Kathleen Wilson is updating and transforming Sybil Rosenfeld's 1939 study of strollers and provincial theatrical circuits. Wilson compares the theaters in five provincial towns—Newcastle, Liverpool, Norwich, Bristol, and Cork—and three imperial outposts—Kingston, Jamaica; St. James, St. Helena; and Fort Marlborough [Benkulen], Sumatra. For her the eighteenth-century stage consisted of provincial nodal points in a network reaching out from the patent theaters as "a collectively created and widely diffused cultural form . . . socializing English and colonial peoples into *recognizing* difference." It helped to refine and inculcate ideas of Englishness in relationship to other ethnicities on a grid of "progress." Wilson concludes, "Theater thus exemplified and was instrumental in a shift in the notion of time from a cyclical to progressive mode that ranked civilizations according to their 'age,' race, and accomplishments."[8] As in the project undertaken by Henry Higgins, progress is associated with the acquisition and mastery of English (ness).

Into such formations over time, the myth of Galatea returns. Between the Ovidian and the Shavian versions of Pygmalion, eighteenth-century artists found self-reflexive inspiration in a myth about an art that seeks to create a perfected form of life. With perfectibility as the condition of her coming into being, Galatea is an Enlightenment effigy. Susan Leigh Foster, in *Choreography and Narrative: Ballet's Staging of Story and Desire* (1996), shows how Marie Sallé's "pantomime-rich" choreography for the Covent Garden ballet of *Pygmalion* (1734) served as a point of departure for the refinement of expressive movement that came to characterize the eighteenth-century *ballet d'action*, a "technique of configuring dichotomous oppositions" such as "Life" and "Art."[9] Gail Marshall, in *Actresses on the Victorian Stage: Feminine Performance and the Galatea Myth* traces the problem of the "sculpture metaphor" into the nineteenth century.[10] Indeed, Eliza's success as a sham duchess echoes that of many flesh-and-blood English actresses before her—working-class girls who learned to pass as great ladies on the stage. One of the greatest of them all, Frances Abington, who created the role of Lady Teazle in *The School for Scandal*, started her workaday life as a lowly flower seller in Covent Garden. Shaw explicitly recognized this well-worn path to refinement in his afterword to *Pygmalion*: "Such transfigurations have been achieved by hundreds of resolutely ambitious young women since Nell Gwynne set them the example by playing queens and fascinating kings in the theater in which she began by selling oranges" (281–282).

"The Garden"—as Covent Garden was known to its intimates, and of these there were many, from Richard Steele to William Hogarth to John Ruskin to Charles Dickens—featured not only transformations of nature into culture, of raw material into finished product, but also of raw material into waste product, which, less frequently remarked but no less significant, doubles the sense of human and material expendability in performance. I mean for the word *waste* to have a dual sense that encompasses opposite extremes of a complex phenomenon: first, it means refuse, as in waste matter, related in fact or in metaphor to excrement; second, it means excessive or superfluous expenditure, the squandering of material substance. These usages converge in commonplace phrases like "filthy lucre" or "filthy rich," and they prompted Thorstein Veblen to speak of "conspicuous consumption" and Georges Bataille of "sacrificial expenditure" when those general economists set out to explicate public demonstrations of waste as a genre of cultural performance. Included in this genre are both the ancient idea of "The Gift," which, as defined by French theorists from Marcel Mauss to Jacques Derrida, is a sacrificial expenditure with the implicit but unenforceable expectation of reciprocity, and its long-surviving, still-thriving siblings, charity and philanthropy.[11] Such practices proliferate in the urban spaces that I have elsewhere called "vortices of behavior."[12] These tend to form at the points in any cityscape where main thoroughfares, called "pathways" by urbanists, intersect at junctures of exchange called "nodes" and "landmarks."[13] Covent Garden has long served Londoners and visitors as a nodal point and landmark: then, puppet booths, flower stalls, exotic bird peddlers on St. James Street, kiosks vending everything from sausages to pornographic prints, mountebanks, drunks, bawds, specialty brothels such as Mrs. Jenkins's "Elysium Flogging House," and down the street, *Pygmalion* at the Theater Royal, Covent Garden; now, popular concerts at afternoon tea, Diana memorabilia, Union Jacks on little sticks, the theater museum, and *My Fair Lady* with Jonathan Pryce at the Theater Royal, Drury Lane.

Among the spectacular elements in the node or landmark must be numbered its inhabitants, categorized and judged by gawking passersby. A behavioral vortex is generally where different kinds of people from all ranks meet and take one anothers' measure. John Ruskin, reconstructing the boyhood of the artist J. M. W. Turner, who was born in Maiden Lane in 1775, contrasts his "Covent Garden training" with that of the Venetian Giorgione, and he vividly assays the importance of this feature of the urban node:

> The second great result of this Covent Garden training was, under-standing of and regard for the poor, whom the Venetians, we saw, despised; whom, contrarily, Turner loved, and more than loved—understood. He got no romantic sight of them, but an infallible one, as he prowled about the end of his lane, watching night effects in the wintry streets; nor of sight of the poor alone, but the poor in direct relations with the rich. He knew, in good and evil, what both classes thought of, and how they dealt with, each other.[14]

Or as Shaw puts it more tartly in the Preface to *Pygmalion*, "It is impossible for an Englishman to open his mouth without making some other Englishman hate or despise him" (191).

Nor is class alone the measure of difference in the behavioral vortex of Covent Garden. For three hundred years the nodal points of London have drawn and redrawn the mental map of the world in action, gesture, and tableau. As early as 1700, the journalist Tom Brown wrote:

> London is a World by it self. We daily discover in it more New Countries, and surprising Singularities, than in all the Universe besides.

There are among the *Londoners* so many Nations differing in Manners, Customs, and Religions, that the Inhabitants themselves don't know a quarter of them.[15]

In making such an ethnoscape, of which a busy market on any given day is a microcosm, race matters. With a population estimated at 20,000 by the mid-eighteenth century (out of a total of 676, 250 Londoners), people of color constituted a small but particularly visible minority.[16] Forbidden to learn trades, they were consigned either to servitude or beggary. In either of those roles, they were called upon to perform in public, a performance in which their skin was, I believe, a stock costume, neither startling to the passersby nor negligible in its supernumerary effect as the moveable scenery of a hemispheric drama of disentitlement. As servants, people of color appeared as ornamental accessories, icons of waste in our second sense of luxury expenditure. *The Character of a Town Misse* of 1675 stipulates that an aspirant to such a character, "hath always two necessary Implements about her, a *Blackamoor*, and a little *Dog*; for without these, she would be neither *Fair* nor *Sweet*."[17] Some of the servants wore metal collars around their necks, engraved with the names of their masters. Decked out in livery, topped off by turbans, they were marked as the lucky ones, when the alternative was to be *waste* in the first sense of the term. Zacharias Conrad von Uffenbach, visiting London in 1710, was shocked by the prevalence of prostitutes and beggars around Covent Garden and the adjacent St. Giles parish, including "Moors" of both sexes: "The females wear European dress," Uffenbach notes, "with their black bosoms uncovered, as we often saw them."[18] St. Giles is the patron saint of beggars, and those who followed that occupation in this parish were known as "St. Giles blackbirds."[19]

A behavioral vortex like Covent Garden, where the ambience of the past exerts its pressure palpably, might be thought of as the kind of hypothetical place that I call a "time port." Like the maritime cities that exist as centers of exchange and social contact, a time port functions as an entrepot, a point of arrival, negotiation, and circulation. The difference is that argosies arrive in the time port from many different places in the past. After they have docked and unloaded, they compete with other arrivals from other pasts to shape the living textures of the cityscape, even as they prepare to embark again for other destinations in the future. The rhythm of these arrivals and departures keeps time, but not the same time for everyone.

Covent Garden is a clock of this kind, one that keeps different kinds of time, following the rhythms of cyclical return by the day or by the season. The painter William Hogarth preceded Shaw in finding it so. In 1738, one hundred years after the construction of the Piazza and nearly two hundred years before Shaw wrote the Covent Garden scene in *Pygmalion*, Hogarth published four engravings done from paintings representing "The Four Times of the Day." The first of these, titled "Morning," is set in the same spot where Freddy Aynsford-Hill upsets Eliza Doolittle's basket and spoils her goods, fatefully drawing Henry Higgins's attention to the overflowing Billingsgate of her speech (Figure 7. 1). In the upper right-hand corner of the engraving, the portico of St. Paul's Church looms austerely, with its clock pointedly surmounted by the figure of Time, bearing a scythe, and subscribed with the warning, "*Sic Transit Gloria Mundi*." The chimes of this clock, in fact, striking ominously at the moment Henry Higgins turns to leave the Piazza, remind the Professor to be more charitable to Eliza Doolittle. He hears the chimes piously as "the voice of God" (*Pygmalion*, 207).

A number of kinds of time are measured here, quite apart from the face time on the clock. Nowhere else in the play is Higgins's piety an issue. Like the antiquity of the Tuscan order that Jones selected for the portico of the church, "the voice of God" arrives into the Covent Garden scene from some place in the past. It moves Higgins to a ritualized performance of spontaneous but self-interested philanthropy that belongs not to the modern economy of exchange but to the ancient economy of the Gift. Two radically different protocols of synthetic behavior, selling and giving, circulate in the same vortex. Higgins leaves without a flower in return for his shower of coins, but in time, the measure of all things, Eliza's sacrifice will return his gift with interest.

As the flower and vegetable market, Covent Garden was a place of the daily transition between wholesomeness and filth, where the morning tide of market-fresh succulents rolled in on carts from the countryside and the afternoon left-overs, once their value had been extracted or exhausted, were tossed in the gutters to rot. Sir Richard Steele, writing in a number of *The Spectator* devoted to London *flanerie*, describes a walk by "Mr Spectator" that begins at dawn on the Thames and takes in the market scenes, measuring the differences between people in them by the fine calibration of the times at which they make their appearances on the stage. In so doing, he describes what I mean by a time port:

> The Hours of the Day and Night are taken up in the Cities of *London* and *Westminster* by People as different from each other as those who are born in different Centuries. Men of Six a Clock give Way to those of Nine, they

Figure 7.1   Hogarth's *The Four Times of the Day*
Source: Yale Center for British Art, Paul Mellon Collection

of Nine to the Generation of Twelve, and they of Twelve disappear, and make Room for the fashionable World, who have made Two a Clock the Noon of the Day. When we first put off from Shore, we soon fell in with a Fleet of Gardiners bound for the several Market-Ports of *London*; and it was the most pleasing Scene imaginable to see the Chearfulness with which those industrious People ply'd their Way to a certain Sale of their Goods. The Banks on each Side are as well peopled, and beautified with as agreeable Plantations, as any spot on Earth; but the *Thames* it self, loaded with the Product of each Shore, added very much to the Landskip. It was very easy to observe by their Sailing, and the Countenances of the ruddy Virgins who were Supercargoes, the Parts of the Town to which they were bound. There was Air in the Purveyors for *Covent-Garden*, who frequently converse with Morning Rakes, very unlike the seemly Sobriety of those bound for *Stocks-Market*.[20]

Consciously or not, Steele echoes an earlier *Spectator* number in which "Mr Spectator" is accosted by a very young prostitute in the Piazza of Covent Garden, elliding the public sale of fresh produce and human flesh. Read together with the allusion to the "Ruddy Virgins" who are arriving from the country with their fresh produce (and as fresh produce) to talk with "Morning Rakes," the earlier number marks a later stage in the transformation of morning into evening and wholesomeness to waste:

> The other Evening passing along near *Covent-Garden*, I was jogged on the Elbow as I turned into the Piazza, on the right Hand coming out of *James-Street*, by a slim young Girl of about Seventeen, who with a pert Air asked me if I was for a Pint of Wine.... We stood under one of the Arches by Twilight; and there I could observe as exact Features as I had ever seen, the most agreeable Shape, the finest Neck and Bosom, in a Word, the whole Person of a Woman exquisitely beautiful. She affected to allure me with a forced Wantonness in her Look and Air; but I saw it checked with Hunger and Cold: Her Eyes were wan and eager, her Dress thin and tawdry, her Mein genteel and childish. This strange figure gave me much Anguish of Heart, and to avoid being seen with her I went away, but could not forbear giving her a Crown. The poor thing sighed, curtisied, and with a Blessing, expressed with utmost Vehemence, turned from me.[21]

In Steele's own reckoning, Covent-Garden Piazza is a kind of clock, measuring with its own manner of precision the passage of time in the diurnal withering of flower petals and the seasonal etiolation of flesh, as girls "newly come upon the Town" sold themselves, infected themselves, exhausted themselves, and finally beggared themselves, when pity was at last the only desire they could engender in the hearts of men. But in the economy of the Gift, pity is no negligible desire. The child's performance of gratitude, punctuated by her delectable curtsey, offers value for value received. Repeating the scene enacted by Mr. Spectator and the Girl, Shaw's stage directions for the performance of charity in *Pygmalion* read (207):

> *The church clock strikes the second quarter.*
> HIGGINS [*hearing in it the voice of God, rebuking him for his Pharisaic want of charity to the poor girl*] A reminder. [*He raises his hat solemnly, then throws a handful of money into the basket and follows Pickering*].
> THE FLOWER GIRL [*picking up a half-crown*] Ah-ow-ooh! [*Picking up a couple of florins*] Aaah-ow-ooh! [*Picking up several coins*] Aaaaaah-ow-ooh! [*Picking up a half-sovereign*] Aaaaaaaaaaaah-ow-ooh!!!

At the extreme edges on either side of the commodity, stand two values: the priceless and the worthless. The giving of alms before the church door, like throwing sops to the poor at medieval banquets, is a synthetic behavior that docks in the time port like a ghost ship from another place in time. Like so much else that happens in "The Garden"—the selling of birds and flowers (or flesh), the drinking of chocolate and coffee, the staging of plays and operas—charity is a luxury expenditure. And like violence, luxury is the performance of waste.

In Hogarth's "Morning," baskets of cabbages and bunches of mushrooms, winter fruits, dot the scene along with the refuse into which they are being transformed. The hasty observer might conclude that sex work begins early in the morning among the English, but closer scrutiny establishes the fact that it runs 'round the clock. In the geometric grouping of the younger prostitutes and their demanding "Captains" on the right, the base of the compositional triangle culminates with a conspicuous figure at its lower left apex, which extends to the center-line of the image: a blind beggar woman of African or West Indian extraction, her hand extended and her mouth opened in unanswered supplication.

A long way from home, we imagine, hunched in her threadbare cloak against the London winter and apparently unwarmed by the meager fire, she is laboring in the superannuated economy of the Gift while everyone around her seems to have something or someone to sell, something or someone to buy, or at the very least something (or someone) to do. Like unsold produce, she is a prisoner of the gutter. Unhearing and unseeing, an overdressed but underwrapped coquette, actually a notorious bawd, passes by the beggar on her pretentious way to church, fan raised to her lips, while her link boy carries her prayer book under his arm so that he can shield his hands from the cold and also stress his unreadiness to give alms. The unmet needs of the blind beggar woman, homeless in the cold, reappear like the repressed in Eliza's musical wish list in *My Fair Lady* (33):

> All I want is a room somewhere,
> Far away from the cold night air;
> With one enormous chair...
> Oh, wouldn't it be loverly?
>
> Lots of choc'late for me to eat;
> Lots of coal makin' lots of heat;
> Warm face, warm hands, warm feet...!
> Oh, wouldn't it be loverly?

This would be uncanny were it not for the fact that it records the same material conditions in the same urban node in an evolved but genealogically related system of social relations. The position of the beggar woman, like that of Eliza Doolittle, suggests that her situation corresponds to that generally allocated by performance theory to the abject: that is, socially marginal but symbolically central.[22] With that centrality comes an excruciating visibility.

In his excursus on nineteenth-century Covent Garden in *Our Mutual Friend*, Charles Dickens represents it as a scene of Hogarthian abjection, a combination of "Morning" and "Gin Lane," to which his Mr. Dolls is compulsively drawn, the beguiling slum that props up the morality of the middle classes as the Ghetto props up the morale of the Gentiles:

> This market of Covent Garden was quite out of the creature's line of road, but it had the attraction for him which it has for the worst of the solitary members of the drunken tribe. It may be the companionship of the nightly stir, or it may the companionship of the gin and beer that slop about among the carters and hucksters, or it may be the companionship of the trodden vegetable refuse which is so like their own dress that they perhaps take the Market for a great wardrobe; but be it what it may, you shall see no such individual drunkards on the doorsteps anywhere, as there. Of dozing women-drunkards especially, you shall come upon such specimens there, in the morning sunlight, as you might seek out of doors in vain through London. Such a stale vapid rejected cabbage-leaf and cabbage-stalk dress, such damaged-orange countenance, such squashed pulp of humanity, are open to the day nowhere else.[23]

At least Hogarth's beggar woman and Shaw's "squashed cabbage leaf" follow trades. The beggar's occupation, soliciting gifts from those better off than she, reciprocating by assuring them of their substance and well-being, in fact at once points toward and effaces the labor that this scene requires for its existence. Coffee and chocolate houses (like Tom King's in the background) flourished in the Covent-Garden area as they did in many neighborhoods of many cities in the circum-Atlantic world, and with the large quantities of sugar that sweetened them, coffee and chocolate as produce demonstrate the importance of West Indian slavery in the development of metropolitan economy and social life, for which the Middle Passage was the actual cost, hidden from view in plain sight.

This context inverts the association of the beggar woman with the deep past and connects her image with a pioneering modernity—that of the black Atlantic. Modernity in this sense is not simply a period of time—it is a *form* of time, one experienced as the fractious, nonsynchronous rhythms of displacement, rupture, and loss but characterized by historians as homogenous, abstract, and empty of everything except progress.[24] It is in this sense that Paul Gilroy argues that Blacks were the "first truly modern people."[25] That Covent Garden was a nodal point in this vast, transoceanic grid of injustice is a theme in Ruskin's commentary on the boyhood of Turner and the way in which the painter of "Slave Ship" developed an early sense of the performance of waste from the Covent-Garden scene. This Ruskin calls "English death," and he notes that it contains no "gentle processions to churchyards among the fields":

> But the life trampled out in the slime of the street, crushed to dust amidst the roaring of the wheel, tossed countlessly away into howling winter wind along five hundred leagues of rock-fanged shore. Or, worst of all, rotted down to forgotten graves through years of ignorant patience, and vain seeking for help from man, for hope in God—infirm, imperfect yearning, as of motherless infants starving at the dawn; oppressed royalties of captive thought, vague ague-fits of bleak, amazed despair.[26]

And for the all the ways in which the experience of a Cockney flower girl who shines at the Embassy Ball can't be compared with that of Gilroy's moderns or Ruskin's dispossessed, her own sense of loss—of being cruelly humiliated and separated forever from her past—comes out in a most revealing turn of phrase: "I'm a slave now, for all my fine clothes" (*Pygmalion*, 277).[27]

Stung by her revolt against his mastery, Higgins would throw her back on the street, "a squashed cabbage leaf" once more, reviling her for her ingratitude in the wake of his magnanimous act of charity, his gift of the English tongue, the language of Shakespeare and Milton, which blinds him utterly to the fact of *her* labor in the process of language-acquisition, not to speak of her feelings. Her skin is not black, true (except for the grime of the streets), but neither is it thick. It is only now that Higgins, belatedly and dimly showing a readiness to acknowledge an injustice, begins to appreciate Eliza's epiphany about the difference between the flower girl and the duchess, which might be paraphrased, in accordance with the materials that I have presented here, in this way: in Covent Garden, as in the wider Atlantic world and even in modernity at large, the fundamental difference is not in how people behave, but in how they are treated.

NOTES

1. *My Fair Lady: A Musical Play in Two Acts*, Adaptation and Lyrics by Alan Jay Lerner, Music by Frederick Lowe (New York: Coward-McCann, Inc., 1956), 30. Subsequent references parenthetical.
2. Bernard Shaw, *Pygmalion: A Romance in Five Acts* (1912), in *Selected Plays with Prefaces*, vol. I (New York: Dodd Mead & Company, n.d.), 278–279. Subsequent references parenthetical.
3. Walter Benjamin, *Illuminations*, ed. Hannah Arendt (New York: Shocken Books, 1968), 261.
4. Michel Serres and Bruno Latour, *Conversations on Science, Culture, and Time* (Ann Arbor: University of Michigan Press, 1995), 62.
5. Henri Lefebvre, *The Production of Space* (London: Verso, 1991); theater historians who have taken up the urban situation of the physical stage include Marvin Carlson, *Places of Performance: The Semiotics of Theater Architecture* (Ithaca: Cornell University Press, 1989); Steven Mullaney, *The Place of the Stage: License, Play, and Power in Renaissance England* (1988; rpt. Ann Arbor: University of Michigan Press, 1995); and Janette Dillon, *Theater, Court, and City, 1595–1610: Drama and Social Space in London* (London: Cambridge University Press, 2000). See my "Space Wars," *Theater* 30 (2000): 128–131.
6. John Dunton, *The Night-Walker: or, Evening Rambles in Search after Lewd Women, with the Conferences held with Them, To be publish'd Monthly, 'till a Discovery be made of all the chief Prostitutes in England, from the Pensionary Miss, down to the Common Strumpet* (London: Printed for James Orme, 1696), 13.
7. Dian Kriz, "Slavery, Sugar, and the Culture of Refinement: Imaging the Colonial Exchange between Britain and the West Indies, 1700–1840," in progress.

8. Kathleen Wilson, "Theater, Culture and Modernity in the English Provinces 1720–1820," in progress.

9. Susan Leigh Foster, *Choreography & Narrative: Ballet's Staging of Story and Desire* (Bloomington: Indiana University Press, 1996), 4.

10. Gail Marshall, *Actresses and the Victorian Stage: Feminine Performance and the Galatea Myth* (Cambridge: Cambridge University Press, 1998), 4. See also Celia Marshik, "Parodying the £5 Virgin: Bernard Shaw and the Playing of *Pygmalion*," *The Yale Journal of Criticism* 13 (2000): 321–341.

11. See Lewis Hyde, *The Gift: Imagination and the Erotic Life of Property* (New York: Vintage, 1979), passim.

12. *Cities of the Dead: Circum-Atlantic Performance* (New York: Columbia University Press, 1996), 28.

13. Marvin Carlson, *Places of Performance: The Semiotics of Theater Architecture* (Ithaca: Cornell University Press, 1989), 10–11.

14. John Ruskin, "The Two Boyhoods," from *Modern Painters*, vol. V, part IX, "Of Invention Spiritual" (1860), in *Unto this Last and Other Writings by John Ruskin*, ed. Clive Wilmer (London: Penguin, 1985), 146.

15. Tom Brown, *Amusements Serious and Comical, Calculated for the Meridian of London*, 2nd edn. "with large Improvements" (London, 1700), 22.

16. Gretchen Holbrook Gerzina, *Black London: Life Before Emancipation* (New Brunswick, N. J.: Rutgers University Press, 1995), 5.

17. Quoted in Gerzina, *Black London*, 17.

18. Zacharias Conrad von Uffenbach, *London in 1710*, trans. and ed. W. H. Quarrel and Margaret Mare (London: Faber and Faber, 1934), 88.

19. Gerzina, *Black London*, 19.

20. *The Spectator*, ed. Donald F. Bond, 5 vols. (Oxford: Clarendon, 1965), IV, 99.

21. *The Spectator*, II, 534–535.

22. Peter Stallybrass and Allon White, *The Politics and Poetics of Transgression* (Ithaca: Cornell University Press, 1986), 5

23. Charles Dickens, *Our Mutual Friend* (London: Penguin, 1997), 710.

24. Ian Baucom, "Introduction: Atlantic Genealogies," *SAQ* 100 (2001): 7.

25. Paul Gilroy, *The Black Atlantic: Modernity and Double Consciousness* (Cambridge: Harvard University Press, 1993), 221.

26. Ruskin, "The two Boyhoods," 152.

27. Tracy C. Davis, in "Shaw's Interstices of Empire: Decolonizing at Home and Abroad," describes the relationship of female dependence of Eliza as that of "master and slave, colonizer and colonized." *The Cambridge Companion to George Bernard Shaw*, ed. Christopher Innes (Cambridge: Cambridge University Press, 1998), 225.

8

"MEN TO MONSTERS": CIVILITY, BARBARISM, AND "RACE" IN EARLY MODERN IRELAND

David J. Baker

"They are blacke Moores, o Queene, wash them as long as you will, you shall never alter their hue."[1] The author of this statement remains anonymous, but was most likely an English clergyman, once of Cork, but driven out of his acquired home in 1598 by Gaelic allies of Hugh O'Neill, Earl of Tyrone. In *The Supplication of the Blood of the English Most Lamentably Murdered in Ireland, Cryeng Out of the Yearth for Revenge*, he seeks to persuade Elizabeth I that the Gaels who have dispossessed him cannot be reformed. There is no more profit to be had in that attempt "then he that endevored with washinge to make a blacke moore white" (60). "[T]hose Englishe-bloode thirsters," he tells her, "murder yore faithfull people: ravishe theire wives and daughters: beate out the braines of their younge children in the armes of their nurses" (72).

The charge that the Gaels were irredeemably degenerate was crucial to the repertoire of arguments deployed by "New Englishmen" as they sought to make a place for themselves in early modern Ireland. These newly arrived English settlers were often locked in controversy with "Old Englishmen," longtime inhabitants whose ancestors had arrived during the Norman invasion under Henry II in 1172. Commentators sometimes frame the debate between these "two competing colonial communities"[2] as a fairly strict opposition: the recent emigres, they say, tended to argue for a radical reordering of England's governance of Ireland on the grounds that the Gaels were, as the author of the *Supplication* puts it, "Malitious, hatefull, bloody: a fitter broode to fill hell, then to people a Cuntry" (74). Moreover, the settlers claimed, these qualities were intrinsic to the Gaels: "It is a nature engraffed in them, will never be ridde out of them" (73). The Old English, by contrast, tended to argue that the existing government would suffice and that the Gaels could gradually be brought round by education and reform.[3] In this essay, however, I suggest that, while this opposition may hold when we contrast New English to Old English writings, it often begins to break down *within* New English treatises themselves. When I look closely at these, I find that many are actually far more unstable than this Old/New distinction implies. Even the virulent *Supplication*, as I will show, is split against itself, propounding not only a deterministic view of the Gaels, but an ameliorative one as well. As so often in such works, the author's ethnic hostilities and political aims are clear enough, but his rhetorical tactics are muddled. Such instabilities, moreover, are endemic to New English texts throughout the early modern period. They can be found not only in Edmund Spenser's much analyzed *A View of the Present State of Ireland*, which is roughly contemporaneous with the *Supplication*, but, as I note, in John Temple's *The Irish Rebellion*, a work of the mid-seventeenth century. My larger argument, then, is that the field of New English writing directed against the inhabitants of Ireland should be read as heterogeneous, conflicted, volatile, and not easily reduced to a particular set of programmatic declarations. Specific claims that New Englishmen advance should not be considered in isolation, but rather in relation to the whole ensemble of sometimes contradictory notions that made up this complex field. We should not be surprised, therefore, when a single work offers claims that undercut its own apparent premises, or even seems unable to decide exactly what its premises might be. Such texts do more than reveal a coherent, anti-Gaelic bias. On the contrary, when read attentively, they reveal the workings of a conflicted *mentalite*, elaborating an ideology out of its own often inconsistent antipathies.

Do New English writings also elaborate early versions of what would later become "racial" typologies, as a growing number of critics assert?[4] Certainly, hostility to the Gaels was interwoven with biases against other peoples in this period. Reaching for a trope by which to emphasize the utter alterity of the Gaels, the author of the *Supplication* arrives at "blackness." Moreover, categorical links of this sort may well have been historically consequential. According to Christopher Ivic, works such as this treatise "participated in the heterogeneous production of proto-racial identities."[5] Although, as he is quick to say, "race" had many meanings in the early modern period itself and usually denoted lineage, genealogy, and social rank—not skin color—he argues that "later biologically informed discourse on race recuperated prescientific imaginings of racial difference."[6] This proleptic relation between early modern and modern "discourses" of race justifies, he says, retrospective readings that uncover contemporary racism in its "pre-emergent" stage. "If 'race' originates as a category that hierarchically privileges a ruling status and makes the Other(s) inferior," asserts Lynda Boose in a similar vein, "then for the English the group that was first to be shunted into this discursive derogation and thereafter invoked as almost a paradigm of inferiority was not the black 'race'—but the *Irish* 'race.'"[7] Again, the *Supplication* suggests not only that "Gaelic-ness" and "blackness" were sometimes conjoined in the minds of New Englishmen, but that the "racializing" of both may have occurred not sequentially, but simultaneously.

I would add the caveat, though, that the heterogeneity of New English writings often makes it difficult to know just which claims are representative of the genre. It is widely acknowledged that applying contemporary notions of "race" to the early modern period can be problematic. Indeed, it is for this reason that the term frequently comes hedged about by quotation marks and amplified by qualifications in recent criticism. " '[R]ace' ... was a highly unstable term in the early modern period," say the editors of an influential volume; it could take on "complex, multiform and even contradictory senses."[8] This was "a moment," says Boose, "when several systems of meaning were clearly still in competition. The discourse of race that the Tudor and Stuart eras produce is written into that gap."[9] We should realize as well that the New English texts in which this "proto-racism" was perhaps partially emergent were often themselves "complex, multiform, and even contradictory." However much they may have made up a "discourse" in the aggregate, not all of these works operate from the same premises about the Gaels. The differences of tenor and argument among them—and within them—are sometimes pronounced. When we investigate "proto-racial" notions in this period, we should pay close attention to where and why these were articulated. Ivic points out, for instance, that in "the writings of New Englishmen, 'race' could function as a term of abuse when it referred to the entire Irish race and, crucially, their inherent nature."[10] As we have seen, the assertion that the Gaels were debased and violent by "nature engraffed in them" is made by, among many others, the author of the *Supplication*. But, as we will note shortly, this claim is launched amid a welter of other declarations, some that militate against it, and in a treatise that seems to be in fundamental contradiction about its own denigrations. Even if we read the *Supplication* selectively, as nothing more than an attack on intrinsic Gaelic vileness, we need to remember that its charges are meant as pointed rejoinders to another, antithetical set of claims—the Gaels were not intractably perverse, but susceptible to reform—and these too made up part of early modern English thinking on Irish ontology. Moreover, the vehemence of the *Supplication* is a bilious effusion of a distinct historical moment, the uprising of 1598, and, while it no doubt contributed to a general animus against the Gaels, its specific influences are not clear. The problem, as it turns out, is not in locating "proto-racial" adumbrations in New English writing of the early modern period. Rather, it is in deciding how these adumbrations are in tension with, and dialectically dependent upon, the other tropes and claims that make up the complex and variegated field of that writing. It is *because* the categories that these texts deploy are at every point imbricated with other categories, and *because* in their denigrations they do not usually proceed from a fixed sense of what "race" might be that establishing them as "prototypical" can be difficult. In practice, thinking about early modern "raciality" will require exacting analyses, both textual and historical. The rhetorical complexities of a work, its immediate history of reception, its later assimilation to larger trends—all will have to be considered equally and jointly.

Obviously, this is a project that can only be opened up in this essay. Here, I mean to look at two works in which "proto-racial" statements are made—the *Supplication* and, more briefly, Temple's *Irish Rebellion*—to attend to their contradictions, and to position them within the repertoire of New English writings. Differences among such texts can be explained, to an extent, by the varying fortunes of English governance in the Irish kingdom and by the circumstances of each author. Andrew Hadfield points out, for instance, that Edward Campion, who in his *A Historie of Ireland* could be quite benign and hopeful in his treatment of Gaelic barbarism, was "writing in 1571, at a time of relative peace and stability, after the defeat of Shane O'Neill and before the disastrous attempts of Essex and Sir Thomas Smith to colonize Ulster."[11] Other New Englishmen, of course, had less cause to feel benevolent. As Nicholas Canny notes, the attempts by the author of the *Supplication* to "decry all elements of the Irish population as an irredeemable people"[12] follow directly from the overthrow of the Munster plantation and from his own expulsion along with other English settlers. Spenser wrote the *View* either in 1590, if recent arguments by some historians are to be accepted,[13] or around 1596, according to most critics, or, even more likely, at various times during this troubled decade, and probably it is to this that some of the "harshness, even ruthlessness" of the treatise can be attributed, as Debora Shuger has suggested. By contrast, Sir John Davies's *A Discovery of the True Causes Why Ireland Was Never Entirely Subdued* (1612)[14] "reflects the success of Mountjoy's Irish campaign, which stamped out the dangerous clan revolts of the 1590s."[15] And so on.

Events alone, however, do not account for the disparate arguments that we find in New English texts. These discrepancies have as much, if not more, to do with the chronic inability of English settlers in the kingdom to come to a consensus on the bases of their collective critique of Gaelic barbarism. They do indeed denigrate Irishmen with a numbing similarity and predictability, and sometimes for their "inherent nature."[16] Gerald of Wales, whom Hadfield identifies as the "ghost-in-the-machine of all Tudor descriptions of Ireland and the Irish,"[17] wrote in 1185 that the Irish were "so barbarous that they cannot be said to have any culture. . . .They are a wild and inhospitable people. They live on beasts only, and live like beasts. . . . All their habits are the habits of barbarians."[18] As Hadfield says, "no Elizabethan writer differed significantly from his 'observations.' "[19] But whether any individual writer in any specific text in any given passage should be seen as entirely possessed by this ghost is a more complicated question. Campion, for example, conceded that the Gaels of the "lewder sort" were prone to "leachery above measure," but held that "[t]he same being vertuously bred up or reformed" could become "such mirrours of holinesse and austeritie, that other Nations retaine but a shewe or shadow of devotion in comparison of them."[20] Consider too how the alternative poles of the fluctuating debate are touched on in a brief exchange between the two interlocutors of Spenser's *View*—Irenius and Eudoxus. The first has a suggestion for reducing the Gaels to civility: change their names. Whereas now each Gael takes his name from his "septe" (clan), which reinforces his dependence on its "heade," Irenius proposes that by statutory law such a man should be required to "take vnto him selfe a seuerall surname ether of his trade and facultye or of some qualitye of his bodie or minde, or of the place wheare he dwelte." In this way, he thinks, the Gael might "in shorte time learne quite to forgett his Irishe nacion." But Eudoxus is sceptical: "I like this ordinaunce verye well," he says, but, sounding rather like the author of the *Supplication*, he wonders: "now that ye haue thus devided and distingushed them what other order will ye take for theire manner of lief"? "[F]or all this thoughe perhaps it maie kepe them from disobedience and disloyaltye yeat will it not bringe them from theire Barbarisme and salvage life."[21]

For Irenius—at least at this moment in the treatise—reform in Ireland is a matter of social engineering. Alter the customs of its people by education and their natures will follow, "ffor Learninge hathe that wonderfull power in it selfe that it cane soften and attemper the most sterne and salvage nature."[22] Here, he sounds like Campion. Gaelic names encode a distinct (and debased) "culture" with its own forms of property, hierarchy, and belonging. Change them and the Gaelic "nacion" will pass into oblivion. Eudoxus, however, is no such nominalist. On the contrary, he claims to believe that the Gaelic "manner of lief" follows from the nature of the Gaels themselves, and that as a people, under whatever epithet they appear, they are barbaric, savage, and prone to treachery. Recategorizing them will not avail much. What's in a name? It's hard, though, to decide which is Spenser's "view." We are so used to thinking of him as an inveterate critic of the Gaels that it comes as a surprise to read that, in one voice at least, he was willing to suppose that their depravity might be annulled by nothing more than a change in nomenclature, albeit one that implies a far reaching reconstitution of Gaelic society along the lines of "civility." What, Irenius seems to ask, is *not* in a name?

To be sure, the *View* is a dialogue, and thus we might expect one position to be played off another, perhaps with the balance eventually shifting this way or that. But the same radical uncertainly about ultimate claims can be found in more virulently monologic texts. In the *Supplication*, it seems even to have infiltrated the author's composition and editing. "Plucke up the fruites," he wrote, and then—or perhaps later—he paused, crossed out "fruites," wrote "roots" over it in his manuscript, and continued the sentence thus: "of rebellion, while god geveth yo*u* leave from other business: be assured the younge Impes that shall grow from thence will never beare better fruite."[23] As I mentioned, the reader whose "leave from other business" would now allow her to attend to the matter at hand was meant to be Queen Elizabeth I, and this sentence was meant to convince her that it is the children of the Gaels who must especially be looked to. They are intractably vicious, and "[n]o education, no bringing up, no tyme will better them. Take a woolves whelpe from the first teate; bringe him up in yo*re* owne house tame; weane him as much as yo*u* can from the condicions of his kinde, he will retourne to his old nature, notw*th*-standinge all yo*re* care, all yo*re* labour" (70). We can see, of course, that one reason the author made his revision was stylistic: he found himself ending with the claim that the Gaelic "Imps" would "never beare better fruite," so, to keep his vegetable metaphor coherent and avoid redundancy, he returned and altered "fruites" to "roots." But, intentionally or (as most likely) not, his editing signals an ongoing contradiction in his argument, one that persists from the *Supplication*'s first invocation of "the high and mightie Princesse, *ELIZABETH*" (13) to its closing blessing, "Soe be it, good god" (90). "[W]hat speake we of the effectes," the author asks early in the treatise, "w*ch* appeare in the sight of all men [?] The cause is rather to be thought upon" (16). Does the malice of the Gaels toward the English take its cause from their "rooted" properties, and it is these that must be "Plucke[d] up," or is this animus rather the contingent "fruite" of conditions in which, perhaps, the settlers themselves are implicated? This is a question to which this New English supplicant— despite himself, we sense—has a double answer.

On the one hand, he wants to show that the crisis in Ireland has come about because the conditions imposed by original conquest of Elizabeth's "noble and valiant ancestors" (47) have deteriorated since the twelfth century. Recognizing that the Gaels were a "people naturalie inclined to rebellion & pininge alwayes at the yoake [that] was laid upon them," these primordial conquerors built cities, erected castles, and imported "their owne people naturall subiectes of y*e* birth of England" (47–8). Had this conquest endured, he tells the Queen, "the [Gaelic] peoples hartes" could not have been "soe...poysoned w*th* malice against us....The offspringe of the first conquest, would never have thought themselves other then Englishe...[and] we should have utterly forgotten them ever to have ben Irishe" (75–6). Despite the author's many condemnations of the "natural" inclinations of the Gaels, therefore, he does not consistently assume that they are or always have been unalterable. The Irish were predisposed to revolt, but they could have been forestalled by the crown's strong and consistent government over the years. Conversely, absent that government, the kingdom and all of its inhabitants were bound to decay. "Weedes they are," he says of the Gaels, and "What wise gardiner," he asks Elizabeth, "would have suffered them soe to have growne?" (45).

Nor were the Gaels the only ones who had degenerated from their first natures. Like many other New English tracts, the *Supplication* is vehement in its denunciation of the Old English who have forsaken their "nation" and declined into Irish savagery. This critique, as in other works, is conducted in a lurid and insistently corporeal rhetoric. As we might expect in a tract with its title, the *Supplication* runs with blood, usually that of New Englishmen tortured, hacked, or cannibalized. We read of English bodies caught in brutal transformations. "The miserable body" of one victim, declares the author, "was first

wounded w*th* the sword...was forct (for the greater torment) to
yeald up the ghost, through the scorchinge heate of the fier, beinge
first roasted on the one side, then on the other" (14). Here and elsewhere, we are called to witness the physical disintegration of coherent
"Englishness." Besides blood, the author is preoccupied with breast
milk, an even more potent sign (and medium) of dissolution. This
was a familiar topic in New English works. In one of the best known
passages in Spenser's *View*, for example, Irenius speculates that "the
Chief Cause of bringinge in the Irishe language amongest" the Old
English was "theire fosteringe and marryinge with the Irishe." "[F]or
firste the Childe that suckethe the milke of the nurse muste of neces-
sitye learne his firste speache of her, the which beinge the firste that
is envred to his tounge is ever the most pleasinge vnto him...
they...drawe into themselues togeather with theire sucke even the
nature and disposicion of theire nurses."[24] In the *Supplication*, the
author uses some of the same lactic imagery, but for him the consequences of Irish nursing are even more far reaching. Interestingly, it
is here that he invokes "race," but in order to put pressure on the
notion that it might be a stable category for anyone. "I, but these [Old
English women] w*th* whom wee marry," he imagines some English
settlers protesting, "are of the race of the Englishe: are sprange of
them...[and] are distinguished...from the Irishe" by statutory law.
"[Y]ee deceyve yo*re*selves, O Bretheren," he counters, "w*th* bare
names." Like Eudoxus, the supplicant is convinced that Irish depravity is more ingrained than nomenclature can represent. But what also
makes the Irish especially depraved to him is their propensity to
become what they "are" not and to transform others from what they
"are." Your wives' English ancestors, he tells his countrymen,
"drowned themselves in Irish puddells...they drewe theire nature
from the corruption of their mothers; they suckte theire conditions
from the teates of theire Irish nurses" (38). We can detect a paradoxical logic at work in the *Supplication*, a logic that might indeed be
"proto-racial," though with all the complications that implies. On the
one hand, according to this author, there should be "races" in
Ireland. (The term, as we know, could have many meanings in his
time, but presumably he intends something like "kinship group.")
On the other hand, bloodlines (and milk lines) have become so intertwined and corrupted in the kingdom that, no matter how much he
upholds it, the very idea of a distinct "race" there seems dubious to
him. "Race"—in the genetic sense—is a fiction by which an incorri-
gibly hybrid people hide their true "nature." The mongrel
Englishmen he addresses are, in effect, being called upon to found, or

even "invent," such a "race" by abstaining from intermarriage with Gaelic and Old English "Paramours" (36). A "race of the Englishe" is an ideal that, to the chagrin of this author, contemporary practice in the Irish kingdom does not support. Simply put, there is too much sex, and too much fluid swapping generally, to keep the English and the Irish "proto-races" distinct.

The effects of this hybridity are registered throughout the rhetoric of the *Supplication*. It's often pointed out that, as in examples offered here, New English works castigate Irish women.[25] It is they who practice their beastly transformations upon the settlers; it is their milk that corrupts English children and later transforms "men to monsters" (38). But, in this treatise, Gaelic infiltration extends beyond the nursery and into the bedroom, and has the effect of turning Englishmen not just into Irish "monsters," but into women. "Shee that at night suckes from yo*re* bosome," the author warns his reader, "what soever the store house of yo*re* harte containeth, laboreth in the morninge (as if she were w*th* childe) untill she have delivered it" to her "kinsmen" (34). Here, we notice that the intended reader seems to have shifted gender from female—Queen Elizabeth—to male, the author's compatriots. But, giving suck to Irish women in the night, how "male" are they? It is not only, the author seems to be implying, that Gaelic women entice New Englishmen into illicit unions where they are figuratively consumed and betrayed. It is that, as these lines suggest, Ireland is one phantasmagory of carnage and copulation in which English mastery, knowledge, and identity are "suckte" out—along with the settlers' literal blood and milk—to be dispersed, altered, and turned back against them by some ghastly "labor" of native reproduction. One Irish traitor, he opines, should have been slaughtered in his cradle: Elizabeth "had avoyded halfe this troble by the death of that one whelpe, who then sucked milke, nowe suckes bloode" (71). This is the "scene" of the *Supplication*'s writing, and even Elizabeth is not exempted from its circuitous flow of bodily fluid. "Lett the splite bloode of yo*re* naturall and true subjects sinke into the depthe of yo*re* harte" (21), the author urges. Only then will she truly know her obligation to revenge them. On this terrain, clearly, there is very little in Gaelic, Old English, or even New English "natures" that is enduring. Instead, it is these very "natures" that are radically contingent and ceaselessly changing.

However, we would misread the *Supplication* if we were to take it only as a confession, perhaps unwitting, of chronic mutability. Driven, no doubt, both by his rage at the Gaels and his own sense that the Old and the New English cannot always be clearly divided from them, the author prosecutes a severe argument for utter Irish "difference." He must demonstrate to the Queen that "there is no hope of subiection, hope of loyalty or alleagaunce in them, from the highest to the lowest; from the noble man to the chorle; from the old to the younge; man and woman...they are all of one disposition" (73). The danger for him, as I have said, is that the Queen will revert to the more conciliatory policies long advocated by the Old English. To prevent this, he must assert that the Gaels are completely unamenable to change. And, to make this plausible in turn, he must insist that they are completely and unalterably dissimilar. Some of the tropes he employs are drawn from the centuries-old repertoire of English invective, some are of more recent coinage. The Gaels, he implies, following Gerald of Wales, are savages, little better than animals. They are, however, also enemies of true Protestant religion. He compares them unfavorably to "Gothes and Vandalles," and also, in the same sentence, to "Turkes" (20). Sometimes they are instead Jews: "The Contention begune betwene C[hriste]ndome and Israell in the wombe is never to be pacified" (36). Sometimes they are more precisely the "Scribes and Pharises whose contentions amonge them selves, could never either by reason, or frindshipe be setled" (66). Sometimes they are rather the foes of the children of Israel, the "very Amalekites, that god hath often given (as he doth nowe) into the handes of England" (68). And it is as he pursues this shifting argument that the author further likens the Gaels to "blacke Moores." He does not, it is true, make these analogies with much consistency, but that, of course, would be mostly beside the point. The author of the *Supplication* is not looking to define fixed equivalencies between these groups. He simply wants to push the Gaels to the farthest extreme of degeneracy and to remind the Queen that "Yo*re* mercy will not change theire manners" (60). He uses "blackness" to signify absolute "otherness," as he makes clear when he reassures Elizabeth that, no matter how rigorously she moves against her Irish foes, she will never be charged with cruelty: "yo*re* princly nature is knowne throughe all the worlde, to be as farre from it, as heaven from hell; as contrary to it, as white to black" (71). Thus, while claims that will seem "proto-racial" to us do emerge in this treatise, the disposition of these claims is first of all tactical: they are meant to turn the Queen's government against the people who have driven the author from his "home" and to promote a "new Conquest amongst a people that will not be woone w*th* lenitie" (77). "They are all crooked," he declares, "into the fire w*th* them" (88). The *Supplication* responds, in a forceful but incoherent way, to the exigencies of one New Englishman's tribulations in Ireland in the year 1598. It is a screed from a man driven to distraction by his recent reversals in the kingdom and rancid with hatred for those who precipitated them.

What was the fate of this work in the years that followed? And how influential were its claims and proposals? We should realize first that, just as the views of New Englishmen were diverse, so too were the fortunes of the tracts they penned. And it was not only or even mostly the pessimistic appraisals of Gaelic "nature" that were historically consequential. One of the most significant works to come from this cohort in the seventeenth century, for instance, was Sir John Davies's *A Discovery of the True Causes Why Ireland Was Never Entirely Subdued*.[26] As James I's attorney general in Ireland, Davies was in a position to implement a comprehensive program of legal (and, thus, as he understood it) cultural reform, and, not surprisingly, he operated from the premise that his policies could effectively transform his Irish subjects. Turning, like many before him, to the shaping powers of education, he told his countrymen in 1612 that the Irish were "for the most part send[ing] their children to schools, especially to learn the English language: so as, we may conceive an hope that the next generation will in tongue and heart, and every way else, become English, so as there would be no difference or distinction but the Irish Sea betwixt us."[27] Moreover, Davies's pronouncements were to have a decisive and lasting effect on the legal doctrines by which the English dealt with subjugated peoples. As Hans Pawlisch has shown, his "juridical stance on Gaelic property right laid the basis for an imperial formula that was fundamental in the creation of the British empire."[28] The *Supplication*, by contrast, was not published, and was instead "left as mail to be collected by the incoming president of Munster, George Carew, who was appointed to that post on March 6, 1600."[29] Whether or how that official read the treatise, we do not know. A case can be made, however, for a very real, though indirect, influence. The Queen's government did take seriously the call for revenge issued by its author and other refugees. An army of 3,000 was dispatched to reimpose English authority, headed up by Carew. As this campaign was to continue until the defeat of Tyrone in 1603, a decisive event in England's struggle to subordinate Ireland, it could be said that though the *Supplication* lay, probably disregarded, among Carew's papers for many years, the anger it vented contributed to the devastation of Gaelic culture in that kingdom inflicted under James I. Whether or not the moments of "proto-racial" ascription that we have located registered with whoever read this tract, or had much to do with whatever influence it had, is an open question.

Certainly, the attitudes that informed the text's vehement denigrations of the Gaels would persist among English settlers in Ireland. The *Supplication*, as its editor points out, "has to be read alongside" other works in an unfolding genre, "English atrocity literature."[30] The best known of these is a work of the mid-seventeenth century, Sir John Temple's *The Irish Rebellion* (1646),[31] a diatribe catalyzed by the Ulster uprising of 1641 and the "massacre" that was said to follow. In his polemic, Temple returns to the years of Elizabeth's reign to consider the origins of the latest Irish revolt, and finds, just as his anonymous predecessor did at the time, that the first cause is the innate "disposition of the [Irish] People, their hatred so implacable, their malice so unappeaseable, to all the English Nation, that no Laws, or gentle Constitutions, would work, no publick benefits attemper, or any tract of time, reconcile, and draw them to any tolerable patience of cohabitation; but they in all Times continued to take all advantages...most perfidiously to rise-up and imbrue their hands in the blood of their English neighbors." Elizabeth's efforts to reform the Gaels, he says, were "all...in vain," since "the matter then wrought-upon was not susceptible of any such noble forms" (17, 19). Although the *Supplication* "prefigures the opinions of the 1650s,"[32] there are differences between it and Temple's *Irish Rebellion*, enough, at any rate, that we can notice slight shifts in English thinking on the Gaels. Both tracts are, finally, exercises in *non*history: the Irish go on a rampage in the middle of the seventeenth century for the same reason they do some forty years earlier: they are inherently vicious and will always be. Both are concerned with English/Irish miscegenation and what Temple calls "a kind of mutual transmigration into each other's manners" (23). But while the author of the *Supplication* is mostly unconcerned with explaining Irish treachery except as it reveals the obvious "Crookednes of their nature" (17), Temple is somewhat more analytical and, at moments, a little more circumspect in his declarations. "Concerning the first original of this great Conspiracy," he acknowledges, "I must ingenuously confess, that I am myself much unsatisfied in the first conceptions of this monstrous birth; and therefore shall not now be able clearly to resolve others therein" (63). The problem that Temple cannot "obtrude every thing as infallible" (5) unsettles much of his treatise. But since such uncertainty must not persist, Temple arrives at a solution. He cannot satisfy his English readers about the causes of the rebellion, he decides, because of the "nature of the Irish." Essential to it is "a kind of dull and deep reservedness, as makes them, with much silence and secrecy, to carry-on their business" (25). "Therefore it is not much to be wondered-at, that the first beginnings (which were so mysterious and obscurely laid,) should remain as yet concealed with so much great *obstinacy*" (63, Temple's emphasis). A weakness in English epistemology is converted into a flaw in Irish ontology. Similarly, Temple is more equivocal than the author of the *Supplication* about the possible causes of Gaelic degeneracy, although, in the end, he is just as convinced of it. His truly is a "proto-racism," slipping uneasily among several notions of intrinsic difference. The inhabitants of Ireland, he says, are and long have been "devoid of all manner of civility… living like beasts, biting and devouring one another" (14). But why? Here, Temple is unsure. Whether this was because of the "malignant impressions of Irreligion and barbarism, transmitted-down, whether by infusion from their ancestors, or natural generation, had irrefragably stiffened their necks, and hardened their hearts against all the most powerful endeavours of *Reformation*" (19, Temple's emphasis) he cannot tell. Notice the range and variety of these possibilities; they are indeed "complex, multiform, and even contradictory." One supposition—the malign influence of Catholicism, "transmitted-down"—runs counter to Temple's general assumption that the Gaels are malevolent by nature and is in fact an historical and cultural hypothesis. Another—"barbarism"—briefly recalls the classical antecedents of New English commentary on the Gaels, of which Shuger has reminded us.[33] Still another—"infusion from their ancestors"—presumes that Gaelic resistance is somehow physically "transmitted" and thus does somewhat resemble "later biologically informed discourse on race."[34] And a final guess—"natural generation"—also holds out a corporeal explanation, but it eschews any notion of lineage and opts instead for some spontaneous "generation" (out of what? by what?) of "Irishness." It's not that the *Irish Rebellion* is any less confused than the *Supplication*; it's that they are confused in different ways. While the *Supplication* seems contradictory because its argument keeps shifting between Old English claims that the Gaels are remediable and New English claims that they are not, the *Irish Rebellion* does not try to accommodate Old English reformism. After the events of 1641, the inborn savagery of the Irish has become the only acceptable premise, and all of the "explanations" that Temple throws out so randomly are meant only to prevent anyone from entertaining any doubt on that score. Temple's contradictions, like those of the *Supplication*, are motivated by a single animus. But the conceptual range of these "explanations" has broadened, even as the range of acceptable opinion has narrowed.

Of course, what *we* immediately notice is that among those claims Temple has briefly inserted a notion—"infusion from their ancestors"—that later periods will see developed into a full blown "racism." Just as we can't help but note that, as he pursues his own bifurcated argument, the author of the *Supplication* finds Gaelic "blackness" an apposite way to make a political point and so anticipates a later "regime . . . of visible difference."[35] This is "proto-racial" thinking, if you will, although it is only in the later work that the argument is tightening slowly around the idea that there is some somatic explanation for Irish duplicity. It is the "loose humours of the natives," (18) says Temple, that account for their continued intransigence. Some critics, it's true, have doubted whether "race" can be an operative concept in the early modern period, and have argued against looking for intimations of it in New English works. Shuger, for example, points out, "[r]ecent criticism of Tudor/Stuart Irish discourses . . . has focussed on their alleged imperialist, racist, and genocidal implications." She insists, however, that when New Englishmen refer to the Gaels as "barbarians," it is not to "conflate the Irish with New World or other non-white peoples." Instead, they mean to "designate . . . them as northern Europeans." The "organizing polarity" of such texts is not race, but "civility versus barbarism," and this should not be reduced to "an emotive equivalent to the trite and pernicious binarism of 'Us' versus 'Demonic Other'."[36] She has a good point, although our look at the *Supplication* and the *Irish Rebellion* suggests that she may have overstated it. New Englishmen do mostly argue for their own "civility" and assail Gaelic "barbarism," and still inchoate "racial" categories figure very little in their writings. But, as we have seen, the "binarism" of " 'Us' versus 'Demonic Other'," now matter how "trite" it has since come to seem, is endemic in the early modern period itself. In both the texts we've considered, it is not only the language, but the logic of "racism" that is being forged, slowly and haphazardly. That this "proto-racism" was *ad hoc* and inevitably emerged in close relation to other typologies of abuse does not imply that it did not exist. Nor does the historical fact that the heat for this forging process was supplied by specific incendiary encounters between New English and Gaels—for example, the attack on the Munster plantation—imply that the "proto-racism" so generated was not consequential, both immediately and then in later periods. These works, after all, make their own claims on the future, and their prognostications, lamentably, are often all too accurate. "They are all runne together to drive yo*u* out of you*re* kingdome, to destroy yo*re* people," the author of the *Supplication* told his Queen in 1598.

"Lett them all drinke of one cuppe together," he pleaded, "Lett them all taste one whipp....Lett the sworde spare none that lightes in [its] way" (86). He could not have known it, but Ireland—a "field of blood" Temple called it (17)—would see such retribution exacted many times over in the century to come.

NOTES

1. *The Supplication of the Blood of the English Most Lamentably Murdered in Ireland, Cryeing Out of the Yearth for Revenge (1598)*, ed. Willy Maley, *Analecta Hibernica*, 36 (1994): 60. All further references are given parenthetically in the text.

2. Andrew Hadfield, " 'The naked and the dead': Elizabethan perceptions of Ireland," *Travel and Drama in Shakespeare's Time*, ed. Jean-Pierre Maqueslot and Michele Willems (Cambridge: Cambridge University Press, 1996), 46.

3. On these debates, see Brendan Bradshaw, *The Irish Constitutional Revolution of the Sixteenth Century* (Cambridge: Cambridge University Press, 1979).

4. See, for instance, Christopher Ivic, "Spenser and the Bounds of Race," *Genre*, 32 (1999): 141–173, *passim*; Margo Hendricks and Patricia Parker, introduction to *Women, "Race," and Writing in the Early Modern Period*, ed. Margo Hendricks and Patricia Parker (London: Routledge, 1994), 1–2; Lynda E. Boose, " 'The Getting of a Lawful Race': Racial discourse in early modern England and the unrepresentable black woman," *Women, "Race," and Writing*, 36–37; Dympna Callaghan, "Re-reading Elizabeth Cary's *The Tragedie of Mariam, Faire Queene of Jewry*," *Women, "Race," and Writing*, 164–165; Willy Maley, " 'This ripping of auncestors': The Ethnographic Present in Spenser's *A View of the State of Ireland*," *The Texture of Renaissance Knowledge*, ed. Philippa Berry and Margaret Tudeau-Clayton (Manchester: Manchester University Press, 2003): 117–134. On the relation between early modern racial categories and those of our own period, see Margaret W. Ferguson's remarks in "Juggling the Categories of Race, Class, and Gender: Aphra Behn's *Oroonoko*," *Women, "Race," and Writing*, 211–212. For a general treatment that locates Ireland in the history of racist thought and practice, see Theodore W. Allen, *The Invention of the White Race, Volume One: Racial Oppression and Social Control* (London: Verso, 1994). Allen argues plausibly for analogies between the treatment of "the Africans, the American Indians, and the Irish" in the early modern period. In Ireland, he says, the English "reduced all members of the oppressed group to one undifferentiated social status, a status beneath that of any member of any social class within the colonizing population. *This is the hallmark of racial oppression* in its colonial origins, and it has persisted in subsequent historical contexts" (32, Allen's emphasis).

5. Ivic, "Spenser and the Bounds of Race," 143. Ivic refers the comparison with which I open as an instance of the "discourse on 'blackness'... surfac[ing] in early modern English discourse on the Irish" ("Spenser and the Bounds of Race," 147).

6. Ivic, "Spenser and the Bounds of Race," 143.

7. Boose, "Getting of a Lawful Race," 36. Boose's emphasis.

8. Hendricks and Parker, "Introduction," 1.

9. Boose, "Getting of a Lawful Race," 37.

10. Ivic, "Spenser and the Bounds of Race," 145.

11. Hadfield, "The naked and the dead," 38.

12. Canny, *Making Ireland British 1580–1650* (Oxford: Oxford University Press, 2001), 163.

13. See David Edwards, "Ideology and experience: Spenser's *View* and martial law in Ireland," *Political Ideology in Ireland, 1541–1641,* ed. Hiram Morgan (Dublin: Four Courts Press, 1999), 143–144.

14. *A Discovery of the True Causes Why Ireland Was Never Entirely Subdued [And] Brought Under Obedience of the Crown of England Until the Beginning of His Majesty's Happy Reign (1612),* ed. James P. Myers, Jr. (Washington D.C.: Catholic University of America Press, 1988).

15. Shuger, "Irishmen, Aristocrats, and Other White Barbarians," *Renaissance Quarterly,* 50 (1997): 506.

16. Ivic, "Spenser and the Bounds of Race," 154.

17. Hadfield, "The naked and the dead," 34.

18. Quoted in Hadfield, "The naked and the dead," 34–35.

19. Ibid., 34.

20. *Ancient Irish Histories* (Dublin: Hibernia Press, 1809), 1, 19.

21. *The Works of Edmund Spenser,* vol. 10 (Baltimore: Johns Hopkins University Press, 1949), 215.

22. Spenser, *Works,* 218.

23. According to Willy Maley, the *Supplication*'s editor, there is a "single complete original text" (Maley, introduction to the *Supplication* 11) of this treatise extant. He also notes that it is "written in a very legible secretary hand. All deletions and insertions are in the same hand as the author" (90).

24. Spenser, *Works,* 119.

25. See, for instance, Joan Fitzpatrick, *Irish Demons: English Writings on Ireland, the Irish, and Gender by Spenser and his Contemporaries* (Lanham: University Press of America, 2000), *passim.*

26. See n. 14.

27. Davies, *Discovery,* 217. On a New English critic of Davies's views and policies, see Eugene Flanagan, "The anatomy of Jacobean Ireland: Captain Barnaby Rich, Sir John Davies and the failure of reform, 1609–22," *Political Ideology in Ireland,* 158–180.

28. *Sir John Davies and the Conquest of Ireland: A Study in Legal Imperialism* (Cambridge: Cambridge University Press, 1985), 14.

29. Maley, "Introduction," 10.
30. Maley, "Introduction," 7.
31. *The Irish Rebellion; or, An History of the Attempts of the Irish Papists to Extirpate the Protestants in the Kingdom of Ireland; Together with the Barbarous Cruelties and Bloody Massacres which Ensued Thereupon* (1646; rpt. London: 1812). All further references will be given parenthetically.
32. Hadfield, "English Colonialism and National Identity in Early Modern Ireland," *Eire/Ireland,* 28 (1993): 83.
33. Shuger, "Irishmen," 497.
34. Ivic, "Spenser and the Bounds of Race," 143.
35. Callaghan, "Re-reading," 165.
36. Shuger, "Irishmen," 495.

9

MUSTAPHA RUB-A-DUB KELI KHAN AND OTHER FAMOUS EARLY AMERICAN LITERARY MAHOMETANS

Philip D. Beidler

One of the most widely told anecdotes about the tragic destruction of the University of Alabama by Union raiders in April 1865 concerns the unusual identity of the single book saved from the burning library. It was a copy of the Koran. A strange fact, you might say; but perhaps not too strange, in a war in which troops fought on both sides uniformed as French-Algerian Zouaves—complete with Fez, sashes, brocaded cutaway jackets, scarlet pantaloons. Scimitars seem to have been optional; but dress wear in some cases did require a turban. Nor was it too great a literary irony especially for the region whose favorite imported reading included Sir Walter Scott's *The Talisman*, with its romantic bookending of Richard Lion Heart with his noble adversary Saladin, or a wildly popular pseudo-oriental verse romance by the Irish poet Thomas Moore, set in Kashmir and detailing the courtship of a Moghul princess by the King of Bokhara, entitled *Lallah Rookh*. Probably one should also note in this connection that Mark Twain, in *Huckleberry Finn*, attempting to put a period on his absolute contempt for antebellum Southern romanticism, sends two steamboats to the bottom of the Mississippi. The first is named the Walter Scott. The second, rendered in the parlance of the region, is the "Lally Rook." Meanwhile, to the north, he also took more than occasional fun in satirizing his Connecticut neighbor, P. T. Barnum, for a pseudo-oriental pleasure dome of a residence erected in Bridgeport and garishly named Iranistan.[1]

In fact, here as elsewhere, the late-eighteenth- and early-nineteenth-century American writer actively mirrored the aestheticized "orientalism"—and I am using the term here both in the sense of how Americans and Anglo-Europeans of the era understood the idea of the "eastern" or "oriental"—that is, what we would call Middle Eastern or Near Eastern, as opposed to the Far Eastern; and in our contemporary Edward Said's classic formulation of traditional self-validating "western" constructions of the "eastern" in just this vein[2]—of admired British and European writers of the era: Montesquieu, Voltaire, Johnson, Goldsmith, Coleridge, Beckford, Byron, and others. They avidly read, for instance, arabesque fantasy ranging from Coleridge's visionary "Kubla Khan" to Byron's swashbuckling "Corsair;" evolving forms of the "eastern" tale, in early cases such as Johnson's *Rasselas* and Voltaire's *Candide*, a form of the philosophical novel, and latter, as in Beckford's *Vathek*, an offshoot of gothicism; and nearly endless variations on the "citizen of the world genre"—sometimes called the philosophical letter—in which an "eastern" visitor encounters, reports on, and frequently satirizes western cultures. Indeed, albeit themselves frequently regarded as rude exotics, primitives, semi-savage frontier dwellers, and the like, early Americans revealed profound fascination with the mysteries of the Moor—Latin-French for Maurus, native of Mauritania, which at the time meant the present Morocco, Tunisia, and Algeria; the Turk—Middle French and English for a speaker of the Turkic languages; the Mahometan—alternatively, as Mohammedan or Muhammedan, follower of the prophet; the Mussulman—Turkish for true believer; the Saracen—Arabian for desert dweller; the Ottoman—from the Arabic Othman, English Osman, founder of the empire bearing his name; the Persian—the Parsee, derived of Farsi; the Bedouin—Arabic Bedawi, desert dweller.[3] Related, although somewhat separate, was also a concurrent Egyptological fascination derived from a Western reawakening of interest, due to Napoleon's campaigns, in the culture of the ancient kingdom of the Nile, and from the discovery of the Rosetta Stone and the claims made by Champollion in the 1820s about the unriddling of the hieroglyphics.[4] Ensuing developments, in Malini Schueller's instructive accounting, would include obsessions with the The Holy Land and the world of the Indic orient. And finally, of course, would come Asian orientalism, and a set of serial obsessions with China, Japan, Korea, Vietnam, and the Pacific Rim, with Americans eventually—by typical linguistic and political fiat—executing an exact cultural reversal in the meaning of the word, making the west east and the east west.

Nonetheless, for most of the antebellum era, it was the orientalism of the earlier Arabs, Persians, and Ottoman Turks that maintained a decided hold on American visions of the East. Travel writing of the era included George William Curtis's *Nile Notes of a Howadji* (1851) and *The Howadji in Syria* (1852); and Bayard Taylor's *A Journey to Central Africa; or Life and Landscapes from Egypt to the Negro Kingdoms of the White Nile* (1854); and *The Lands of the Saracen; or Pictures of Palestine, Asia Minor, Sicily, and Spain* (1855). N. P. Willis's earlier *Pencillings by the Way*, detailing a cruise in the eastern Mediterranean, "fascinated readers with its raptures over Mediterranean sunsets, twilights, and veiled women (Schueller, 31). And John Lloyd Stevens gained overnight popularity (and abundant royalties) for *Incidents of Travel in Egypt, Arabia Petraea, and The Holy Land* (1837)[5]—a work known to have been a great favorite of Poe. In a more familiar literary vein, Melville's Fedallah in *Moby-Dick*, playing the beturbaned, glittering-eyed, fire-worshipping Mephistopheles to Ahab's Faust, is a Parsee. In *The Blithedale Romance*, Hawthorne is at pains to name his alluring nineteenth-century feminist femme fatale Zenobia, at once recalling the fabled queen of the Nile but also obviously traceable in a more direct popular culture lineage to William Ware's *Zenobia* (1837), in which a missionary attempts to put off oriental corruption. Earlier, Koranic influences had lent their peculiar exoticism to Poe's early poems such as "Israfel" and "Al Araaf." It was by no accident at all that he elected to call his first collection of verse *Tamerlane and Other Poems* and a major short-story volume, working the twinned strains of the gothic and the oriental, *Tales of the Grotesque and the Arabesque*. Before that, Washington Irving, in the wake of such international best-sellers as *The Sketch-Book* and *Tales of a Traveller*, had helped cement his status as the first American writer of trans-atlantic reputation with wildly popular studies of the Moorish legacy in Spain including *The Conquest of Granada* and *Legends of the Alhambra*. Earlier, in the *Salmagundi* papers, he and his waggish collaborators—Lancelot Langstaff, Anthony Evergreen, Pindar Cockloft, and the lot—had assigned to a pseudonymous Tripolitan prisoner and cosmopolite, one "Mustapha Rub-a-Dub Keli Khan," the peculiarly abrasive task of satirizing parochial American pride in the politics of democratic "logocracy." And late in life, along with biographies of Goldsmith and Washington, he would complete a volume-length life of the Prophet. Before that, one of the most popular early American novels had been Royall Tyler's 1797 *The Algerine Captive*, the picaresque adventures of an American sailor, one Updike Underhill of New Hampshire, from his boyish rovings to his eventual rescue by a western privateer from enslavement at the hands of the Barbary Pirates. In fact, to this day, celebrating American military resistance to such depredations, when people sing the Marine Corps anthem, those are "the shores of Tripoli" they are talking about, right after "the Halls of Montezuma."

Indeed, again as revealed by Malini Johar Schueller, a spate of such texts responded to the experience of the "Barbary" orient, mixing the genre of the captivity narrative—itself by then distributing itself out of the "white" Indian captivity genre and into the "black" slave narrative—with the literature of travel, adventure, and exploration. Besides Tyler's novel, these included Susanna Rowson's earlier drama *Slaves in Algiers* (1794); James Ellison's *The American Captive* (1812); and Joseph Steven Jones's *The Usurper* (1841). An early popular history was Matthew Carey's *A Short Account of Algiers and Its Several Wars* (1794). And a contribution to an emerging, distinctly American vein of the philosophical letter tradition—contemporary, for instance, with Crevecoeur's *Letters from an American Farmer*, and anticipating Irving—was Peter Markoe's *The Algerine Spy in Pennsylvania* (1787).[6]

Thus in the early republic there existed a substantial array of texts in which early modern Islam is viewed in an extended way through American eyes. Further, the view came at the intersection of a number of nascent republican forms, with a set of racial politics frequently as diverse and strangely evolving as those of the new nation. Tyler and Rowson, for instance, contain inside views of a slave system, as shown below, in which Americans and Anglo-Europeans—caucasians—were enslaved by cultures of what would be now, by American estimation, the nonwhite. Yet in Tyler, the narrative ranging of the titular protagonist into cultural exotica frequently makes the American experience of Algerine slavery read as much like travelogue as captivity tale—although the experience of being a quarry slave, exacted as punishment for striking an overseer, is dire enough to make him momentarily consider conversion to Islam, as is the witnessing of a would-be escapee's death by impalement sufficiently horrific to deter him from any further plans of the sort. Further, on the explicit matter of race and slavery, his status as captive ambassador of a new religion of democracy is complicated by our knowledge of his previous service as surgeon on a slave ship, during which he has excoriated the horrific cruelties of the evil trade with a passionate recognition that it is nothing less than a crime against humanity, a curse he somehow realizes his own enslavement may have been designed to expiate. Yet once he himself is enslaved, while American enslavement of Africans and Arab enslavement of Americans may remain paired in the narrative as comparable injustices, the narrative suggests that slavery as a cultural practice is now conceived of in Underhill's case as mainly a crime against American liberty. Indeed, if anything is revealing in this respect it is his very use of the term "race," whereby Underhill reveals at best a republican variation on a set of early modern attitudes in evolutionary ferment. His proto-abolitionist outrage at the horrors to which he finds enslaved Africans subjected is crowned by his reference to them as "MY BRETHREN OF THE HUMAN RACE."[7] On the other hand, the Algerines who enslave him are "a ferocious race" (xii), and the Jews who persistently play false with his hopes of emancipation are a "cunning race" (II, 167). To put this more directly, on matters of race and slavery, like most of his American contemporaries, Underhill—to his credit, at least, without the evasions of a Thomas Jefferson—is still struggling to endow national politics with a moral vocabulary. Similarly, Rowson's drama seems to trace out a contemporary form of "white" slavery as an account of the Algerine captivity of two American women, Rebecca and Olivia, that should possibly lead us back to analogies concerning the racially ordered mirror image of the American "peculiar institution." Yet again, as to early American issues of race and, in this case, gender and the politics of American liberty, this picture of slavery from the outset proves immensely complicated as well. To begin with, the play itself, accompanied by music by the prominent American composer Alexander Reinagle, seems to have been conceived of as comic opera.[8] Further, even within any critique of slavery as a historical institution—let alone as a cross-cultural problematic of racial difference with distinct American implications—here it is the specter of sexual menace, albeit attended with visible emphasis, as Jenny Franchot observes, on "American liberty and women's rights" (257), that trumps all other thematic concerns. That is, if, as for Tyler, Barbary slavery is a crime against American liberty, for Rowson it is not only this—with the issue fairly trumpeted in the play's opening verse argument—but also a crime against republican chastity and/or womanly purity. Rebecca, a mature woman, has been taken for ransom by Ben Hassan, a Jew. Her son Augustus has been enslaved to another master. Olivia, the text's ostensible ingenue, has been kidnapped by an Algerian ruler to be part of his harem. Further, as Schueller astutely observes, such matters of race, gender, and enslavement become perplexingly involuted by the presence of "Fetnah, the most racially and culturally ambiguous woman in the play" (64). She is actually the first character we meet: "British and Jewish by birth," as Schueller summarizes, "but Algerian and Moslem by rearing (her father having moved to Algiers and converted to Islam) and Christian by conviction."

Accordingly, throughout, the play here does seem to make its one concession to the idea of racial difference: she is thus technically a white Christian woman, while, in a potentially "fallen" status as one of the Dey's enslaved mistresses, she also anticipates the familiar figure in subsequent fiction, of the tragic mulatta. Meanwhile, a number of other matters contend for thematic interest. Two young American captives, Fredric and Henry, plot escape with Ben Hassan, Fetnah's father, a heavily caricatured comic Jew. Olivia, beloved of Henry, recruits the Moorish beauty Zoriana, a secret Christian convert, as her accomplice in the design. They are all assisted by Sebastian, a Spanish slave. When the plot goes awry, Olivia agrees to consider conversion to Islam and marriage to the Dey so that the others may be freed. Rebecca, who turns out to be her mother, volunteers to remain with her. Meanwhile a general slave uprising occurs. Fetnah turns up in the last scene to receive her freedom as well. In turn "Mrs. Rowson" accepts a prompter's invitation to deliver an epilogue celebrating female heroism generally. "Women were born to universal sway;" she asserts, "Men to adore, be silent, and obey" (94).

The dramas by Ellison and Jones are generally less problematic, affirming, as did Carey's earlier account of a new nation's victory over its Tripolitan enemies, the values of republican freedom and goodness over oriental despotism and immorality (Schueller, 13). So Markoe's use of the citizen-of-the-world narrative recast as espionage drama, becomes basically "a political conversion narrative" in which the oriental traveler, "Mehmet," chooses at the end to make the new nation his permanent home.

Despite what strikes the reader of today as a good deal of reverse cultural and racial gyration on many of the oppositions between "slave" and "free" values it purports to affirm, Tyler's novel of all the texts mentioned is the best remembered. This would seem to be on the basis of its appeal to an audience not displeased by the integration of the captivity narrative and the literature of travel and exploration with a topical reference to some contemporary international muscle flexing by the young republic.[9] The ironies of course are not lost on us now: in a quick, decisive, surgical strike against Islamic terrorism, America had established its signature upon the world stage as an international maritime and military power. Barbary—derived from Berber—in turn linked to the Greek root for barbarian, meaning foreign, outsider—was yet another word signifying the world of Islam. For all that we called it by many names, however, we still clearly didn't know much about it; what we did know we frequently used to our own cultural purposes; and what we did or didn't know did not really seem much to matter in any event, with the whole business rapidly receding into the realm of popular culture cliche. Nor should one have been surprised on the foregoing literary and cultural record. Indeed, in much of pre-revolutionary American writing, Islam seemed to served mainly just as a kind of available metonymy for the non-Western, the strange, the exotic, the outlandish. Franklin repeatedly used references to the religion, for instance, as a stock image for describing the capaciousness of his anti-sectarianism. The design of the nondenominational meeting house erected in Philadelphia by a committee of trustees was such, he bragged, "that even if the Mufti of Constantinople were to send a Missionary to preach Mahometanism to us, he would find a pulpit at his service."[10] (To his later credit, during the debate on the Constitution, he also compared a proslavery speech in Congress to the Divan of Algiers defending the "plundering and enslaving of Christians." Albeit this from a man who had earlier owned and sold Negro slaves.) Franklin's fellow deist, the Virginian William Byrd, had recourse to a similar vein of figuration in a famous passage from the *History of the Dividing Line* reflecting on conversations conducted on natural religion with a faithful Indian guide. Said individual, Bearskin, he pronounced a veritable Shaftesbury in warpaint, even down to a restoration rake's dream of a heavenly afterworld filled with nubile, compliant maidens and a hell of shrewish, sexually demanding Mrs. Loveits and Lady Wishforts. Perhaps, he concluded—it seems now a good deal disingenuously— "the Indian notion of a future happiness" may strike the English reader as "a little gross and sensual, like Mahomet's paradise." Still, "how can it be otherwise in a people that are contented with Nature as they find her and have no other lights but what they receive from purblind tradition?"[11] Correspondingly, even the arch-puritan Cotton Mather could use the figure in *The Christian Philosopher* to tout the merits of a wise eclecticism—not to mention justify his own rapacious pedantry. Even "the great Alstead instructs me," he says, "that we Christians, in our valuable Citations from them that are Strangers to Christianity, should seize upon the Sentences as containing our Truths, detained in the hands of *Unjust Possessors*; and he allows me to say, Audite Ciceronem, quem Natura docuit. However, this I may say, God has thus far taught a Mahometan! And this will I say, Christian, beware lest a Mahometan be called in for thy Condemnation."[12]

More to the point of our concerns, aside from the relatively isolated handful of Barbary "slave" texts responding to particular and violent historical events, the constructions of Islam by seventeenth-, eighteenth-, and nineteenth-century American writers would surely have seemed the stuff of increasingly disembodied religious and aesthetic troping to fifteenth- and sixteenth-century English voyagers, as well as their counterparts in Spain, France, Italy, Portugal, and every other Atlantic seafaring nation, for whom Islam was a major historical and military presence across the whole of the oceanic world. Captain John Smith, for instance, among the most prolific producers of narratives of New World adventure, honed his fighting skills against the Turks on the plains of central Europe. He had also, one should add, rehearsed his famous American captivity scene with the experience of having himself been sold in a Turkish slave market. Similarly, Hakluyt's Voyages more generally speak not only of new world adventuring but of encounter with the Persian, the Bokharan, the Turk. Having conquered Constantinople, Asia Minor, the Fertile Crescent, North Africa, and much of Iberia, Islamic peoples of a host of ethnic and geographic origins operated freely upon sea and land as Corsairs, Pirates, Plunderers, and Raiders—with a reputation it would seem now, not unlike the dreaded Northmen of the late Middle Ages or their predecessors, the Vandals. Most important to purposes of *our* understanding, they were legendarily feared as notorious enslavers of Europeans—the fact notwithstanding, of course, that the same Europeans had been taking them captive in substantial numbers since the crusades. In 1617, for instance, Muslim pirates extending a long practice of enslaving Christians along the coasts of Spain, France, Italy, and even Ireland, captured 1,200 men and women in Portuguese Madeira. In 1627, pirates from the Barbary coast of North Africa raided Iceland and went home with 4,000 slaves. As late as the 1640s, it is probable that there were many more English slaves in Muslim North Africa than there were African slaves under English control in the Caribbean. Cumulatively, according to one historical estimate, between 1580 and 1680, there may have been as many as 850,000 Christian Europeans taken by Muslim slavers, with the number possibly rising to a million if we take matters down to the late eighteenth and early nineteenth centuries when such depredations were brought to a halt.[13] Meanwhile, since the ninth century, Muslim slavers had made the enslavement of black, subsaharan Africans "a fundamental part," as recently noted by David Brion Davis, of Islam's "remarkable expansion."[14] Accordingly, when European nations became part of the African trade, they in some degree buried emergent definitions of racial subordination by justifying the enslavement and Christianization of subsaharan Africans—as did the Portuguese, for example, as a just part of the centuries-long reconquest of Iberia and crusade against the Moor—and as would other Christian nations, including, eventually, the Confederate States of America, more generally, all the while establishing distinct and even biological racial hierarchies, come to enumerate the benefits of salvation among their sundry justifications. The point of all this, however, I hasten to say, is not to overplay Islam and underplay European implication in the slave cultures of the early modern Atlantic and Mediterranean worlds. Nor is it to ignore the fact that Islamic slave cultures, in their particular reponses to the presence of subsaharan Africans, generally devised and enacted categories of race and color analogous to those in the west.[15] Rather, it is simply to make us more aware than we may have been before of how the ongoing war between Islam and the West institutionally created a climate whereby, in Davis' persuasive judgement, "the continuing enslavement of Christians by Muslims and of Muslims by Christians actually conditioned both groups to accept the institution of slavery on a wider scale and thus prepared the way for the vast Atlantic slave system" (51). To put this more simply, there existed a geo-political climate in which the idea of just or unjust ownership of other human beings became almost infinitely adjustable depending on what racial or ethnic culture you happened to be passing through, albeit voluntarily or involuntarily, yourself free or yourself enslaved, at the time.[16] Accordingly, complex Anglo-American definitions of and justifications for African slavery on the basis of race—theories, successively, of religious, cultural, ethnic, and finally biological superiority/inferiority— seem to have undergone their own complex, essentially ad hoc, evolutions as the demands of ideology required that certain political fictions be hardened into certain racial myths. In short, during the colonial and early republican periods in America, as in contemporary England, racism as we know it was decidedly a work in progress, literally forming its own categories and writing its own vocabulary.[17] The complicated cultural emanations of this in both literary and historical narrative of the era are manifold—and in themselves worth a book. To complement the newly nationalistic narratives of Algerine captivity cited earlier with a classic British analogue enjoying sustained popularity with American readers in the decades before the Revolution, Defoe's *Robinson Crusoe*, for instance, begins its oceanic saga with the titular hero aboard a mid-seventeenth-century English slaver bound for Guinea. Off the coast of Africa, he himself is captured and enslaved by seafaring Turks. After undergoing Turkish slavery for two years, he finally escapes, and, anticipating Tyler's

Underhill, is rescued by a Portuguese slaving captain. He is then conveyed to Brazil, where for four more years he becomes modestly wealthy as himself a slaveholding planter. Nor, in a bizarre American reconnection, can one resist a brief analogous recounting of the actual story of one David Levy Yulee, the descendant of an English Jewish grandmother and a Portuguese Jewish father, with the latter serving, until his untimely death in the sultan's dungeons, as First Councillor Grand Vizier to the King of Morocco. By way of Gibraltar and the West Indies, the young Levy/Yulee—he seems to have used the names interchangeably—eventually found his way to early-nineteenth-century Florida where, as a U. S. representative, albeit only after a major lawsuit contesting his qualifications because of the Danish citizenship of his father, he saw to the passage of funding finance bills for final Indian removals from the territory and helped secure Florida's admission as a slave state to the Union. For this he was rewarded with election as the state's first U. S. Senator. A large slaveholder and ardent secessionist, he was indicted after the war for treasonous "plotting to capture the forts and arsenals of the United States, and with inciting war and rebellion against the government" while still a sitting Senator (173). He was then imprisoned for a year, only to emerge as a railroad tycoon responsible for construction of the first line connecting Florida's east and west coast, finally dying in Washington, D. C. in 1886.[18]

To be sure, it is tempting here as elsewhere to go for the easy anecdotal irony. And from there it is just as easy to go on to the slavery blame game, the orgy of geo-political finger pointing that has gone on as long as slavery has had a history in the west. Early modern Christians blamed the Muslims and vice-versa. The Portuguese and Spanish blamed the Arabs. The English blamed the Portuguese and Spanish. Revolutionary Americans—albeit excising such objectionable content from the Declaration of Independence for fear of alienating Southern representatives—blamed George III. Antebellum northerners, for whom slavery quickly proved unprofitable on land while simultaneously a boon to the shipping trade, blamed the Southerners. In turn, accused Southerners recalled generations of New England sugar, slave, and rum traders plying the infernal Atlantic triangle. Meanwhile, there is the whole separate school of historical inquiry—matching historical evidence with autobiographical slave texts such as Olaudah Equiano's and others less famous—that spotlights the role of African slavers of the coast preying on the hapless peoples of the interior and/or entire "kidnapper kingdoms" such as Dahomey and the Oyo state trafficking in subjugated ethnic enemies.[19] In fact, considerable work has been done on how the spread of Islam into Africa, itself creating new sets of subsaharan tribal identities and alliances on the basis of Muslim and non-Muslim, played into such rivalries. Conversely, volumes now exist detailing how the culture arising from slave experience in the new world was in many cases deeply influenced by the roles of antebellum African Muslims, who themselves left behind a substantial body of personal narrative.[20]

Whatever its implication in these matters, we do know that for a variety of reasons—political, military, geographic—Islam at last seems to withdraw from the boundaries of the Euro- and Anglo-American Atlantic world in the eighteenth century. For Americans, specifically, the Barbary pirates provide the last time Muslims figure significantly in early American history—and as well, a final set of contacts whereby the image of the white American slave in Africa might have been paired with that of the black African slave in America as a critique of the disparity between American political, economic, and racial practice and an abstract rhetoric of universal human liberty. Part of this was simple imperial geography. While Anglo-European visions of empire continued to project themselves mainly eastward through the Islamic Mediterranean and the land mass of Asia Minor to the Indian subcontinent, American eyes turned westward toward an ever extending frontier and finally to the vast Pacific rim. As late as 1924, for a Briton like E. M. Forster, the title *Passage to India* by definition incorporated as part of the cultural drama an eastward sea voyage circumnavigating the mediterranean and African dominions of Islam that Vasco da Gama would have understood. By the mid-nineteenth century in America, on the other hand, the use of an identical title by Walt Whitman extended both the transcendentalist and the imperialist imperatives of an earlier cosmic skirting of the Sierras duly westward across the vast Pacific that lay beyond. Part of it was also due to the peculiar concentration of Americans on the discrete racialisms that claimed historical attention in the antebellum republic. Much cultural energy was devoted to rationalizations, for instance, of the final removals of native peoples from the lands east of the Mississippi. Meanwhile, in response to increasing abolitionist pressures, slavery interests formulated myriad new forms of racial explanation—political, economic, religious, even scientific—to defend their increasingly embattled institution.

As to cultural images of Islam and Islamic peoples themselves, references involving tropes of difference became increasingly aestheticized, and distinctly lacking, for instance, the sense of cultural engagement maintained in Anglo-European "orientalist" representations of the same period. Aside from the literary references mentioned above, perhaps the strongest vestiges of the former strength of Islamic figurations would continue to exist, ironically, in the residual ritual and paraphernalia of Freemasonry—throughout the early republic, in its connection with figures as diverse as Franklin, Paine, Hamilton, Jefferson, and even the revered Washington, already suspect as a form of atheism and by the 1820s, through new political proliferations combined with a secrecy born of lingering connections with founding elites, actually suspected of fomenting an overthrow of democratic government. And of course there remains the mighty dollar—an idea no doubt especially shocking both to God-fearing Americans who take pride in the nation's immense wealth and global economic supremacy *and* to anti-American fanatics around the globe, willing to commit acts of mass terror because such filthy lucre has rendered us Godless—with the mystic symbology of freemasonry continuing today to blazon the inheritance of Islam on its very face.

In terms of physical demographics, a muslim cultural and ethnic presence in the United States remains negligible until the late nineteenth and early twentieth centuries, when there occur two main migrations. The first, between 1875 and 1912, brought a substantial group of immigrants from what was then called Greater Syria, including the contemporary Syria, Jordan, Palestine, Israel, and Lebanon. Initially these included numerous Arabic and Middle Eastern Christians. The second took place at the end of World War I, with the breakup of the Ottoman Empire. Still, in 1970, Muslims in the United States numbered only half a million. With the last three decades, growth had amounted to eight million.[21] Meanwhile, in a media age, as Americans of all ages we still mainly continue to see them in the images of our given ages: the romantic Riff bandits of *The Desert Song*; The Sheik of Araby; Sinbad the Sailor; The Thief of Baghdad; The Sultan of Swat; Aly Khan; King Farouk; The Shah of Iran; Rudolf Valentino in *The Sheik*; Alfred Drake in *Kismet*; Omar Sharif playing his noble falcon of the desert to Peter O'Toole's Lawrence of Arabia; Shriners and their Mosques; Sam the Sham and the Pharoahs; Johnny Carson's Karnak the Magnificent; Walt Disney's Aladdin; Ray Stevens' Ahab the Arab. And now the new images—what we just can't help ourselves from seeing as the fanatical, obsidian-eyed, basilisk faces staring at us from the pages of newspapers and from our television screens. We still don't know who they are. Meanwhile we newly envision ourselves as slayers of Afghans, Saudis, Iraqis, or of Islamic members of shadowed networks with Arabic names we can barely pronounce, let alone keep up with— Al Qaeda, Fatah, Hamas, Hezbollah, Islamic Jihad. We worry about getting on airplanes with them. We wonder where ideological profiling ends and ethnological profiling begins. What is a religion and what is a race? If we are committed to a killing war on the ground, how and when will such distinctions begin to blur?

Having begun these summary meditations with a historical anecdote, let me conclude with a popular culture one of more recent origin that, by way of retracing earlier matters, may bring us back around to something of a topical currency. It concerns a phone conversation I had some years back with a favorite nephew, a teenager at the time, who was telling me how much he'd enjoyed seeing the movie *Robin Hood*. What had he liked the most, I asked. He said he really liked the character played by Morgan Freeman. Silence on my end. Robin Hood, I'm thinking. Kevin Costner. Twelfth-century England. Morgan Freeman. "Don't tell me, let me guess," I said. "He's quote 'a Moor.'" "Yeah," he answered excitedly. "How did you know that?" I said that it would take much too long to explain. I see now that I was wrong. Moors, Ottomans, Saracens, Mussulmans, Mahometans. How *does* one explain the cinematic lifting-out of a distinguished African American actor from character roles in the context of historical American representations of race in which he has played a faithful chauffeur to Jessica Tandy's Miss Daisy and a faithful sergeant major to Mathew Broderick's Robert Gould Shaw and transplant him to the Age of the Crusades as the faithful sidekick of Kevin Costner's Robin Hood. Make him a Moor. That should take some explaining, but for Americans it doesn't, any more than it does when they think that because Othello is a "Moor" and is described in the play as "black," it's natural that he be played by somebody of visibly subsaharan African descent. To put it simply, we make Blacks into Moors and Moors into Blacks at the convenience of cultural categories devised to suit us. As with so many of the other racial constructions of self and other we in the west have managed to put on the shelf in the American museum, there's no time like the present to start explaining, because we're already centuries too late.

NOTES

1. In *A Connecticut Yankee in King Arthur's Court*, Hank Morgan, newly arrived in medieval England, is being carried captive by a knight who has claimed him by right of conquest. He sees a glistening edifice of towers and turrets in the distance. "Bridgeport?" he asks his captor. "Camelot," is the answer.

2. To use Said's exact formulation, "Orientalism is a style of thought based upon an ontological epistemological distinction made between the "Orient" and (most of the time) the "Occident." As a cultural discourse, it constructs "a Western style for dominating, restructuring, and having authority over the Orient." *Orientalism* (New York: Vintage Books, 1979), 2–3.

3. These are current dictionary etymologies, appearing in Webster's Tenth Collegiate Dictionary. Since the age of Johnson in England and Webster in America, they have passed in and out of lexicographical currency, often with no discernible historical logic. Mahomet, for instance, seems to have been the preferred reference to the Prophet in a number of major early American writers, although Mohammed and Muhammed were equally well known in standard usage.

4. Among canonical writers of the American Renaissance, Egyptological references form their own vast web of discourse. In "The Prairie" chapter of Melville's *Moby-Dick*, contemplating the enigmatic visage of the great sperm whale, Ishmael famously concludes, "Champollion deciphered the wrinkled granite hieroglyphics. But there is no Champollion to decipher the Egypt of every man's and every other being's face" (380). (New York: Penguin, 1992.) Of his celebrated foleaceous railroad bank in spring thaw, Thoreau similarly asks in *Walden* "What Champollion will decipher this hieroglyphic for us, that we may turn over a new leaf at last?" (203). Owen Thomas, ed. *Walden and Civil Disobedience* (New York: Norton, 1966). "What is the grass," Whitman similarly inquires, answering "...I guess it is a uniform hieroglyphic,/ And it means, Sprouting alike in broad zones and narrow zones,/ Growing among black folks as among white,/Kanuck, Tuckahoe, Congressman, Cuff, I give them the same, I receive them the same" (34) *Leaves of Grass*, ed. Harold W. Blodgett and Sculley Bradley (New York: Norton, 1965). One could extend the string of citations through Emerson, Hawthorne, Dickinson, and a host of lesser literary devotees of what Schueller calls Egyptomania.

5. This gathering of titles appears in Malini Johar Schueller's *U.S. Orientalisms: Race, Nation, and Gender in Literature, 1790–1890* (Ann Arbor: University of Michigan Press, 1998), to which much of my subsequent discussion of "Barbary" orientalism is deeply indebted. Further page references are parenthetical in the text.

6. Numerous personal narratives of the Barbary slave experience, further revealing the ubiquitousness of the genre in early American writing, have recently been collected by Paul Baepler in *White Slaves, African Masters: An Anthology of American Barbary Captivity Narratives* (Chicago: University of Chicago Press, 1999).

7. Royall Tyler, *The Algerine Captive*, ed. Jack B. Moore (Gainesville, FL: Scholars' Facsimiles and Reprints, 1967), 169–170. Further page references are parenthetical in the text.

8. The intention is noted in Rowson's preface to the print text. The version cited here appears in *Plays by Early American Women, 1775–1850*, ed. Amelia Howe Kritzer (Ann Arbor: University of Michigan Press, 1995), 55–95. For details on Reinagle, see Jenny Franchot, "Susanna Haswell Rowson," *American Writers of the Early Republic*, ed. Emory Elliott (Detroit: Gale, 1985), 257.

9. The publication dates of the three editions published during Tyler's lifetime actually parallel crucial stages in what were called the "Barbary wars." The 1797 first edition appeared, as Jack Moore points out, in the same year Joel Barlow negotiated the release of captured Americans in Algeria (xvi–xvii). The 1802 London edition appeared in the midst of the 1801–1805 war; and the 1817 edition followed opportunely upon the victorious punitive expedition by naval forces under Captain Stephen Decatur whereby a peace treaty favorable to U. S. interests was finally secured.

10. *Autobiography*, ed. Leonard W. Labaree (New Haven: Yale University Press, 1964), 176. In "A Dialogue Between Two Presbyterians," Franklin used the same figure to defend a minister fallen afoul of local orthodoxy. "I would only infer," says one of the speakers, "that if it would be thought reasonable to suffer a Turk to preach among us a Doctrine diametrically opposed to Christianity, it cannot be reasonable to silence one of our own Preachers, for preaching a Doctrine exactly agreeable to Christianity, only because he does not perhaps zealously propagate all the Doctrines of an Old Confession" [*Papers of Benjamin Franklin*, II, 32, ed. Leonard W. Labaree (New Haven: Yale University Press, 1960)].

11. William Byrd, "History of the Dividing Line," *The Prose Works of William Byrd of Westover*, ed. Louis B. Wright (Cambridge: Harvard University Press, 1966), 248.

12. *Cotton Mather: Selections*, ed. Kenneth B. Murdock (New York: Hafner, 1965), 292.

13. Robert C. Davis, "Counting European Slaves on the Barbary Coast," January 5, 2001 paper, American Historical Association, Boston, MA. Cited by David Brion Davis, "Slavery—White, Black, Muslim, Christian," *New York Review of Books*, July 5, 2001, 51.

14. Indeed, as early as 869 CE, Davis reminds us, "the Arabs had transported enough black slaves from East Africa to the Persian Gulf to ignite an extensive revolt in the Tigris-Euphrates delta in what is now Iraq." Before they were defeated in 883, the insurrectionists themselves "killed thousands of Arab men, enslaved countless women and children, and even threatened Baghdad" (51). Davis's summations derive from his own massive research in the field, forming the basis of his classic study *The Problem of Slavery in Western Culture* (Ithaca: Cornell University Press, 1966). Islamic slave practices are also treated in authoritative detail in Orlando Patterson, *Slavery and Social Death* (Cambridge: Harvard University Press, 1982). In the context of the present argument, it

should be noted that both writers remark significantly on racist attitudes developed by Muslim slavers against subsaharan Africans.

15. See Ronald Segal, *Islam's Black Slaves: The Other Diaspora* (New York: Farrar, Straus and Giroux, 2001). Following Bernard Lewis, Segal asserts that Islamic culture evolved from early attitudes with no particular negative associations attaching to blackness to distinctly negative ones attached to slavery. "Finally," writes Segal, citing Lewis directly, " 'the large-scale importation of African slaves influenced Arab (and therefore Muslim) attitudes to the peoples of darker skin whom most Arabs and Muslims encountered only in this way' " (46).

16. To evidence the persistence of such attitudes of acceptance among Anglo-Europeans in their encounters with Islamic slavers, see Karl E. Meyer & Sharleen Blair Brysac, *Tournament of Shadows: The Great Game and the Race for Empire in Central Asia* (Washington, D.C.: Counterpoint, 1999). An explorer in 1832 noted, for instance, "that it was common practice for Uzbek man-hunters to capture Russians for sale in Bokhara's markets." "The Mahometans are not sensible of any offense in enslaving the Russians," he explained, "since they state that Russia herself exhibits the example of a whole country of slaves, especially in the despotic government of their soldiery" (81).

17. A frequently adduced example of this is the interchangeability of the words "slave" and "servant" in early America when applied to both indentured whites and enslaved African Blacks. Orlando Patterson, for instance, notes this cultural practice (6–7), in turn citing Winthrop D. Jordan, *White Over Black* (Baltimore: Penguin Books, 1969), 45–48. One might also adduce, from major texts of antebellum American writing, the depiction of polite slaveowners' preferences for the ongoing use of the euphemism "servant" in referring to their chattel. See, for instance, conversations between Mr. and Mrs. Shelby on their Kentucky plantation in *Uncle Tom's Cabin* as they prepare to sell Tom and Eliza's son Harry to a slave trader.

18. Mills M. Lord, Jr., *David Levy Yulee: Statesman and Railroad Builder*. Unpublished M. A. History thesis, University of Florida, 1940.

19. For a succinct account of such tribal policies and practices during the early modern era, see Felipe Fernandez Armesto, *Millennium* (New York: Touchstone, 1995), 271–273.

20. Allen D. Austin, ed. *African Muslims in Antebellum America: A Sourcebook* (New York: Garland, 1984).

21. Jane I. Smith, *Islam in America* (New York: Columbia University Press, 1999), 51–53.

NOTES ON CONTRIBUTORS

Philip Beidler is Professor of English at the University of Alabama, where he has taught American literature since 1974. His recent books include *The Good War's Greatest Hits: World War II and American Remembering* (University of Georgia Press, 1998), and *First Books: The Printed Word and Cultural Formation in Early Alabama* (University of Alabama Press, 1999). Recent essays appear in *Virginia Quarterly Review, Georgia Review*, and *Michigan Quarterly Review*. His new book is *Late Thoughts on an Old War* (University of Georgia Press, 2004).

Gary Taylor is Director of the Hudson Strode Program in Renaissance Studies at the University of Alabama. He is general editor of the *Complete Works* of Shakespeare (Oxford University Press, 1986) and the *Collected Works* of Thomas Middleton (Oxford University Press, forthcoming), and author of *Buying Whiteness: Race, Culture, and Identity from Columbus to Hiphop* (Palgrave, 2005), *Castration: An Abbreviated History of Western Manhood* (Routledge, 2000), *Cultural Selection* (Basic Books, 1995), and *Reinventing Shakespeare: A Cultural History from the Restoration to the Present* (Grove Weidenfeld, 1989).

David J. Baker is Professor of English at the University of Hawaii. He is the author of *Between Nations: Shakespeare, Spenser, Marvell, and the Question of Britain* (Stanford University Press, 1997) and the editor of *British Identities and English Renaissance Literature* (Cambridge University Press, 2002). His essays have appeared in such publications as *ELR* and *Critical Inquiry*.

Benjamin Braude teaches Middle Eastern history and courses on racism and anti-Semitism at Boston College. He is also a research associate of the Department of Religion and Biblical Literature at Smith College and the Center for Middle Eastern Studies at Harvard University. In addition to his forthcoming *Sex, Slavery, and*

Racism: The Secret History of Noah and His Sons, his other publications include *Christians and Jews in the Ottoman Empire: The Functioning of a Plural Society,* reissued in 2001 as a one-volume paperback. Recently he has contributed to *William and Mary Quarterly, Annales: Histoire, Sciences Sociales,* and the *UNESCO History of Humanity.*

Barbara Fuchs, formerly Associate Professor of English and Adjunct Associate Professor of Spanish at the University of Washington, where she worked since receiving her Ph.D. from Stanford University in 1997, is now an Associate Professor of Romance Languages at the University of Pennsylvania. Her research specialties include sixteenth- and seventeenth-century English and Spanish literature and culture, imperialism and national identities in a Mediterranean and transatlantic context, and postcolonial theory. Recent publications include "Empire Unmanned: Gender Trouble and Genoese Gold in Cervantes' 'The Two Damsels'," *PMLA*, March 2001; "Faithless Empires: Pirates, Renegadoes, and the English Nation," *English Literary History,* Spring 2000; and *Mimesis and Empire: The New World, Islam, and European Identities* (Cambridge University Press, 2001). Current essays appear in *New Centennial Review, Modern Philology, Studies in English Literature,* and *Passing for Spain: Cervantes and the Fictions of Identity* (Illinois University Press, 2002).

Kim Hall holds the Thomas F.X. Mullarkey Chair in Literature at Fordham University. The author *of Things of Darkness: Economies of Race and Gender in Early Modern England* (Cornell University Press, 1995), she has published numerous articles on race in Renaissance/early modern culture and has lectured nationally and internationally on Shakespeare, race theory, Renaissance women writers, visual arts, material culture, and pedagogy. She is currently working on two books: *Othello: Texts and Contexts* (contracted with Bedford/St. Martin's Press) and *The Sweet Taste of Empire: Gender and Material Culture in Seventeenth-Century England.*

Karen Ordahl Kupperman is Professor of History at New York University. Her scholarship focuses on the Atlantic world in the sixteenth and seventeenth centuries, particularly contacts and ventures between Europe and North America and the Caribbean. Her most recent book is *Indians and English: Facing Off* (Cornell University Press, 2000), winner of the American Historical Association's Prize in Atlantic History and a History Book Club selection. Her book *Providence Island, 1630–41: The Other Puritan*

Colony (Cambridge University Press, 1993) won the Albert J. Beveridge Award of the American Historical Association for the best book in American History, including Canada and Latin America. She has written *Settling with the Indians: The Meeting of English and Indian Cultures in America, 1580–1640* (1980); *Roanoke: The Abandoned Colony* (1984, reissued 1991); and has edited *Captain John Smith: A Select Edition of His Writings* (1988) and *America in European Consciousness* (1995). Kupperman's current project combines Eurohistory and environmental history in an Atlantic context. It examines competition between Christian leaders and Indian priests over controlling the natural world and forecasting, even controlling the weather. This project draws on Kupperman's recent work in Indians and English, and on new scientific work in the history of climate. She is also engaged in a scholarly edition of Richard Ligon's *True and Exact History of the Island of Barbados* (1657, 1673).

Joseph Roach is Charles C. and Dorathea S. Dilley Professor of Theater and English at Yale University. He has chaired the Department of Performing Arts at Washington University in St. Louis, the Interdisciplinary Ph.D. in Theatre at Northwestern University, and the Department of Performance Studies at NYU. His books include *Cities of the Dead: Circum-Atlantic Performance* (Columbia University Press, 1996), which won the James Russell Lowell Prize from MLA and the Calloway Prize from NYU, and *The Player's Passion: Studies in the Science of Acting* (University of Michigan Press, 1993), which won the Barnard Hewitt Award in Theater History. His essays appear in *Theatre Journal, Theatre Survey, The Drama Review, Theatre History Studies, Discourse, Theater, Text and Performance Quarterly, South Atlantic Quarterly,* and other journals.

Francesca Royster is Assistant Professor of English at DePaul University. She received her Ph.D. from the University of California-Berkeley in 1995. Her areas of research include Shakespeare Studies, Women's Studies, and Queer Theory. Her book, *Becoming Cleopatra: Race, Gender and the Politics of Reinvention,* is forthcoming from Palgrave Press. She has recently published essays in *Shakespeare Quarterly, Shakespeare Studies,* and *Transforming Shakespeare,* ed. Marianne Novy (St. Martin's Press, 1999).

Gordon Sayre is Associate Professor of English at the University of Oregon, where he teaches courses in Colonial and nineteenth-century American Literature and Native American Literature. He is the author of *"Les Sauvages Americains": Representations of Native*

Americans in French and English Colonial Literature (1997) and editor of the anthology *American Captivity Narratives* (2000). He has also published articles about natural history and anthropology in eighteenth- and nineteenth-century America, such as "The Mammoth: Endangered Species or Vanishing Race," in *Journal of Early Modern Cultural Studies*, 1:1.

Index